ATLANTIS:
THE EVIDENCE OF SCIENCE

ATLANTIS:
THE EVIDENCE OF SCIENCE

EMMET SWEENEY

Algora Publishing
New York

Library of Congress Cataloging-in-Publication Data —

Sweeney, Emmet John.
    Atlantis : the evidence of science / Emmet Sweeney.
        p. cm.
    Includes bibliographical references and index.
    ISBN 978-0-87586-771-7 (trade paper: alk. paper) — ISBN 978-0-87586-772-4 (hard
cover: alk. paper) — ISBN 978-0-87586-773-1 (ebook) 1. Atlantis (Legendary place) I.
Title.
    GN751.S94 2010
    001.94—dc22
                                2010009921

Printed in the United States

TABLE OF CONTENTS

FOREWORD

The discovery in 1992 of tobacco and cocaine, American narcotics, in an Egyptian mummy, and the finding, in 1998, of ancient European DNA in Native Americans, should have reignited debate on the question of Atlantis: That it did not was due to several widely-held assumptions about human and natural history. (a) It is assumed, by the great majority of scientists, that no catastrophes of the type described by Plato, which sank Atlantis to the depths of the ocean in a single "day and night" of misfortune, have ever occurred — not at least within the memory and experience of mankind. (b) It is believed, by virtually all researchers, whether mainstream or "alternative," that no large islands, far less a continent, ever existed in the Atlantic Ocean, and that the geological evidence has demonstrated this in a most convincing manner. (c) It is accepted by virtually all historians that the civilizations of the New World are much less ancient than those of the Old, and that, consequently, the parallels observed between the cultures of the Old World and the New are purely coincidental: such features must have developed independently on either side of the ocean. By the time the peoples of the New World began to build pyramids, it is held, pyramid-building had long ceased in Egypt and elsewhere in the Old World, and by then the Egyptians, Greeks and Babylonians were in possession of the wheel and had developed an advanced Iron Age technology. Since none of these are found in the New World, there can have been no cultural interaction.

All three of the above statements are regarded as unassailable fact; so unassailable indeed that not even the discovery of European DNA in Native Americans and tobacco and cocaine in Egyptian mummies could shake them. Yet it is the contention of the present author that all three are utterly false, and that they made their way into the textbooks through a series of errors committed by scientists and historians over the past two centuries.

It will be a goal of the present study to refute these assumptions, these articles of faith which have wiped Atlantis from the history books just as surely as Plato had it wiped by nature from the face of the earth. Essentially, I hope to demonstrate that: (a) From the Old Stone Age through to the New Stone Age and the Early Bronze Age the earth was struck by a series of natural catastrophes of a violence far greater than anything in the experience of modern man. During these catastrophes, which were marked by vast earth tremors and tidal waves, large areas of inhabited land in various parts of the globe sank into the sea. (b) The overwhelming evidence of geology and biology proves that a large mountain range ran down the middle of the Atlantic Ocean during the Old and Middle Stone Ages, and that part of this landmass survived above water into the New Stone Age and Early Bronze Age. (c) The great civilizations of the Old World were not thousands of years older than those of the New. All the ancient civilizations arose simultaneously and were in fact profoundly influenced and shaped by the cosmic catastrophes then occurring. In short, the Early Bronze Age of Egypt and Mesopotamia was contemporary with the Early Bronze Age of Mexico and Peru, and the destruction of Atlantis at the end of this epoch terminated the transatlantic cultural exchange.

INTRODUCTION

I would not consider myself justified in inflicting another book on Atlantis on the public were it not for the fact that over the past few decades, and even within the last few years, tantalizing new evidence has appeared which, though well-enough known within the relevant scholarly disciplines, is not yet widely known outside. I must confess that before the appearance of this evidence I myself was a skeptic. To me, Atlantis was best left alone, the preserve of the "lunatic fringe" who have, over the past few decades, filled the libraries and bookshops with their wild speculations, placing the Lost Island everywhere from Antarctica and the Pacific to the Moon and Mars. A major source of my skepticism was the knowledge that continents or continent-sized landmasses cannot sink into the ocean — not without destroying the entire human race, at least. Yet the weight of the new evidence, which curiously enough seems to have largely escaped the attention of the "Atlantean" enthusiasts, is such that it caused this skeptic to reconsider. It is, as we shall see, material which simultaneously solves the problem of the so-called "Lost Continent" and casts a dramatic new light on every aspect of the whole question, opening before us fresh and astonishing vistas.

The most important facet of the new evidence involves the question of transatlantic contact.

One of the central tenets of all research into Atlantis has been the proposition that in ancient times men made voyages across the Atlantic, and the Old and New Worlds interacted with each other: This because Plato had placed Atlantis "opposite the Pillars of Hercules" (Gibraltar) and mentioned a string of islands leading from Atlantis to the "opposite continent." This has been taken to be the first mention of America in western literature. The proposition that such trans-atlantic contacts existed has always been vigorously opposed by mainstream academia, one of whose guiding principles has been the virtually complete isolation of the Americas prior to Columbus. But the idea of a culturally isolated America is now officially dead and buried. Evidence from various sciences, but most particularly from archaeology, forensic pathology and genetics, has proved beyond question that there was contact across the North Atlantic in antiquity. This contact began in the Old Stone Age (Paleolithic) and continued into the period of the great civilizations, the civilizations of Egypt and Babylonia. The only question now remaining is this: By what means and through what channels did these early voyagers cross the ocean?

An examination of this new evidence, from the perspective of the Atlantis question, is urgently needed. And this is all the more pressing when we consider the geological evidence, generally ignored in mainstream populist scientific literature, of a recently-submerged landmass (post-Glacial, according to some authorities) in the middle of the Atlantic Ocean.

In addition to this, there is the need to integrate my own findings, and those of Professor Gunnar Heinsohn, dramatic in their own way, into the general Atlantean narrative. These findings are founded firmly upon two of the most fundamental principles laid out by Immanuel Velikovsky in the 1950s. That: (a) Cosmic catastrophes, of exactly the type described by Plato in his description of Atlantis and its destruction, really did occur: and (b) That the last of these catastrophes occurred within historical times; and in fact, as I contend in my various publications, they took place near the middle of the ninth century BC.

Over the past century and a half, and ever since the revival of the Atlantean debate by Ignatius Donnelly, the most important objection to the idea is the almost universally-held conviction that catastrophes of the type said by Plato to have destroyed the island-civilization in a single "day and night of misfortune" simply do not happen. According to conventional wisdom, the earth's geology has evolved at an astonishingly slow rate, and the forces of erosion, of wind, rain and sun, year by year effect small changes in the landscape which over the millennia and indeed over the hundreds of millennia, build up to large changes. More dramatic events, such as earthquakes and volcanic eruptions, do occur; but these are a rarity and, in any case, they do not as a rule produce dramatic alterations to the landscape. On occasion, a particularly powerful volcanic eruption may effect big local changes. A volcano might blow itself to pieces and may kill thousands of people in the process, but its effects do not extend beyond its own immediate vicinity. If tidal waves, or tsunamis, are involved, then great numbers of people might lose their lives. Nonetheless, the eruption, no matter how powerful, will rarely have a major impact outside a thirty mile radius; and, in the conventional view (this being the crucial point), no volcanoes of the past could have been any more violent than those observed at work today.

Volcanoes and earthquakes aside, the building of important geological features such as mountain ranges, is now said to proceed at an exceedingly slow rate. The earth's tectonic plates are continually pressing against each other, or else moving apart; and when they move together they build mountain ranges, slowly but surely, over millions of years. It is held, for example, that the raising of the Andes or the Himalayas took many millions of years, and was accomplished at a rate of no more than a few centimeters per century. Where the earth's plates move apart, it is conceded that land might be sunk into the sea; yet this would apply to only tiny sections of coastline at a time.

The above notion, described as uniformitarianism, was first popularized by Darwin's friend and colleague Charles Lyell. Lyell was concerned to provide Darwin with the enormous stretches of time apparently necessary to produce new species through his proposed slow-acting evolutionary mechanism of natural selection. As such, Lyell rejected the earlier theory of catastrophist (at that time widely endorsed by some of the greatest minds of Europe and North America), which held that in the past volcanic and other types of catastrophes, of an intensity much greater than anything experienced in modern times, had occurred. And so Lyell began to speak of a world millions of years old and to pour scorn on the ancient traditions — found throughout the globe — of epoch-making upheavals of nature in the not-too-distant past. He poured scorn too on the great quantities of geological and paleontological evidence which had emerged in the course of the eighteenth and nineteenth centuries which pointed in exactly the same direction.

Yet any honest appraisal of the uniformitarian principle can only cause one to wonder how such an idea could have found its way into the textbooks, far less have been elevated to the status of scientific orthodoxy. Consider what Lyell was actually saying: Only those forces observed operating today could have operated in the past — and only at the same intensity. In short, if it's not happening now, it couldn't have happened in the past. But this is not science: this is faith! We might as well imagine a future historian, say in a thousand years, proclaiming; "World wars don't happen now, therefore they could not have happened in the past."

In fact, the earth's history, both recent and not-so recent, was not nearly as peaceful as is now imagined. Catastrophes, involving massive movements of the planets' tectonic plates, occurred only a few thousand years ago; and these "super-eruptions" left their mark on human and natural history. Indeed, as we shall see, the last of these events shook our world as recently as the beginning of the first millennium BC.

The above statement, dramatic though it may appear, will be defended in detail in the course of the present volume. For Atlantis, we shall find, was a Bronze Age society, a civilization of the recent and not the distant past, which was swallowed by the ocean less than a century before the Greeks celebrated their first Olympiad. It was indeed a world and culture that can be firmly anchored in history.

Yet this statement should not delude the reader into believing that the present writer subscribes to the now commonly-held belief that Atlantis represents a distorted memory of the Cretan or some other Aegean civilization. The evidence to be examined in the present volume, some of it astonishing and new, some of it old and reasonably well-known, will leave the reader in no doubt that Atlantis, the real Atlantis, was located precisely where Plato said it was — in the middle of the Atlantic Ocean, due west of Gibraltar, in the region now occupied by the Azores. The latter archipelago might indeed be described as the vestiges of Atlantis — a name which, by the way, the Portuguese still apply to the group.

In our quest for the truth we shall be often pleasantly surprised by the quantity of the evidence. We shall find, for example, that all the nations of western Europe and North Africa told of a lost island in the ocean, and that the peoples of North-west Africa in particular, who apparently still called themselves "Atlantians" in the time of Diodorus of Sicily (first century BC), spoke of a mighty power emanating from a volcanic island in the ocean which overwhelmed all of North Africa and Egypt. This account, similar in many ways to that of Plato, nevertheless clearly owed nothing to the Greek philosopher and provides powerful independent corroboration for him.

One of the skeptics' most cherished myths — that the story derives solely from Plato — is thus demolished.

The next such myth to receive the same treatment is the geological. As we have seen, this is perhaps the skeptics' strongest weapon; yet it is just as weak. For, as we shall see in Chapter 2, the evidence shows that catastrophes much greater than anything experienced by modern man did happen in the past; and the last of them happened only a few thousand years ago. Even worse, we shall find that the related myth — that geology says no sunken landmass existed around the Azores — is manifestly untrue, that the geological evidence says the exact opposite; that a substantial landmass, which consisted largely of sial (the building blocks of the continents) and sedimentary rocks, existed quite recently in the Azores region, and that this landmass was sunk to the bottom of the sea in a relatively recent age: Postglacial, according to some sources. These are not the conclusions of the author, or of other Atlantean true believers, but of professional geologists and biologists, many of whom are utterly hostile to the whole Atlantis notion. It is now even admitted that the Azores rest upon their own continental plate — a tiny one, admittedly. This feature, actually termed the Azores Microplate, clearly at one time formed part of the Eurasian or African Plate. It is, as we shall see, around the size of Ireland, and its contours almost certainly are those of the ancient island spoken of by legend.

The next myth to be overturned is the proposition that no sure evidence of transatlantic contacts prior to Columbus (aside from the very brief foray of the Vikings) exists. This indeed is one of the perennial canards of the skeptics. For years, they have argued that the parallels observed by Donnelly and others between the ancient cultures of the Old World and the New were merely coincidental and diffusion was not in any way needed to explain them. They dismissed too the persistent accounts of "white" Native Americans, as well as the value of Native American traditions which spoke of white culture-bearers who, in a far-off time, had left their island-home in a great canoe and sailed west to the Americas, there to instruct the peoples they met in the sciences of astronomy etc. How shocking then for these skeptics when west-European mitochondrial DNA was found in Native American populations! This discovery, made by a team of geneticists in the early 1990s, has still to be fully taken on board by the wider scientific community. So unexpected and so problematic was the finding that for a while academics were unsure how to react. In the end, it was admitted to be true, though still not "fully understood." Atlantis, of course, could not be countenanced as the missing link (though Plato had stated specifically that a chain of islands leading from Atlantis acted as bridge to a mysterious western continent). Instead, it was postulated that Ice Age adventurers, in small kayak-like canoes, had made their way across the North Atlantic ten or twelve thousand years ago!

And this is still the explanation proffered in the scholarly journals.

But science hadn't delivered its final shock. A couple of years before the European DNA was found in Native Americans, another team of scientists, this time toxicologists, was discovering traces of tobacco and cocaine, two American narcotics, in Egyptian mummies. Once again, the findings shocked the scientific community; and once again, the initial reaction was incredulity. There had to be some mistake. Either that or the findings were fraudulent — a charge actually leveled at the team's leader on more than one occasion. But the tests were repeated by the first team and by others, again and again and again. Finally, it was admitted: the cocaine and tobacco were there. How they got there is said to be unknown, but there they most assuredly are.

How to make sense of all this without Atlantis? We are rapidly approaching the point where, even if an Atlantis story never existed, we would perhaps need to invent one.

But there is yet one major proviso. For some reason, both believers and skeptics have been bewitched by the figure of 9,000 years said by Plato to have elapsed between the destruction of Atlantis and the time of Solon (sixth century BC). It is perhaps understandable why skeptics would be keen to emphasize this figure, for it so neatly undermines everything else Plato says. But why the defenders of a historical Atlantis should hold by it is more difficult to understand. One possible explanation is that 9,500 BC seems to tie in with the date now provided by geologists for the end of the Ice Age, or the end of the Pleistocene. And so, although those same geologists still deny any catastrophic event linked to the end of the Pleistocene, Atlantean theorists, from Donnelly and Spence through to Graham Hancock and Colin Wilson, have seized on this as a possible "scientific" verification of Plato's account. But the simple fact is, the society described by Plato is one of the Bronze Age, and the 9,000 years mentioned by the Egyptian priests to Solon is explained by the fact that ancient peoples, including both Egyptians and Mesopotamians, had no idea of real historical timescales and regularly gave grossly inflated estimates of their own antiquity. One hundred years after Solon, Egyptian priests were telling Herodotus that their civilization began around eleven thousand years earlier!

But uncritical acceptance of the date provided by Plato has blighted all attempts to solve the mystery. The legends of Wales and Ireland, for example, speak of lands submerged beneath the sea only a few centuries before the dawn of the Christian era. Traditions from all over Europe and the Near East speak of similar events at the same time. Thus the founding of Rome by Romulus and Remus, in the eighth century BC, is associated with catastrophic disturbances of nature. Yet none of these traditions could be utilized by Donnelly, Spence, Hancock or Wilson, or any of the host of other researchers who have put pen to paper over the last hundred years. In the same way, ancient monuments of South America, most notably Tiahuanaco, seemed to provide abundant evidence of recent cataclysms as well as a colossal upraising of the Andes Mountains. But the civilizations of the Americas are known to have commenced around 1000 BC, and Tiahuanaco is clearly related, in terms of general culture, to the other civilizations of the region. This has meant either (a): Rejecting any link between the catastrophe of Tiahuanaco and Atlantis or (b): Redating the entire civilization of Tiahuanaco to 10,000 BC. And this is exactly the course taken by Hancock, Wilson and many other modern writers in a futile attempt to hold onto the ten thousand year old civilization of Plato's account.

So, the 9,000 year-old Atlantis needs to be forgotten. We are dealing with a civilization of the Neolithic and Early Bronze Age; a civilization that we might expect would have left its signature throughout the Atlantic seaboard of Europe and North Africa; a civilization like the "Megalithic" culture of those very regions! But this brings us to another difficulty. The pyramid-building/mound-building civilization of Western Europe is dated to the third and early second millennia BC. How then can this have influenced the Native American Bronze Age civilizations, which did not commence until the beginning of the first millennium BC? The answer to this question is stunningly simple: As I have proved in great detail in my previous publications, the Bronze Age civilizations of the Old World had no 2,000-year head-start over those of the New. They all rose, almost simultaneously, in the wake of a great cataclysm which devastated the entire earth in the middle of the second millennium BC.

The final piece of the jigsaw fits into place.

As might be expected, the work to follow is a highly interdisciplinary exercise. My job has been rather like that of a detective, sifting through the evidence and following every possible clue. This of course is necessary, in view of the fact that the island home of this people and culture has been sunk beneath the ocean. I could not, in such circumstances, scorn to look at the evidence not only of archaeology, but also of geology, mythology, botany, zoology, comparative linguistics, genetics, forensic pathology, and many other fields. It may be, by some miracle, that a Neolithic axe-head or carved megalithic stone may someday be dredged from the sea bed near the Azores. But in lieu of such a happy result, about as likely as locating the proverbial needle in the haystack, we must be prepared to look at whatever is available, whatever is not at the bottom of the ocean.

I am of course indebted to all the scholars and specialists, in all the above fields, whose meticulous work has helped, often in ways they perhaps could not have imagined, to fill out the picture. I have however been most influenced by, and am most indebted to, the following: Ignatius Donnelly, who reignited the Atlantis debate and made the first attempts to tie-in the story with the findings of modern science; Immanuel Velikovsky, who gave us a new respect for ancient myths and who, almost single-handedly, proved that great natural cataclysms, of the type described by Plato, actually did happen in the recent past; and Gunnar Heinsohn, the Bremen academic who demonstrated that ancient history is not nearly as old as claimed in the textbooks, and whose ideas, ultimately, brought together the world of the megalith-builders with that of the Celts, and thus finally reintegrated the former into the historical narrative. That is just what the present work intends to do. The first megalith-builders were the Atlanteans, but they were not a people removed by millennia from the other ancient civilizations; they came just immediately prior to them. And, as we shall see, having understood this, we are able, finally, to take Atlantis out of the realm of half-forgotten myth and legend and put it, finally, back into the realm of history.

One result of this is the discovery and identification of an actual Egyptian reference to the war with the Atlanteans.

CHAPTER 1. LEGENDS OF A LOST WORLD

A PERENNIAL OBSESSION

The legend of Atlantis has become one of the obsessions of modern popular culture. Quite literally dozens of books appear every year, in the English language alone, each of them promising dramatic new revelations; each of them claiming to have finally solved the riddle of the Lost Continent. Yet it was not always thus. Until the publication of Ignatius Donnelly's *Atlantis: the Antediluvian World* in 1882, few paid much attention to the strange story which had first appeared two thousand years earlier, in Plato's political dialogues, the *Timaeus* and *Critias*. In these documents Plato provides an all-too brief description, reproduced below, of the mythic island, its history and culture, and its final destruction. In Plato's account, the end of Atlantis is presented as illustrative of a number of beliefs expounded by the Greek philosopher himself, most important of which was the theory of the cyclic nature of civilizations and the notion of how excessive arrogance (Greek, *hubris*) is an indicator of a civilization's impending collapse.

It is true that in the immediate aftermath of the publication of Plato's story, a good deal of interest was generated. There was, for a while, a fairly intense debate, some (including, apparently, Aristotle) seeing the story as fiction, others seeing it as true. The philosopher Crantor, for instance, a student of Plato's student Xenocrates, tried to find proof of the sunken island's existence. His work, a commentary on Plato's *Timaeus*, is lost, but another writer, Proclus, reports that Crantor travelled to Egypt and was actually shown a written account of Atlantis' history inscribed in hieroglyphics on the walls of the temple of Neith in the Delta.

After the third century BC, interest in the lost island diminished. By the start of the Christian age, it was generally assumed that Atlantis represented the arrogant pre-Flood generations whom God had destroyed in the time of Noah. By the Middle Ages the story was more or less forgotten. Only with the dawning of the modern age, in the fifteenth century, did interest in the lost island reawaken. So for example Plato's story inspired the utopian works of several Renaissance writers, most famously perhaps Francis Bacon's *New Atlantis*. Renaissance authors also began to comment on the traditions of other lands, which seemed to offer support for Plato. Writers of the time noted that a number of peoples of western Europe (the Irish, Welsh, Bretons, Spaniards etc.) had a legend of a lost island in the ocean, and it was generally assumed, almost in passing, that these must have been references to the lost island of Plato's dialogues. This was of course the Age of Discovery, and it was to bring many more such stories to the attention of the scholarly community. The natives of the Canary Islands, for example, the Guanches, whom the Spaniards subjugated during the course of the fifteenth century, had a similar tale, and it was found that even the peoples of the Americas possessed like traditions.

In spite of the general reawakening of interest in Atlantis during the Renaissance, it was not until the latter years of the nineteenth century that it became a popular obsession. Without question, the man most responsible for this was Ignatius Donnelly, a colorful Irish-American, whose restless nature made him in many ways a typical representative of nineteenth century America. Donnelly was to achieve recognition as a politician, but it was as a writer that he gained widespread acclaim and notoriety. In his *Atlantis: the Antediluvian World*, published in 1882, Donnelly went more or less on the word of Plato, and, like the early Christian commentators, saw in the destruction of the island-empire a reflection of the biblical Deluge. He followed Plato, however, rather than the Bible, when it came to dating. According to him, Atlantis was destroyed around 9,500 BC, when an enormous comet gave the earth a near miss, raising vast tidal waves and causing mass extinctions. In Donnelly's view, the extinction of the mammoths, as well as the other Pleistocene megafauna, was brought about by the same upheaval of nature that sank Atlantis to the bottom of the ocean.

A great deal of *Atlantis: the Antediluvian World*, was concerned with an examination of cultural parallels between the ancient civilizations of the Old World and the New: for Donnelly took seriously the statement of Plato that beyond Atlantis there lay a series of other islands which acted as stepping stones to a continent on the other side of the ocean. From this, it was obvious that should the story be true, there must have been transatlantic cultural links in the distant past; and, sure enough, Donnelly was able to identify a whole plethora of apparently precise parallels between the ancient cultures of the Old World and the New. Chief amongst these were traits that have since become the stock-in-trade of "Atlantean" researchers: pyramids, mummification, dragon-worship, star-worship, etc. He also was the first to highlight other, less well-known hints of contact, such as the occurrence of plants like the banana, an Old World fruit, in the New World.

Donnelly's book produced a storm of controversy, and ignited the debate, which really has never, to this day, drawn to a conclusion. Since his time, the number of publications, which more or less followed his lead, has become legion; and they continue appearing to this day. Yet the reaction of the scholarly establishment to Donnelly was, from the very beginning, almost universally negative. Two points were raised against him which, one way or another, are raised till the present day and which are widely believed to have utterly "debunked" the whole Atlantis idea.

The first of these was catastrophes and cosmology. Even though Donnelly placed the end of the Pleistocene and Ice Age around 9,500 BC, he nevertheless invoked a catastrophe of cosmic dimensions to do so. Yet by his time, the general weight of scientific opinion had moved decisively against the whole idea of catastrophes, especially world-wide catastrophes of the type described by Donnelly.

The second objection concerned dates. If the transatlantic bridge, which Atlantis formed, was destroyed over eleven thousand years ago, how could it still act as a connecting-link between the Old and New Worlds in the time of the ancient civilizations? These did not arise until around 3,000 BC (in the Old World), and around 1,000 BC (or even later) in the New. Therefore, Atlantis could not be invoked as providing a path for the diffusion of Old World ideas, such as pyramid-building. Furthermore, by the time pyramid-building commenced in the New World, it had long come to an end in the Old. Therefore, the parallels could not, in any case, be the result of cultural diffusion.

And so, in the decade following the appearance of Donnelly's book, the academic establishment decided decisively against him; and all subsequent attempts to resurrect the idea have received the same cold reception. Even more damning evidence, it is now said, has been brought to bear; and so, for example, it is suggested that Wegener's idea of Plate Tectonics proves beyond question that a large island, of the type described by Plato, could never have existed in the middle of the Atlantic. There is, indeed, a very active volcanic zone in that area, the mid-Atlantic volcanic ridge. This is a major tectonic fault-line; but it is said that here in fact the seismic pressure is upwards, and that, if anything, land is being built in the region (e.g. the Azores) rather than sunk.

And so the matter has been, as it were, laid to rest. Indeed, the idea that Atlantis could ever have existed, has been sunk deeper even than Plato's legendary island. Yet it is the contention of the present writer that the "debunkers" have been less than honest in their approach. None of the objections raised against Donnelly, or indeed against Plato, were insurmountable, and all are easily answered. For, as we shall see in the pages to follow, the overwhelming weight of evidence shows that catastrophes did happen; that Atlantis was destroyed in the Bronze Age (not 9500 BC); and that the geology of the mid-Atlantic, far from rebutting the Atlantis story, confirms it in the most dramatic way possible.

Yet before considering any of this we must look at what legend and history has to say. It is from ancient story, after all, that we know of the lost island in the first place.

PLATO'S ACCOUNT

The most important (though, as we shall see, not the only) source of the Atlantis story is Plato; and it is worthwhile repeating here what he said; for in many ways it is a thrilling and colorful narrative. Plato is said to have learned the story from Critias, a friend and colleague of his own teacher, Socrates. We are told that Critias heard the story from his grandfather, also called Critias (then nearly ninety years of age), who in turn heard it from his own father Dropidas, a friend and relative of Solon, the Athenian lawmaker and poet. Solon was an extraordinarily active and inquisitive personality. He is known to have travelled to Egypt around 570 BC, and, if we are to believe the accounts given by Plato and Plutarch, there immersed himself in the lore of the country. After spending some time at Heliopolis, he travelled to the Delta city of Sais, where there stood a famous temple to the goddess Neith, a deity believed by both Greeks and Egyptians to be identical to Athena, the patron goddess of Athens. Here Solon made enquiries of one of the priests (according to Plutarch his name was Sonchis), about the history of mankind. We are told that the Greek poet took notes of what the priest told him, and that these notes later came into the possession of Plato. Upon his return to Greece, Solon was said to have conceived the idea of writing an epic poem about Atlantis and its destruction, to be called the *Atlantikos*, but he died before the project could be completed.

In any event, Plato used Solon's notes for his own purposes, and embedded the story in two of his most important political dialogues, the *Critias* and the *Timaeus*. Written in 360 BC, these works were clearly intended to serve as illustration for the philosopher's own political ideas. He never completed the *Critias*, and it is worth noting that Benjamin Jowett, among others, argued that he had originally planned a third dialogue titled *Hermocrates*. After describing the origin of the world and mankind in *Timaeus*, as well as the allegorical perfect society of ancient Athens and its successful defense against an antagonistic Atlantis in

Critias, Plato may well have intended to make the strategy of the Hellenes during their conflict with the Persians a subject of discussion in the *Hermocrates.*

The *Timaeus* begins with an introduction, followed by an account of the creation and structure of the universe and ancient civilizations. In the introduction, Socrates muses about the perfect society, described in Plato's *Republic,* and wonders if he and his guests might recollect a story which exemplifies such a society. Critias mentions an allegedly historical tale that would make the perfect example, and follows by describing Atlantis. In his account, ancient Athens seems to represent the "perfect society" and Atlantis its opponent, representing the very antithesis of the "perfect" traits described in the *Republic.*

In the *Timaeus,* we read how Solon, wishing to lead the Egyptians onto the topic of history, recounts to them some of the earliest legends and traditions of Greece, of Phoroneus, the first man, of Deucalion, who survived the Flood and of the genealogies of his descendants. These tales were said to have elicited this response from the Egyptian priest: "Oh Solon, Solon. You Greeks are always children — there is not such a thing as an old Greek." To which Solon replied: "What mean you by this saying?" The priest at this point continued, giving Solon a brief lesson in natural history and the meaning of mythology:

> You are young in soul, every one of you. For therein you possess not a single belief that is ancient and derived from old tradition, nor yet one science that is hoary with age. And this is the cause thereof: There have been, and there will be, many and diverse destructions of mankind, of which the greatest are by fire and water, and lesser ones by countless other means. For in truth the story that is told in your country as well as ours, how once upon a time. Phaethon, son of Helios, yoked his father's chariot and, because he was unable to drive it along the course taken by his father burnt up all that was upon the earth, and himself perished by a thunderbolt — that story, as it is told, has the fashion of a legend, but the truth of it lies in the occurrence of a shift of the bodies in the heavens which move round the earth and a destruction of the things on the earth by fierce fire, which recurs at long intervals. At such times all they that dwell on the mountains, and in high and dry places, suffer destruction more than those who dwell near to rivers or the sea; and in our case the Nile, our saviour in other ways, saves us also at such times from this calamity by rising high. And when, on the other hand, the Gods purge the earth with a flood of waters, all the herdsmen and shepherds that are in the mountains are saved, but those in the cities of your land are swept into die sea by the streams; whereas in our country neither then nor at any other time does the water pour down over our fields from above, on the contrary it all tends naturally to swell up from below.
>
> Hence it is, for these reasons, that what is here preserved is reckoned to be the most ancient; the truth being that in every place where there is no excessive heat or cold to prevent it, there always exists some human stock, now more, now less in number. And if any event has occurred that is noble

or great or in any way conspicuous, whether it be in your country or in ours or in some other place of which we know by report, all such events are recorded from of old and preserved here in our temples; whereas your people and the others are but newly equipped, every time, with letters and all such arts as civilised States require; and when, after the usual interval of years, like a plague, the flood from heaven comes sweeping down afresh upon your people, it leaves none of you but the unlettered and the uncultured, so that you become young as ever, with no knowledge of all that happened in old times in this land or in your own. Certainly the genealogies which you related just now, Solon, concerning the peoples of your country, are little better than children's tales; for, in the first place, you remember but one deluge, though many had occurred previously; and next, you are ignorant of the fact that the noblest and most perfect race amongst men were born in the land where you now dwell, and from them both you yourself are sprung and the whole of your existing city, out of some little seed that chanced to be left over; but this has escaped your notice because for many generations the survivors died with no power to express themselves in writing. For verily at one time, Solon, before the greatest destruction by water, what is now the Athenian state was the bravest in war and supremely well organized also in other respects. It is said that it possessed the most splendid works of art, and the noblest polity of any nation under heaven of which we have heard tell.

The above passage, coming immediately before the first mention of Atlantis, is of immense importance to the whole question; for it presents to us a natural history in which cosmic catastrophes, caused by disturbances within the Solar System, really do happen. It is a cosmology which is of course nowadays completely rejected by the scholarly establishment. Yet the story of Atlantis is inexplicable without it; and if this Egyptian/Platonic explanation of mythology and cosmology is correct, then events like the destruction of Atlantis become entirely plausible.

Having spoken to Solon of his native country, the priest, as we learn from the *Critias*, then began to relate its illustrious past to the story of an aggressive and mighty empire which had sought to enslave the known world: Atlantis:

Many great and wonderful deeds are recorded of your state [Athens] in our histories. But one of them exceeds all the rest in greatness and valour. For these histories tell of a mighty power which unprovoked made an expedition against the whole of Europe and Asia, and to which your city put an end. This power came forth out of the Atlantic Ocean, for in those days the Atlantic was navigable; and there was an island situated in front of the straits which are by you called the Pillars of Heracles; the island was larger than Libya and Asia put together, and was the way to other islands, and from these you might pass to the whole of the opposite continent which surrounded the true ocean; for this sea which is within the Straits of Heracles is only a harbour, having a narrow entrance, but that other is a real sea, and the surrounding land may be most truly called a boundless continent. Now in this island of Atlantis there was a great and wonderful empire...

It is at this point that the description of the lost island begins. According to the narrator, in ancient times the gods had divided the earth so that each might own a lot; Poseidon being appropriately bequeathed the island of Atlantis. The island was described as larger than Libya and Asia (i.e., Asia Minor) put together, though the dimensions actually provided are of an island roughly the size of Ireland. We are told it was approximately 700 kilometers (435 miles) across, comprising mostly mountains in the northern portions and along the shore, and encompassing a great plain of an oblong shape in the south "extending in one direction three thousand *stadia* [about 600 km or 375 miles], but across the centre inland it was two thousand stadia [about 400 km or 250 miles]." Fifty stadia inland from the coast was a "mountain not very high on any side." Here there lived a native woman with whom Poseidon fell in love and who bore him five pairs of male twins. The eldest of these, Atlas, was made king of the entire island and the ocean (called the Atlantic Ocean in his honour), and was given the mountain of his birth and the surrounding area as his fiefdom. Atlas' twin Gadeirus or Eumelus in Greek, was awarded the extremity of the island towards the Pillars of Heracles. The other four pairs of twins — Ampheres and Evaemon, Mneseus and Autochthon, Elasippus and Mestor, and Azaes and Diaprepes — were also given "rule over many men, and a large territory."

We are then told that Poseidon carved the inland mountain where his love dwelt into a palace and enclosed it with three circular moats of increasing width, varying from one to three stadia and separated by rings of land proportional in size. The Atlanteans then built bridges northward from the mountain, making a route to the rest of the island. They dug a great canal to the sea, and alongside the bridges carved tunnels into the rings of rock so that ships could pass into the city around the mountain. They also carved docks from the rock walls of the moats. Every passage to the city was guarded by gates and towers, and a wall surrounded each of the city's rings. The walls were constructed of red, white and black rock quarried from the moats, and were covered with bronze, tin and orichalcum, respectively.

After this description, the narrative, put into the mouth of Critias, returns to the subject of the war waged by the Atlanteans against Athens. The Atlanteans are said to have made an unprovoked attack against all the nations who surrounded the shores of the Mediterranean. They conquered the parts of Libya (North Africa) as far as Egypt and the European continent as far as Tyrrhenia (Italy), and subjected the peoples of these regions to slavery. At this point the

Athenians led an alliance against the Atlanteans, and as the alliance disintegrated, stood alone against the invaders, liberating the occupied lands. "But later there occurred violent earthquakes and floods; and in a single day and night of misfortune all your warlike men in a body sank into the earth, and the island of Atlantis in like manner disappeared in the depths of the sea."

This then is the earliest and most complete account of the volcanic island-empire that in the ancient past occupied the middle of the Atlantic Ocean. But what are we to make of it?

OBJECTIONS TO PLATO

Aside from the oft-quoted charge that Plato was merely inventing the story of a lost civilization and its demise as a vehicle for expressing his own political views, the three main criticisms leveled at the above narrative are as follows:

1. Cataclysms of the type described by Plato, which sunk Atlantis to the bottom of the ocean in "a day and night of misfortune," simply do not happen.

2. In the epoch said by Plato to be that in which Atlantis flourished, 9,500 years before Christ, there were no high civilizations of any kind, Atlantean or otherwise, and certainly no city of Athens or Egyptian kingdom that could have opposed them.

3. Plato's is the only account of Atlantis that we possess and all others are ultimately based on his. Therefore, it probably was an invention of his.

None of these objections, we shall see, provide any serious argument against Plato and, on the contrary, there is much, very much, within his account which constitutes powerful circumstantial evidence in its favor. Before looking at this, however, the objections need to be answered.

Objection (a), which states that cataclysms do no happen, is an immense topic in itself, and shall be examined in the two chapters to follow.

Objection (b), which concerns the chronology of civilization, is of crucial importance for a number of reasons. The Atlantean narrative will never be properly understood unless this question is dealt with properly. It is true, of course, that Plato places Atlantis sometime in the tenth millennium BC; and it is equally true that no civilizations of any kind existed at that time. Many modern investigators, beginning with Ignatius Donnelly, have ruined their argument by taking Plato and his Egyptian sources too much on their word on this issue. But we should note, to begin with, that it is highly likely that the priest really did claim a 9,000-year gap between his own time and that of Atlantis. The Egyptians, as well as the other civilizations of the ancient Near East, were in fact notorious for claiming vastly long histories. Just over a century after Solon, the Greek historian

Herodotus was told by another priest that the Egyptians could count three hundred and forty-five generations of kings from the beginning of their history. Allowing about 25 years to a generation, this would mean that the first pharaoh had reigned around 8,625 years before Herodotus, i.e., around 9,000 BC. If we accord 30 years to a generation, which is more in line with what the Egyptians might have had in mind, then we arrive at an estimate of 10,350 years before Herodotus! In like manner, we now know that the ancient peoples of Mesopotamia, the Sumerians and Babylonians, claimed they could trace their histories back many thousands of years, much longer even than claimed by the Egyptians.

The estimates made by ancient peoples regarding the lengths of their histories are thus now known to be fictitious, and treated as such by all scholars. In saying that Atlantis launched a war against Egypt and Greece around 9,500 BC, the priest was claiming an equally long span for Egypt's history; thereby augmenting the venerability and priority of his own culture. Modern historians know that no civilizations of any kind existed at that time; and it is equally clear, from the description provided by Plato, that Atlantis, as well as her Greek and Egyptian opponents and contemporaries, was a Bronze Age, probably an Early Bronze Age, society. As such, we must ignore the figure of 9,000 years. It is utterly meaningless and misleading. Nor is there any need, as has been done, to argue that Solon somehow added an extra zero and turned 900 into 9,000. (Mathematically there were, of course, no zeros at that time, yet people did think in terms of hundreds and thousands). Thus it has been argued that Atlantis was destroyed 900 years before Solon; i.e., around 1,460 BC. But such a solution is unnecessary. The priest almost certainly did speak of 9,000 years to Solon, as we may judge from the experience of Herodotus, and thus attempts to shear a zero off the figure are meaningless. The simple and most logical solution is that the figure represents nothing but an illustration of the Egyptians' complete lack of understanding of historical timescales.

But, if such be the case, then we are led to the question: If Atlantis did exist, in what era should it be placed?

Here we are involved in a question of fundamental importance. Ignatius Donnelly, as well as a host of imitators, could point to numerous parallels between the cultures of the Old World and those of the New as proof of an early transatlantic link. Such precise parallels between Egypt on the one hand, and Peru/Mexico on the other, as dragon-worship, pyramid-building, mummification, etc., seemed to speak eloquently of an early link between the two worlds, and a very real mutual influence. Yet Donnelly's detractors were quick to point out that no one, neither Egyptians nor Peruvians, were building pyramids or practicing mummification in the era designated by Donnelly as that of Atlantean civilization, the tenth millennium BC. If Atlantis was destroyed around 9,500 BC, it could not be invoked as a link between the civilizations of the two worlds, which only commenced building pyramids in the third millennium BC (in the case of Egypt) and the first millennium BC (in the case of Mexico and Peru).

What then is the solution? The Atlantis described by Plato, with its worship of Poseidon (the god of earthquakes) and its interaction with Egypt and Greece, was clearly a Bronze Age culture. If we look for Atlantis in archaeology we must look to the Bronze Age. But in suggesting that Atlantis belonged to the Bronze Age we are also implicitly suggesting that cataclysms of the type described in Plato's dialogues occurred in the Bronze Age. The two cannot be separated. Even worse, if Atlantis was real, and if it was located in the place described by Plato — the middle of the Atlantic Ocean — and if it was anything like the size Plato claimed, then we are also suggesting that during the Bronze Age, during an age of world history not too far distant, immense catastrophes of nature occurred; catastrophes involving massive movements of the earth's tectonic plates, which could consign very large landmasses to the depths of the ocean in a very short time.

Now, it is well-known that great natural catastrophes did occur during the Bronze Age. The French archaeologist Claude Schaeffer for example counted a total of six, which, in his opinion, had devastated the entire Near East during the Bronze Ages. These disasters, he said, were of such violence that "compared with the vastness of these all-embracing crises and their profound effects, the exploits of conquerors ... would appear only insignificant."[1] The violence of catastrophes during the Bronze Age in the Aegean region is now widely documented, and the eruption of the volcanic island of Thera, which left an enormous volcanic crater, or caldera, has led to widespread speculation on the part of some archaeologists that this could have been the historical event behind the Atlantis legend.

We shall discuss the natural catastrophes of the Bronze Age at a later point, and shall identify the proper chronology within which these events should be placed. For the moment, however, we shall confine ourselves to noting, in passing, that the identification of Thera, or Crete, with Atlantis, flies in the face of what Plato actually said and completely robs the story of its logic. We do not doubt that the catastrophic earthquakes and volcanic eruptions discovered by archaeologists within the ruins of Bronze Age Aegean cities were contemporary with the catastrophic earthquakes that destroyed Atlantis. But they cannot have been the same events, a fact which is proved, beyond all reasonable doubt, by an overwhelming body of evidence, much of it to be presented in the present volume.

---

[1] Claude Schaeffer, *Stratigraphie comparée et chronologie de l'Asie Occidentale (IIIe et IIe millénaires)* (Oxford, 1948) p. 565.

If the Old and New World parallels described by Donnelly and others do hint at early transatlantic links (as the present writer does), and if those links were by way of Atlantis and the archipelago of islands connected to it (as the present writer believes), then an Atlantis in the Aegean makes no sense at all.

And it is just at this point that we must mention the powerful circumstantial evidence found in Plato's account which clearly supports the veracity of the story. Consider the following: Plato said that: (a) The island lay due west of Gibraltar, presumably near the middle of the Atlantic. (b) The island was volcanic and it contained many hot springs. (c) From the island there stretched an archipelago of smaller islands leading to a continent on the far side of the ocean. (d) The Atlanteans visited this continent and interacted with its peoples.

Each of these statements is astonishing in its accuracy and utterly inexplicable if Atlantis was a fiction deriving solely from Plato's imagination. For sure enough, we now know (though we didn't until the 15th century AD), that due west of Gibraltar, in the middle of the Atlantic, there is indeed a volcanic region, including to this day a small archipelago of islands, the Azores, with their own hot springs. We know the Azores exist, because the Portuguese found them in the 15th century. But where did Plato get this knowledge? Next, Plato tells us quite unequivocally, that beyond Atlantis, on the other side of the ocean, there lay an enormous continent. We now know, of course, that there is an enormous continent (two actually) on the other side of the Atlantic, because Christopher Columbus stumbled upon it in 1492. But how did Plato know about it? Finally, we know that many cultural features found in the ancient cultures of the Americas show clear evidence of influence from the Old World. (This evidence, incidentally, has now received definitive confirmation by the discovery of West European DNA within pre-Columbian Native American populations, of which topic more will be said at a later date). But how did Plato know this?

These factors, not often considered in the Atlantis debate, provide very powerful circumstantial evidence, even on their own, that Plato was talking about something real. Even without the other supportive evidence which will be presented as this study proceeds, it would constitute a very powerful argument in favor of Plato and his story.

LOST ISLANDS IN EUROPEAN TRADITION

The third objection to Plato is that he is ultimately the sole source of our knowledge of Atlantis and that, one way or another, all subsequent accounts of the island civilization depend upon him. This idea, asserted again and again in mainstream academic literature, is quite simply untrue. The fact is that every people of Western Europe had a legend of a sunken island in the ocean. True, they did not call it Atlantis, but this is almost beside the point. Belief in a great island which had formerly stood in the Atlantic Ocean was widespread throughout the continent, as well as in North Africa; and this belief owed nothing whatsoever to Plato or his writings.

In addition to these legends, which we shall examine shortly, there are tantalizing hints from Greek tradition itself, from sources earlier than Plato, of a mysterious sunken island in the Atlantic Ocean.

Fig. 1. Phoenician coins from Tyre, showing the Pillars of Hercules (Melkarth) and the Garden of the Hesperides, with the sacred tree guarded by the dragon Ladon (Lotan).

The first hint comes in Homer, about two or three centuries before Plato. In his *Odyssey*, Homer has the hero Odysseus shipwrecked on an island named Ogygia, an island inhabited by the nymph Calypso. The latter is described as the "daughter of Atlas," which would suggest a connection with Atlantis, as does the fact that Hesiod, coming shortly after Homer, describes Calypso as the daughter of Oceanus and Tethys. Calypso's island home is described by Homer as rich and fertile, and Odysseus loiters happily there in a cave with his semi-divine host for seven years. The name of the island, Ogygia, further reinforces the Atlantis connection, since Ogyges of Greek mythology was a king who reigned during a great deluge. It needs to be stressed here that the whole story of the *Odyssey* stands apart from the rest of Greek tradition. Whereas archaeologists found abundant confirmation of Homer in the other sites mentioned by him, Ithaca, the home of Odysseus, stands strangely apart. "Other mythological seats," says one writer, "led archaeologists to the discovery of ancient cultures, which made it possible to establish the historical basis of the saga; Ithaca proved to be a false trail."[1] Indeed,

---

1   Commentary by I. M. Trotsky on Russian translation by V. A. Zhukovsky, of Homer's *Odyssey* (Moscow, 1935) p. xix.

for centuries it has been understood that the *Odyssey* has nothing to do with the Trojan War, or with Greece for that matter. The whole tale has an altogether more ancient, more mythic quality. Whilst the story of Troy could almost be taken as normal history, the story of Odysseus' adventures could never be taken as such. All the evidence points to it being an account of a journey through the North Atlantic; a traveler's tale, or the journey of a non-Greek and probably pre-Greek hero, which Homer grafted onto the life of a hero who fought at Troy. In the words of one authority, "Very probably...the story of Odysseus contains echoes of a more ancient historical reality than the culture of the Mycenaean period."[1]

Even in antiquity there was a general understanding that much, if not all, of the *Odyssey* took place in the Atlantic. Homer himself mentions again and again that his hero had been lost on the wide abyss of the "Ocean Stream," whilst Plutarch mentioned that Ogygia lay five days' sail to the west of Britain,[2] and Tacitus referred to the common belief in his time that the voyage was in the Atlantic.[3] If, as Plutarch says, Ogygia was five days' sail to the west of Britain, it is worth noting that there is no dry land in this position nowadays, which is roughly in the region of the North Atlantic Ridge. Interestingly, he goes on to claim that beyond Ogygia there were other islands, and that, further on, one "comes to a great continent, which surrounds the ocean." Is this, we must ask, the second reference (after Plato) in western literature to America? The remoteness and isolation of Ogygia is emphasized on more than one occasion. Thus the god Hermes, sent by Zeus to the island, travels there only reluctantly: "Zeus sent me here, I came against my will; who would choose to cross such an immense expanse of sea? There is not even a town of mortals around here (*Odyssey*, v, 99-102). This remoteness is confirmed by Odysseus, who says to Calypso; "You want me to cross the fearful immense abyss of the sea in a raft" (*Odyssey*, v, 174-75).

The North Atlantic setting is implicitly accepted even by modern commentators. Thus Robert Graves, a writer averse to placing any of the action in Greek myths outside the Mediterranean, nevertheless casually remarked on Odysseus' encounter with the cannibal Laestrygonians, whose homeland, named Telepylus ("distant gate"), "lies in the extreme north of Europe, the Land of the Midnight Sun, where the incoming shepherd hails the outgoing shepherd. To this cold region, 'at the back of the North Wind', belongs the Wandering, or Clashing, Rocks, namely ice-flows, and also the Cimmerians, whose at noon supplemented their midnight sun in June.... The Laestrygonians ('of a very harsh race') were perhaps Norwegian fiord-dwellers of whose barbarous behaviour the amber mer-

---

1 Ibid. p. xx.
2 Plutarch, *De facie in orbe lunae apparet*, xxvi.
3 Tacitus, *Germania*, iii, 2.

chants were warned on their visits to Bornholm and the Southern Baltic coast."[1] The incident with Scylla and Charybdis, the terrible whirlpool, has for centuries been linked to the mighty maelstrom (Moskoestrom), the giant whirlpool at the southern tip of the Lofoten Islands.[2] The same impression is gained by Odysseus' experiences after the encounter with the Laestrygonians, when he arrives in the island of the enchantress Circe. There are strong clues that this lay north of the Arctic Circle. Thus for example Odysseus mentions that on the island he could "perceive neither where darkness is nor where dawn is, nor where the sun shining on men goes down underground nor where it rises" (Odyssey, x, 190-192). Furthermore, his reference to the "early rising" dawn's "dances" has been taken by many commentators as a description of the sun's behavior as it prepares to rise again after the long Arctic night. It quite literally does a circular "dance" round the entire horizon.

If the voyage of Odysseus was originally undertaken by a western hero, and if his legend is older than Troy, we might look with renewed interest at the lands and peoples he encounters in the ocean. After leaving Ogygia, the hero sets out for the land of the Sea Kings, or Phaecians. Their island Scheria is eighteen days' sail from Ogygia. The details of that journey, such as the information that the hero had the constellations Auriga, Pleiades and Ursa Major constantly on his left, and the latter revolved overhead, never descending to the horizon, seem to indicate that Ogygia must have been in the north-western part of the Atlantic. On these grounds, O. Rudbeck sited it between the 51st and 64th parallel.[3] From there the hero clearly sailed east for eighteen days, during which time he encountered no land. An Atlantic setting is clearly indicated. His next landfall, the island of Scheria, is of the greatest interest. Here he encounters a people — the Phaecians — who are recognized "masters of the sea." Their ships are said to be the swiftest on earth. They are without peer in their knowledge of the sea. Furthermore, they inhabit a land subject to volcanic and seismic disturbance. Angry at the assistance they had given Odysseus, Poseidon, the "Shaker of Earth," threatens to "surround their city with a range of high mountains." This in fact is a threat he carries out. Furthermore, there is an astonishing similarity between the stronghold of the Phaecians and the main metropolis of Atlantis, as described in Plato's *Critias*. So clear are the parallels, in fact, that more than one commentator

---

1 R. Graves, *The Greek Myths*, Vol. 2 (Penguin, 1955) 170.4.

2 Scandinavian writers have long identified Homer's whirlpool Charybdis with the Maelstrom. Thus Olaus Magnus' *Sea Chart* of the 16th century names the Maelstrom "horrenda Charybdis," whilst Norwegian writer Jonas Ramus of the 18th century located Scylla and Charybdis near the Maelstrom.

3 O. Rudbeck, *Atlantica, sive Manheim very Japhete posterorum sedes ac patria* (Uppsala, 1675).

has suggested Plato copied Homer or used him to "fill-out" his description of the Atlantean capital.

In the scheme which I shall be proposing in the present volume, the island of Atlantis sank during the Early Bronze or Copper (Chalcolithic) Age, disappearing only about a century or a century and a half before the Trojan War. Thus it is quite possible, even probable, that the Odysseus story is a hero-tale dating from before the destruction of the Atlantic civilization. But who then was the original "Odysseus"? That he was not Greek is fairly obvious. That he belongs to a western, Atlantic, culture, is equally clear. That his story included a detailed knowledge of the farthest and most inhospitable regions of the North Atlantic is also evident. We ask ourselves: What nation from before the time of Homer (7th or 6th century BC) could have sailed the entire Atlantic, even as far north as the Arctic Circle, and could have incorporated an intimate knowledge of these regions in the tale of one of their heroes? And what nation of master-sailors would have equally been in contact with the peoples of the Mediterranean, transmitting their legends and their heroes to the peoples of the Aegean?

Other hints in the same direction are found throughout Greek legend. Thus for example, in his Eleventh Labor Hercules (Herakles) fetches the golden apples of the Hesperides, the "daughters of the evening," who dwell in an enchanted garden or island far to the west, near to Mount Atlas. The Hesperides were actually the daughters of the titan Atlas, and it seems that their land, connected to the mythic Island of the Blessed, belonged to him. Tradition said that Hercules asked Atlas to fetch the apples from the tree that grew in the garden. He did so, and in the meantime the son of Zeus supported the sky on his own shoulders. Upon returning with the apples, Atlas was said to have been unwilling to resume his task of holding up the sky, but was tricked by Hercules into doing so.

The despoiling of the Garden or Island of the Hesperides by Atlas, who "knew the depths of the ocean" could well have been an allusion to the island's destruction. This is made all the more likely when we note that certain features of the Garden are strikingly reminiscent of Atlantis as described in Plato. Thus Atlas was said to have constructed a wall around the Garden, to protect the Tree, just as Poseidon surrounded the central shrine of Atlantis with walls and channels. Furthermore, the dragon Ladon, who guards the sacred Tree in the Garden of the Hesperides is identical in name and nature to the goddess Leda or Latone, the mother of Apollo. Yet she seems to be identifiable too with Cleito, the goddess who inhabited the sacred precinct in Atlantis and with whom Poseidon sired the ten kings of the country.

It is interesting to note that Phoenician coins from the fifth century BC onwards show the Garden of the Hesperides, complete with the entwined dragon, which the peoples of the region named Lotan, between twin pillars, evidently the Pillars of Hercules. The Phoenicians established many colonies in Spain, from which region they journeyed to the "tin isles" of Britain; and there is little doubt that this trade in metals and metal ores was one of the primary sources of Phoenicia's wealth. So much did the symbol of twin pillars with an entwined serpent become associated with money and coinage, that it passed into common usage in Spain, whence many centuries later it was taken across the Atlantic, to become the symbol of America's currency, the dollar ($).

Another of Hercules' Labors, the Tenth, also centers upon a mysterious Atlantic island which may be yet another reference to Atlantis. In this Labor, Hercules fetched the famous cattle of Geryon from Erytheia, an island near the Ocean stream. Geryon, the owner of the cattle, was the king of Tartessus in Spain, and reputedly the strongest man alive. Geryon's shambling red cattle, beasts of marvelous beauty, were guarded by the herdsman Eurytion and the two-headed watchdog Orthrus, formerly the property of Atlas, a beast born of Typhon and Echidne. It was during the performance of this task that Hercules erected the two pillars, Abila and Calpe, on either side of the Strait of Gibraltar that henceforth bore his name. We are told that whilst performing this deed, the hero was oppressed by the excessive heat of the sun. Stringing his bow, he let fly an arrow at Helios, who protested loudly. Hercules apologized to the god for his ill-temper and Helios, not to be outdone in courtesy, lent the hero his golden goblet, in which he sailed to Erytheia.[1] It was said that the titan Oceanus made the goblet pitch violently upon the waves and Hercules again drew his bow, which frightened Oceanus into calming the sea.

The cosmogonic component of these myths needs no stressing.

On his arrival at the island, Hercules ascended Mount Abas, where he was attacked by the dog Orthrus. The beast was immediately struck lifeless by the hero's great club, whilst the dog's keeper, the herdsman Eurytion, met a similar fate. Geryon himself fell to one of Hercules' magical arrows.

The whereabouts of Erytheia, whose name means "red," has been disputed since antiquity. Some located it beyond the Ocean Stream; others said it was due west of Lusitania (modern Portugal). It is generally believed that the island was named "Red" on account of the color of the setting sun, yet we recall here that in Plato's story, Atlantis, which was located to the west of Portugal, was distinguished by its red and black rocks.

We would be remiss if we failed to mention the account of Aelian (*Varia Historia*, iii, 18), who, although coming after Plato, refers to a work of Theopompus

---

1 See Apollodorus, ii, 5, 10; also Pherecydes, quoted by Athenaeus, xi, 39; and Servius on Virgil's *Aeneid*, vii, 622 and viii, 300.

(400 BC), in which there is mentioned an interview between Midas, King of Phrygia, and Silenus the satyr. Silenus was said to have told Midas of a great continent "beyond the Atlantic, larger than Asia, Europe, and Libya together." The land was inhabited by a race of stalwart men called Meropes who dwelt in large cities and enjoyed a high level of culture. They were persuaded that their country alone was a continent. Out of curiosity however some of them crossed the ocean and visited the Hyperboreans (identified by the Greeks either as Britain or, more probably, Scandinavia), but were so disgusted by the low level of culture they encountered that they returned immediately to their own land.

Although this story seems like an independent corroboration of the Atlantis myth, it has to be admitted that it too may be traced to Solon. It has been pointed out that Silenus, the satyr who relates the story to Midas, has a name very similar to Solon, and Robert Graves suggested that the account might owe its origin to a satirical comedy by the dramatist Thespis. We know that Solon had quarreled with Thespis who, in his plays about Dionysus, put ludicrous speeches apparently full of topical allusions into the mouths of satyrs. Solon was said to have asked: "Are you not alarmed, Thespis, to tell so many lies to so large an audience?" According to Graves, Aelian, our source for the story, "seems to have had access at second or third hand to a comedy by Thespis, or his pupil Pratinas, ridiculing Solon for the Utopian lies told in the epic poem [i.e., Solon's *Atlantikos*], and presenting him as Silenus, wandering footloose about Egypt and Asia Minor."[1] If this is correct, and it seems likely that it is, then we must discount Aelian's and Theopompus' story as a source independent of the tradition utilized by Plato. Both go back to Solon. Nevertheless, it does offer very powerful evidence that Plato at least did not invent the story, and that he was telling the truth when he said it came from Solon. Furthermore, it should be noted that the Aelian/Theopompus version contains striking details which are not contained in Plato, such as an apparent allusion to the use of narcotic plants by the inhabitants of the Lost Continent, and by the assertion that the warlike inhabitants of the region — named Maximos — used only clubs and weapons tipped with stone. Both these were in fact characteristic of the natives of the Americas.

Interestingly, Graves remarks on the parallels between Aelian's Atlantis and the Irish legend of Tir na nÓg (the Land of Youth), the mystical land in the western ocean where Niamh of the Golden Hair took Oisin and whence he returned centuries later on a visit to Ireland. Oisin was apparently disgusted by the degeneracy of his own people compared to Niamh's (they were much smaller than the inhabitants of Tir na nÓg) and bitterly regretted having come back.

---

1 R. Graves, op. cit., Vol. 1, 83.5.

Perhaps our most arresting information comes from the Greek writer Marcellus, whose now lost *Ethiopic History* provided an account of Atlantis which claimed to be entirely independent of Plato. Some of Marcellus' material was used by the Neoplatonist Proclus in his *Commentaries on the Timaeus of Plato*. He writes:

> That such and so great an island once existed, is evident from what is said by certain historians respecting what pertains to the external sea [the Atlantic]. For according to them, there were seven islands in that sea, in their times, sacred to Persephone, and also three others of immense extent, one of which was sacred to Pluto, another to Ammon, and the middle (or second) of these to Poseidon, the magnitude of which was a thousand stadia. They also add that the inhabitants of it preserved the remembrance of their ancestors, or the Atlantic island that existed there, and was truly prodigiously great; for which many periods had domination over all islands in the Atlantic Sea, and was itself likewise sacred to Poseidon. These things, therefore, Marcellus writes in his *Ethiopic History*.[1]

The above Greek allusions to Atlantis are important only insofar as they apparently predate Plato and can be proved to owe nothing to him. Nevertheless, they provide us with little information, and it is to the peoples of Western Europe, as we might expect, who we must look if we wish to fill in more of the details. All of the peoples of the Atlantic seaboard, without exception, possessed a legend of a lost island. It is true that these stories, in the form they have come down to us, are highly mythologized; yet this is to be expected, given the fact that they were handed down by word of mouth for many generations before being committed to writing. And even allowing for such shortcomings, it is evident that by their very existence they provide powerful independent corroboration of Plato.

Some of the best-known stories are from the Celtic fringe. Indeed, knowledge of a lost land was inherent all through Celtic literature and history. Since the conquest and colonization of the Celts by Romans and then Germans, much of their lore has been lost. Nevertheless, they did survive on the Atlantic coasts, where the Irish, Welsh, and Bretons all preserved stories of a sunken island.

Irish legend named the lost island Hy-Brasil, (from *Hy*, or Ó, meaning "island" and *Brasil* or *Breasal*, meaning "mighty" and "beautiful") located somewhere in the Atlantic. This island, which is said to have been named after a primeval king of Ireland, Bressal, was believed in local folklore to become visible once every seven years. It is closely related to another mythical land of the west, Tir na nÓg, the "Land of the Young," a mysterious region across the ocean inhabited by fairy-like immortals. As related above, Tir na nÓg plays a central role in one of the best-

---

1 Proclus, *Commentaries on the Timaeus of Plato* (trans. A. E. Taylor, London, 1820).

known Irish myths, that of Oisin, who resides in the magical land for many centuries without growing old.

Perhaps the most thorough description of Hy Brasil is provided by Irish historian O'Flaherty, writing in 1685. Here we find a vague memory of a land that once existed, a lost paradise somewhere in the ocean, a paradise which periodically may still appear.

> From the Isles of Arran and the west continent often appears visible that enchanted island called O'Brasail and, in Irish, Beg Ara.

> Whether it be real and firm land kept hidden by the special ordnance of God, or the terrestrial paradise, or else some illusion of airy clouds appearing on the surface of the sea, or the craft of evil spirits, is more than our judgments can pound out.

> There is now living, Murrough O'Ley, who imagines he was himself personally in O'Brasail for two days and saw out of it the Isles of Arran, Golam Head, Iross-beg Hill, and other places on the western continent which he was acquainted with. The manner of it he relates, that being in Iross-Ainhagh, in the south side of the Barony of Ballynahinshy, about nine leagues from Galway by sea in the month of April, A.D. 1668, going alone from one village to another in a melancholy humour upon some discontent of his wife's (!) he was encountered by two or three strangers and forcibly carried by a boat into O'Brasail, as such as were within told him — and they could speak both English and Irish. He was ferried out hoodwinked in a boat, as he imagines, till he was left on the seaside by Galway, where he lay in a friend's house for some days after being very desperately ill, and knows not how he came to be there.

> In the western ocean, five or six leagues from the continent there is a sand bank about thirty fathoms deep in the sea. It is called in Irish, Imaire Bay, and in English, the Cod-fishing Bank. From this bank about twenty years ago, a boat was blown southwards by night; next day about noon the occupants spyed land so near them that they could see sheep within it, and yet durst not, for fear of illusions, touch shore, imagining it was O'Brasail, and they were two days coming back towards home.

> Some few generations ago, the crew of a fishing boat passing an island which they did not know, landed thereon to refresh themselves. They had no sooner landed than a man appeared and told them they had no business there as the island was enchanted. They therefore returned to the boat, but as they were going away the islanders gave one of them a book with directions not to look into it for seven years. He complied with the request and when he opened and read the book he was able to practice surgery and psychic with great success. This man's name was Lee, and the book remained as an heirloom with his descendants.

The reader should note the strange transformation of the island into a mythical land of fairy enchantment, a land whose inhabitants possessed secret lore unknown to the modern world. Precisely the same has been done with Plato's Atlantis by modern proponents of various New Age theories.

Nevertheless, as we shall see, the belief that the inhabitants of the mystic lost isle possessed arcane knowledge has a very ancient pedigree.

The rich body of ancient and medieval Irish literature is in fact replete with allusions to a lost island. Thus in the romance of the *Fate of the Children of Turenn*, the sons of Turenn were condemned, for the slaying of Cian, to procure certain magical objects. Setting sail in Manannan's (the Sea God's) boat, they come first to the Garden of Hisberna (evidently the Hesperides) where they took the shape of hawks and seized upon the golden apples which grew there. After other adventures, they landed in the realm of Asol, king of the Golden Pillars, from whom they received seven magical swine. It would appear that the "Golden Pillars" are those of Hercules, whilst the name Turenn looks suspiciously like a variant of "Atlan" ('l' and 'r' being readily confused, we might easily have Tulenn).

The saga of the "Voyage of Maildun" also refers to a number of magical islands in the Atlantic. One of the first encountered by Maildun and his crew was the "Terraced Isle of Birds." This was "a large, high island, with terraces all round it, rising one behind another," and heavily populated with bright-plumaged birds.

Welsh and Cornish tradition also preserve their own stories of sunken lands, and it is evident that Arthur's mystical island of the west, Avalon, must be more or less identical to the Irish Tir na nÓg and Hy Brasil. Incidentally, Avalon (meaning "of apples") bears close comparison with the Greek Garden of the Hesperides, where, as we have seen, there grew a magical apple tree. Hercules, with the help of the titan Atlas, stole these apples, a feat we shall return to at a later stage. In Welsh legend, as opposed to medieval English and French, Arthur is clearly a Celtic deity identifiable, as I have demonstrated elsewhere in detail with Artos, "the Bear," a Celtic version of Hercules, who originally was portrayed with a bearskin over his head and shoulders and holding in his right hand an oaken club.[1] In these accounts, Arthur and his companions visit a mysterious region named Caer Sidi, the circular or revolving Castle. In an ancient poem attributed to Taliesin, Caer Sidi is clearly located under the ocean:

> Perfect is my chair in Caer Sidi:
> Plague and age hurt him not who's in it
> They know, Manawydan and Pryderi.
> Three organs round a fire sing before it,
> And above its parts are ocean's stream,
> And the abundant well above it,

---

[1] See my *Arthur and Stonehenge* (Domra Publications, 2001).

Sweeter than white wine the drink in it.[1]

In the medieval Arthurian legend of Peredur, the hero stumbles upon the Revolving Castle, Caer Sidi, though this time it is portrayed above the ocean, in a well-forested and fertile paradisial region. At some point, however, the circular fortress begins to revolve.

> And they rode through the wild forests, and from one forest to another until they arrived on clear ground outside the forest. And then they beheld a castle coming within their view on level ground in the middle of a meadow; and around the castle flowed a large river, and inside the castle they beheld large spacious halls with windows large and fair. They drew nearer towards the castle and they beheld the castle turning with greater speed than the fastest wind they had ever known.... At the gates were lions, in iron chains, roaring and howling so violently that one might fancy the forest and the castle uprooted by them.[2]

Lewis Spence was of the opinion that this circular citadel, clearly depicted as under the ocean in other accounts, with its surrounding circular moats, may have been a memory of the great settlement of Atlantis herself, described by Plato as being located on a small hill sacred to Poseidon and surrounded by concentric circles of walls and canals.[3] The sudden revolving of the castle, together with the earth-shaking roars of the lions, seemed to suggest Caer Sidi's destruction in seismic disaster.

Welsh tradition is full of references to catastrophic disasters which saw the submergence of large tracts of land. Thus for example in the *Book of Caradoc of Nantgarvan*, which dates from the twelfth century, are found certain of the verses known as the "Triads of Britain." Under the caption of "The Three Awful Events of the Isle of Britain" we find that these consisted of:

> First, the bursting of the lake of waters, and the overwhelming of the face of all lands, so that all mankind were drowned, excepting Dwyvan and Dwyvach, who escaped in a naked vessel (without sails) and from them the Isle of Britain was re-peopled.

> The second was the consternation of the tempestuous fire, when the Earth split asunder, to Annwn (the lower region) and the greatest part of all living was consumed.

---

1 Quoted from Lewis Spence, *History of Atlantis* (London, 1927) p. 132.
2 Ibid.
3 Spence was of the opinion that many of the cities of the ancient Mediterranean, as well as the monuments of the Atlantic west, were inspired by the Atlantean citadel. He cites Carthage as an important example, and there is little doubt that monuments such as Stonehenge, with its concentric standing-stone circles, are reminiscent of the general outline of Plato's metropolis.

> The third was the scorching summer, when the woods and plants were set on fire by the intense heat of the Sun, and multitudes of men and beasts and kinds of birds, and reptiles, and trees, and plants were irrecoverably lost.[1]

The reader will note here the striking parallels between these Welsh verses and the words spoken to Solon by the Egyptian priest, where we heard of successive destructions of the earth by fire and water. The Welsh told of a large area to the west of the country, Cantref Gwaelod, submerged in a terrible catastrophe. In various accounts, the deluge is caused by a lake overflowing when the waters of a bottomless well were unleashed; a legend which has its parallels in Irish tradition. Thus an Irish legend told how Lough Neagh overflowed, deluging the whole earth. This has a parallel in the Welsh story of Gwydno's plain. The name of the woman who had charge of the well in the Irish story was Liban "which is in Welsh Llion, and occurs in the Welsh account of the deluge resulting from the bursting of Llyn Llion, or Llion's Lake. Further, it is this lady's name probably in the same one of its forms, or a derivative from it, that meets us in Malory's *Liones*."[2] The genius of this country, we are told, is Dame Liones, the owner of Castle Perilous, hard by the Isle of Avalon. In Spence's words, "The name Liones or Lyonesse, of course, equates with that of the mythical lake, Llyn Llion, which was supposed to have overwhelmed the world in its bursting...."[3] The connection with both Avalon and the Cornish Lyonesse, the sunken land, is extremely important. According to Sir John Rhys, in Wales "each mere [lake] is supposed to have been formed by the subsidence of a city, whose bells may even now be at times heard merrily pealing." Lewis Spence comments: "That the memory of a submerged land should be so universal in Wales surely indicates a tradition most ancient and deep-seated."[4]

We shall have more to say of these Welsh accounts at a later stage; suffice for the moment to note that all of them place the catastrophic events they describe no more than eight or nine centuries before the dawn of the Christian Age.

The Bretons too had a legend of a sunken land, that of Ys. The earliest written Breton records date of course only from the medieval period, so there is much Christian imagery and localization of the story. Nevertheless, its primeval pedigree is all too apparent:

> According to the legend, Ys was built below sea level, protected from inundation by a dam. The only keys of the gate in the dam were held by

---

1 Rev. Edward Davies, *Celtic Researches* (London, 1804); cited from Lewis Spence, op. cit. pp. 122-3.

2 Sir John Rhys, as quoted by Lewis Spence, Ibid. p. 136.

3 Ibid. p. 137.

4 Ibid. p. 123.

Gradlon, but Satan made Dahut steal them and give them to him. He then opened the gate and Ys was flooded. In some versions of the story, Satan was sent by God to punish the city, whose inhabitants were becoming decadent. Other versions of the story tell that Dahut stole the keys either at her lover's request or in order to open the gates of the city to let her lover in. The only survivor was the King Gradlon, who was advised to abandon his daughter and Saint Winwaloe by Saint Winwaloe himself. Everyone who lived in the city died, while the souls of the dead children were then swallowed by the ocean as a punishment. According to the legend, one can still hear the bells of Ys, warning of a storm. Gradlon then founded Quimper and on his death, a statue representing him on horseback looking in the direction of Ys was erected on the Saint Corentin Cathedral and still stands there. Bretons said that Ys was the most wonderful city in the world, and that Lutèce was renamed Paris after Ys was destroyed, because "Par-Is" in Breton means "Similar to Ys."[1]

According to Breton tradition, king Gradlon actually rode out of the sea on a white horse, which makes him identical to Trevelyan in the Cornish legend of Lyonesse who similarly escaped the destruction of that lost region on a white horse.

The peoples of France, Spain and Portugal also, of course, had their legends of a lost island. To the French, the mythic country was known as l'Île Verte and to the Portuguese, *Ilha Verde* ("the Green Isle"). Spain too had its Antillia, or Isle of the Seven Cities, a rectangular country of the far west which appears not just in story but in the maps of cartographers of the fourteenth and fifteenth centuries. Antillia played the role somewhat of Avalon in British legend, for it was said that Roderick, the last Gothic king of Spain, had there found a refuge from the conquering Moors, remaining, like Arthur, in his island paradise until Spain needed him again. It may well be that Antillia represents a corruption of "Atlanta".

We cannot forget, at this point, that the Iberian Peninsula was part of the Roman Empire for over five centuries, during which time its culture was thoroughly Latinized. As such, we should almost expect the native stories of a lost or sunken or enchanted island to be influenced by or even subsumed into Graeco-Roman legends of the same thing. And this of course is what we do, to a certain degree, find. Medieval Spanish accounts are full of allusions to the "Island of the Blessed" or the "Island of the Hesperides," both of which are clearly influenced by classical ideas. Nevertheless, we should not delude ourselves into imagining that such stories were not genuinely Spanish. In fact, the idea of a lost land in the ocean was central to Iberian culture, and, as we shall see, greatly influenced the phenomenal movement of exploration launched from the Peninsula during the fourteenth and fifteenth centuries.

---

1 "Ys," in Wikipedia. http://en.wikipedia.org/wiki/Ys.

From the beginning of the fourteenth century, Spanish and Portuguese cartographers were producing maps of the Atlantic showing a mysterious landmass variously described as the "Island of the Blessed," "Antillia," "Brasil," or "San Borondón." The last of these, like "Brasil," was influenced by Irish tradition, and it is clear that San Borondón was connected with the Irish story of Saint Brendan and his legendary journey across the Atlantic. Yet Saint Brendan is admitted to be more or less a Christianization of the Celtic god Bran, who obviously also visited a lost island. This appropriation of Celtic gods by early Christians is a well-recognized phenomenon, and a whole host of supposed medieval Irish saints are now known to be Celtic deities. An Irish monk named Brendan may indeed have made epic journeys by sea (the seafaring abilities of the early Irish took them at least as far as Iceland and perhaps even Greenland), but in every detail, the story of Brendan, who meets fire-breathing monsters and floating crystal pillars, is clearly derived from pre-Christian myth. In the medieval *Book of Lismore*, Brendan is said to have sought "for traditions of the Western Continent" and to have, on one occasion come to an island "under the lee of Mount Atlas," where he sojourned for many years.

In Spanish tradition, the legendary island of San Borondón became closely associated with the Canaries, where it is encountered among locals to this day.

So prevalent were these Irish-influenced tales of lost islands among the Spaniards and Portuguese that many of the early voyages of exploration were launched specifically to find them, and the land of Brazil, it now seems certain, was named after one mythical island, Hy-Brasil, whilst the Antilles were named after another. Here again the reader might be tempted to see in this proof that the Iberians lacked their own stories of a lost island, and merely copied from others. Yet this is not the case. Rather we should view it as indicating the existence of a common Hiberno-Iberian culture. Let me explain.

Spain and Ireland, archaeologists and ethnographers now agree, were intimately connected as far back as historical memory goes. Indeed, there is a tradition found in both Galicia (north-west Spain) and Ireland that the Irish were originally migrants from that region; an idea that seems to be confirmed by the very real and continuous cultural contact discovered by archaeologists dating from the start of the Megalithic period. The Q-Celtic dialect of Ireland found its closest European counterpart in the Celtic speech of north-western Spain, where it survived, apparently until well into the Middle Ages. The myths and legends of Celtic Spain, therefore, would have been virtually identical to those of Celtic Ireland — far more closely related to each other than to those of their P-Celtic-speaking cousins the Welsh and Bretons. So, the Spanish and Portuguese obsession with stories of lost islands named Brasil and San Borondón do not imply simple copying from the Irish. These tales were probably as much Iberian as Irish.

We should not finish without mention of a Basque legend, the *Aintzine-koak*, which tells how the seafaring forefathers of this ancient people arrived in the Bay of Biscay after the "Green Isle," Atlaintika, sank under the waves. *Atlantida* is a Basque poem describing their ancient greatness in Atlaintika, its fiery collapse, and the voyage of the survivors to southwestern Europe. Although composed in the 19th century, the poem is, according to *The Readers Digest*, "based on age-old folk belief and oral traditions." We should perhaps list this as a certain independent corroboration of the veracity not only of the Atlantis story, but also the name; yet the striking agreement with Plato's account, plus the 19th-century composition (the 19th century was a great age of romantically-inspired forgery) makes us suspicious. At best, we might say that the *Atlantida* is a romantic creation of the 19th century which was, nevertheless, inspired by genuine ancient beliefs among the Basques.

An important linguistic clue, which may give some support to the *Atlantida*, is found in "Atlaya," the name of a prehistoric ceremonial mound in Biarritz, a town of the French Basque country. "Atalaia" is also a site in southern Portugal featuring a Bronze Age tumulus. Another "Atalya" is found high in the central mountains of Gran Canaria and is evidently a native Guanche term, cognate with the North African/Berber "Atlas." But "Atalya" is also the name of a holy mountain in the Valley of Mexico, venerated by the Aztecs. Apparently, "Atalya" carries the same meaning in Basque, Iberian, Guanche (the ancient Berber-like language of the Canaries), and Nahuatl (the Aztec language); namely, the description of a sacred mountain, mound, or mound-like structure. This sacred mound, or island-hill, is connected in the traditions of these lands with the story of a great flood that preceded the establishment of their own civilization.[1]

Before moving on, we shall note here the occurrence of the word *atl* meaning "water" amongst both Aztecs and Berbers. Apparently, it served the same function as the Egyptian "Nun," meaning both the watery abyss and the hill or mound which appeared first above the water.

---

1 The mysterious Basque language, though not related to Berber, contains many Berber words, indicating close cultural interaction between the two peoples in times past. The Berbers of north-west Africa, as we shall see, called themselves "Atlantians" even as late as the first century BC, and they told of a great volcanic island beside the ocean whose inhabitants had, in an earlier age, conquered their own ancestors on the African mainland.

TRADITIONS OF THE BERBERS

When we consider the history and traditions of North Africa, then we come, as it were, to the very crux of the Atlantis question. For it would appear that the peoples of this region were ethnically and linguistically identical to the Atlanteans, and if we seek the modern descendants of the Atlanteans, we must search among the Berbers.

The connection between North Africa and Atlantis comes of course right at the beginning. Plato himself tells us that the Atlanteans ruled the whole of North Africa, which he calls Libya, as far as the borders of Egypt. But even before Plato the two regions were connected. Herodotus, almost a century earlier, provides a detailed description of the important peoples of the area. After describing the Garamantians, a nation located thirty days' journey to the west of Egypt, and whose capital city Garama exists to this day as the small village of Germa, in the Fezzan Mountains (near the border of modern Libya and Algeria), he mentions a people named the "Ataranteans." These are said to have lived a ten days' journey to the west of the Garamantians. It is evident that the Ataranteans, whose name (given the interchangeability of "l" and "r") could equally well be written as Atalanteans, are little more than a branch of the next people, found a further ten days to the west.[1] These are the Atlantioi, or "Atlantes," said by Herodotus to have their home near a huge mountain called "Atlas," which was regarded by the Atlantes as the "Pillar of Heaven".

Aside from these intriguing comments, Herodotus, sadly, supplies us with little other information. From other sources we know that the ancient Libyans shared many features in common with the Egyptians, and that their language (commonly described as "Hamitic") was closely related to Egyptian. A number of Egyptian gods, but most especially Amon and Neith (Nit) were found among the Libyans, and Neith was even portrayed by the Egyptians wearing the Libyan feathered headdress. Greek sources indicated that the Libyans, but most especially those around the Atlas region, were among the earliest people to practice the arts of civilization, and it was suggested that many fundamental skills of importance to a civilized nation were derived from them. They were, for example, accredited with being the first people to domesticate the dog, and to raise bees for honey. They were also said to have been the discoverers of wine. The deity

---

1 The word *Atlantis* denotes, in Greek, the possessive "of Atlas," and Atlas is said by some to be derived from a Greek word meaning "to uphold." *Atlantic* is the adjective. Yet the North Africans themselves must have used a word like *Atlanta* or *Atlan*, as Herodotus' use of the word "Atarantian" to describe one of the peoples of north-west Africa goes to prove. Evidently the Greek writer simply wrote down what he heard. Had he simply been translating into Greek a foreign word given him by the Egyptians, he would undoubtedly have written "Atlantian."

who bequeathed this knowledge to the Libyans was known, among other things, as Agreos, the father of agriculture, and the beloved son of the goddess Neith. All these "teachings" came to the Greeks from North Africa.

The significance of this reputed Libyan or "Atlantean" wisdom will become apparent as we proceed.

Herodotus himself tells us little, though even what he does say makes it clear that the whole Atlantis and Atlantean story is intimately connected with northwest Africa. So intimate indeed that not a few writers have recently suggested locating it in modern-day Morocco and Algeria, and denying the very existence of an "island" Atlantis. Yet such a position can be defended only by ignoring what Plato said and ignoring also what the ancient peoples of the area, the Atlantes or Atlantians, themselves said. For although Herodotus was remiss in providing us was a history of the Ataranteans and Atlantes, the omission was made good by Diodorus of Sicily, in the first century BC. According to him, the "Atlantians" inhabited a rich country bordering the Atlantic Ocean. They were, he said, notable for their hospitality to strangers and boasted that the gods were born among them. They claimed that Uranus was their first King, and it was he who had civilized the people, causing them to dwell in cities. After his death, Uranus' forty-five children divided the kingdom between them, with Atlas (one of the Titans) receiving the area of Atlantis and naming it for himself. According to Diodorus, Atlas was a wise ruler and like his father also a great astrologer. Since he was the first one to discover the knowledge of the sphere, the people (according to Diodorus) created a legend saying that he bears the world upon his shoulders (Diod. iii, 56-60).

Diodorus in fact goes into much detail of Atlantian/Atlantean history, telling, for example, of a great war with an Amazon queen named Myrine, who conquered the country. These Amazons were said by Diodorus to have originated in a great island far to the west, near the Atlantic Ocean, named Hespera:[1]

As mythology relates, their home was on an island which, because it was in the west, was called Hespera, and it lay in the marsh Tritonis. This marsh was near the ocean which surrounds the earth and received its name from a certain river Triton which emptied into it; and this marsh was also near Ethiopia [Africa] and that mountain by the shore of the ocean which is the highest of those in the vicinity and impinges upon the ocean and is called by the Greeks Atlas. The island mentioned above was of great size and full of fruit-bearing trees of every kind, from which the natives secured their food. It contained also a multitude of

---

1 Reminiscent, we should note here, of the Greek Hesperides, the Daughters of the Evening who dwelt in a Garden or Island by the Ocean Stream. The connection is significant, as we shall see, and implies also a matriarchal cult or culture in the Atlantic regions.

flocks and herds, namely, of goats and sheep, from which the possessors received milk and meat for their sustenance; but grain the nation used not at all because the use of this fruit of the earth had not yet been discovered among them.

> The Amazons, then, the account continues, being a race superior in valor and eager for war, first of all subdued all the cities on the island except the one called Mene, which was considered to be sacred and was inhabited by Ethiopian Ichthyophagi, and was also subject to great eruptions of fire and possessed a multitude of the precious stones which the Greeks call *anthrax, sardion,* and *smaragdos;* and after this they subdued many of the neighboring Libyans and nomad tribes, and founded within the marsh Tritonis a great city which they named Cherronesus after its shape (Diodorus, iii, 53).

It is evident, from any perspective, that Diodorus' account of the Atlanteans is quite different to that of Plato, and is independent of it. There is no question of him having copied from Plato, or even having been influenced by him. Diodorus places the island, evidently volcanic, in a marsh he calls Tritonis. This is obviously a reference to Lake Triton, a geological feature said at one time to have watered the entire Sahara. Placing the island within Lake Triton is almost certainly a mistake, made either by Diodorus or his sources, for the lake is said to have been near the ocean, i.e., the Atlantic. But connecting Lake Triton with the mysterious island of the west is not accidental, for the Greek legend of Phaeton (which the Egyptian priest actually mentioned to Solon, before recounting to him the story of Atlantis), tells how the lake was destroyed during a cataclysm which burned the whole earth and turned the Sahara into a desert. It would appear that the lost island and Lake Triton were confused because they were destroyed in one and the same catastrophe.

Having described the island-home of these Amazons, Diodorus then goes on to tell how they conquered the Atlantians and then every people of northern Africa, finally invading Egypt herself.

It would appear that Diodorus' story of the Amazon war of conquest is identical to the Atlantean war of conquest described earlier by Plato. Yet the great differences between the details of the two stories leave no doubt that they are two separate traditions and that one has not influenced the other. Evidently, from at very least the time of Herodotus, the peoples of north-west Africa called themselves Atlanteans and spoke of a great island in the ocean which they or their ancestors had earlier inhabited. But why, by the time of Diodorus, would the natives of the region have transformed the Atlanteans into Amazons, and have made the Atlanteans the victims, not the perpetrators, of the aggression? The answer lies in the word Amazon. The modern natives of the region, the Berbers, to this day call themselves, collectively, Imazighen, "free men" (singular, Amazigh), and it is evident that Diodorus derived the word "Amazon" from this. It is also possible that the ancient Berbers worshipped a goddess figure or were said to have been ruled by a queen. This would have reinforced the Amazon idea in Diodorus or his informant's mind. It seems clear that the ancient peoples of north-west Africa, whose modern ancestors are the Berbers, called themselves both Atlantioi and Amazigh, and the mighty island empire, which both Plato and Diodorus agree was volcanic and stood in or near the Atlantic Ocean, was inhabited by the Atlantioi/Amazigh, who are seen as both aggressors and victims in the account of Diodorus.

In this context, we might reflect on the fact that any imperial power, in whatever region of the world, always begins by subduing its neighbors, people of related stock.

As we have said, the modern descendants of these ancient North African Atlanteans are the Berbers. Contrary to what is often imagined, the Berbers are not Arabs, nor are they even closely related to the Arabs. True, nowadays most of them speak Arabic, and are all Muslim. In addition, many of them have Arab blood, and look somewhat Arab. But that was not the case with the original Berbers, and there exists, to this day, populations of Berbers, particularly those inhabiting the remoter regions of the Atlas Mountains, who are relatively unmixed with Arab immigrants and who look very much like the original inhabitants of the region. In short, they are white-skinned, blue-eyed and often fair-haired. These traits are most common, in modern times, amongst the Rifs of Morocc, many of whom could be mistaken for northern Europeans.

At one time, the Berbers/Amazigh occupied the whole of North Africa, stretching from the borders of Egypt to the Atlantic coast. Those living closest to Egypt were known as the Meshwesh or Tehenu. They made war against Egyptians on many occasions; and are faithfully portrayed, in full color, on Egyptian monuments. Here they are clearly shown to be pale-skinned, like Europeans.

In Greek legend Atlas, the father of the Atlanteans, was the son of a titan named Iapetus, who was himself the son of Uranus. It is of interest, perhaps, that in biblical tradition the father of the white peoples, the Europeans, is named Japhet.

The Berbers, the modern descendants of these ancient Libyans, or Atlantians, still have a legend of a great island, their original homeland, that stood in the Atlantic Ocean. Contemporary Berber story-tellers, particularly in regions less touched by the modern world, will recite this legend to anyone wishing to hear it. It is a story that could almost have been written by Plato himself.[1]

The Canary Islands lie off the western coast of Morocco. Today, they are part of Spain, but at the start of the fifteenth century they were still inhabited by a mysterious white-skinned and frequently blue-eyed people called the Guanches. Much has been written of the Guanches, yet there is little that is certain. There seems little doubt that their language was a branch of the Berber tongue, and that they themselves were a surviving relic of the ancient Libyan/Atlantean race. When discovered by Europeans in the fourteenth century, they were said to have lost the ability to travel by sea, and the various islands of the archipelago existed completely isolated from each other. Some of them, it is said, were greatly surprised when they saw the Europeans, believing as they did that the rest of humanity had been destroyed in the catastrophe that had earlier brought ruin to their own homeland, a great island in the ocean.

1 Lewis Spence refers to these accounts. See e.g., *History of Atlantis*, p. 209. "I recently received a letter from a lady who knows North-West Africa well, in which she states that many traditions of Atlantis are still to be found among the native population. An Arab Emir of her acquaintance is quite an authority on the subject, and has even written a book on Atlantis in Morocco."

CHAPTER 2. EARTH'S RECENT CATASTROPHIC HISTORY

THE THEORY OF CATASTROPHES

It is widely believed, especially amongst those with a little knowledge, that catastrophes of the type described in legends such as the Flood and Atlantis never happened, and that these beliefs can be attributed to the abject ignorance of ancient man with regard to the world he inhabited. It is held that unusually heavy rains might have caused local flooding, and primitive man, in his naivety, believed that the whole world was being drowned.

This, then, is the modern academically-acceptable "explanation" for cataclysm stories, and it is an explanation repeated in one authoritative publication after another. At a stroke, the belief of virtually all ancient and traditional peoples, that there had been a world-wide flooding of the planet, is dismissed.

Yet it was not always thus. Almost until the publication of Darwin's *Origin of Species*, in 1859, it was assumed by the great majority of geologists and paleontologists that the earth had been struck repeatedly by immense natural catastrophes. This conviction came not so much from a reverential regard for tradition, but from interpretation of the observed geological facts. Indeed, Georges Cuvier, the French founder of paleontology, as a child of the Enlightenment, was decidedly anti-biblical in his views; and yet he regarded it as proven that great upheavals of nature, of a planet-wide scope, had struck the earth repeatedly. He was led to this conclusion both by his observations of geology and by the study of faunal history. Cuvier performed much field-work and was first to identify and classify many species of extinct animals. Invariably, he was led to the conclusion that their destruction, both in manner and speed, could only be explained by immense paroxysms of nature. Cuvier held that human tradition, as found in the various Flood legends, did refer to the last — and only the last — of these events. He thus found corroboration for his views in myth and legend, but had already reached his conclusions quite independently of these.

By the late 18th century these ideas, under the general heading of "catastrophism," had reached the status of given fact among Europe's intelligentsia. Indeed, they found an important place in Diderot's *Encycopaedia*.

It should be noted here that "catastrophism," or something approximating to it, had always been the accepted view of the past, in every culture. As we saw in the previous chapter, the Egyptians of the sixth century BC had already, or so it seems, begun to look at catastrophes in a scientific or at least rationalistic manner. If the conversation between Solon and the Egyptian priest, as recorded by Plato, actually took place, then it would appear that by that time the Egyptians were explaining natural catastrophes on the earth as being the result of disturbances in the cosmos. Of course, we now know that should a comet or large asteroid strike the earth, or should a planet-sized body such as the moon come reasonably close to the earth, then the result would be, just as the priest said, a great "destruction by fire and water" of all things on the earth. Vast tides would be raised, showers of meteorites would bombard the planet, the earth's tectonic plates would go into convulsions, and there would be a general destruction of animals and people, so general indeed that some species might fall into extinction.

By late antiquity many philosophers and thinkers were in agreement with the Egyptian/Platonic notion, and it was generally assumed that these events were in some way or other related to comets. Indeed, in all cultures, comets had always been regarded with terror, and their appearance in the sky viewed as a harbinger of evil. In Roman times, and again during the Renaissance, many of the supposed miracles of the Old Testament, such as the Plagues of Egypt and the opening of the Red Sea, were being explained by natural causes. Thus the Roman writer Pliny spoke of a "terrible" comet named Typhon which had appeared in Egypt and had caused the drowning of an Egyptian pharaoh by the same name. This theme was taken up by a number of Renaissance scholars who apparently had access to ancient texts now lost. Among these were Hevelius, whose *Cometographia* (1668) made reference to works of Calvisius, Helvicus, Herlicius and Rockenbach, all of whom spoke of the Ten Plagues as being the result of the encounter between the earth and the comet Typhon.[1] Rockenbach's ideas were expanded further by

---

1 Abraham Rockenbach, *De cometis tractatus novus methodicus* (Wittenberg, 1602) According to him: "In the year of the world two thousand four hundred and fifty-three — as many trustworthy authors ... have determined — a comet appeared which Pliny also

Isaac Newton's student and successor William Whiston, whose 1696 book *The New Theory of the Earth, from its Original to the Consummation of all Things*, sought to explain the biblical Deluge as the consequence of an encounter between the earth and a great comet. Although condemned as a heretic, Whiston was influential in pointing the way for the savants of the 18th century, who would in time place the study of geology and paleontology on a scientific basis.

It thus came about that by the mid-18th century and the appearance of the *Encyclopédie*, that "catastrophism" occupied an honorable place in the endeavor, and by the end of the century the young Georges Cuvier was refining and building upon the work already done. As we have said, Cuvier was by no means motivated by religion, and in fact never so much as mentions the biblical Flood. His work was based purely on scientific observation. The earth, he conceded, does present to the scientist an apparently calm and pacific demeanor, yet this impression changes immediately as one digs beneath the surface.[1] Cuvier was instrumental in the discovery of many extinct species and was the first to postulate an epoch during which reptiles (dinosaurs) were the dominant animal-life on the planet. He had no doubt that these successive faunal ages were terminated by great catastrophes, and this was an opinion shared by almost all the important earth scientists of the time. The most recent faunal extinction in particular, that of the Pleistocene, was viewed as being the consequence of gigantic tidal waves which swept the planet, leaving millions of mammoths and other such beasts, as well as uprooted forests and rocks and gravel, heaped in the Arctic tundra: "It was conceived that somehow and somewhere in the far north a series of gigantic waves was mysteriously propagated. These waves were supposed to have precipitated themselves upon the land, and then swept madly over mountain and valley alike, carrying along with them a mighty burden of rocks and stones and rubbish. Such deluges were styled 'waves of translation'; and the till was believed to represent the materials which they hurried along with them in their wild course across the country."[2]

This was the situation right up almost until the publication of Darwin's famous book. True, in the decades before *The Origin of Species*, there had been vocal

---

mentioned in his second book. It was fiery, of irregular circular form, with a wrapped head; it was in the shape of a globe and was of terrible aspect. It is said that King Typhon ruled at that time in Egypt.... Certain [authorities] assert that the comet was seen in Syria, Babylonia, India, in the sign of Capricorn, in the form of a disc, at the time when the children of Israel advanced from Egypt toward the Promised Land, led on the way by the pillar of cloud during the day and by the pillar of fire at night" (translated from the Latin by Velikovsky, *Worlds in Collision*, 1950).

1   G. Cuvier, *Essay on the Theory of the Earth*. (English trans. of *Discours sur les révolutions de la surface du globe, et sur les changements qu'elles ont produits dans le règne animal*).
2   J. Geikie, *The Great Ice Age and Its Relation to the Antiquity of Man* (1894), pp. 25-6.

---

and vociferous criticism of the catastrophist paradigm. This was led, to begin with, by James Hutton, a Scottish lawyer and medical doctor (*Theory of the Earth*, 1795), and later by Charles Lyell, another Scottish lawyer (*Principles of Geology*, 1830-33). Both men had their own reasons for criticizing catastrophism, but it is important to remember that these were based not primarily on science, but on ideology. Hutton's opposition found its source in his trust in an all-good and pre-scient God, who would not, he thought, create a world only to destroy it again. Lyell's opposition came from his radicalism. As an opponent of the church, he had an interest in proving the Bible to consist of myth rather than history. He also, like Hutton, had an almost visceral fear of upheaval and uncertainty.

In the end, the theory of uniformitarianism was endorsed by academia and catastrophism rejected. This was at least in part due to the fact that for Darwin's explanation of evolution (i.e., through the process of random natural selection) to be true, enormous expanses of time were necessary. Darwin's theory relied on the existence of rather small differences between individual animals, differences which could (so the theory said), under the pressure of very slowly changing environmental conditions, produce changes in species, small changes which would, in course of vast eons of time, become big changes.

All the evidence which spoke of catastrophes was therefore dismissed: Neither the writings and traditions of the ancients, nor the field-work of catastrophist geologists and paleontologists such as Cuvier, were held to have any value. Why the ancients should all have spoken of great floods, of vast earth tremors, of islands and landmasses disappearing under the sea, was never really explained. In a general sense, it was suggested that since ancient peoples were ignorant of the principles of science and of the geography of the earth, they tended to exaggerate so that a localized flood or earthquake was made into a destruction or an inundation of the whole planet. The paleontological evidence was likewise brushed aside. The extinction of successive genera of animals and plants, at different epochs in the earth's history, was admitted to be somewhat mysterious, though it was suggested that changing climatic conditions must have had something to do with it.

UNIFORMITARIANISM CHALLENGED

By the latter years of the 19th century all mention of past catastrophes was thus being written out of the textbooks and the evidence for them systematically ignored. There were, it is true, a series of maverick figures, beginning with Ignatius Donnelly, who continued to rake up this evidence and present it to the public. These efforts usually elicited great interest, and the books became bestsellers, but they were ignored by the scientific establishment, who now seemed to be possessed of an almost crusading zeal to terminate the debate.

In his *Atlantis: the Antediluvian World* (1882) and *Ragnarok: the Age of Fire and Gravel* (1883), Donnelly introduced a number of themes which were to become the stock-in-trade of these maverick catastrophists over the next few decades.

The first of these, actually a revival of an old idea, as we have seen, going back to antiquity, is that ancient catastrophes had been caused by comets. This theme is most fully developed in *Ragnarok*, where Donnelly takes a fairly detailed look at well-known geological features such as the Drift, the great layer of clay — often mixed with rounded rocks and boulders as well as gravel — which covers a very substantial part of the earth's surface. The evidence presented by Donnelly was quite ingenious and very well argued; and yet his overall thesis was rejected. The intellectual tide had moved, in the twenty years previous, decisively against catastrophism. Although widely popular with the public, Donnelly was ignored by the elite.

In the half-century after the publication of *Atlantis* and *Ragnarok* there appeared various books, usually by outsiders and non-specialists, which attempted to revive the debate. On occasion, archaeological discoveries, such as that of Leonard Woolley at Ur in Mesopotamia, briefly revived talk of catastrophes even within mainstream academia. At the lowest level of literate civilization, Woolley found a nine-foot deep layer of water-borne silt and, famously, asking his wife what she thought it might mean, received the answer, "It's the Flood." But such revisitations were brief. At Ur, and elsewhere, the establishment quickly recovered its composure, and the Flood of Ur was decreed to be a local event caused by heavy rainfall in the upper reaches of the Tigris and Euphrates rivers. This event may have been the origin of the biblical Flood story, but it most certainly was not the world-wide Deluge described in the pages of the Scriptures. Evidence of ancient catastrophes was in fact emerging everywhere during the 1920s and 30s; but the public at large was rarely made aware of this material; and even when it was, the upheavals were quickly explained-away as local disasters, very much as had occurred at Ur.

The real challenge to the new uniformitarian paradigm appeared only in 1950, with the publication of Immanuel Velikovsky's highly controversial *Worlds in Collision*. This book, the result of ten years' research, laid out before the reader an astonishing array of evidence, from the traditions and legends of early peoples everywhere, pointing to an immense natural catastrophe, or rather series of catastrophes, that had occurred just three and a half thousand to two thousand seven hundred years ago. Velikovsky was able to show, in impressive detail, that ancient accounts of catastrophes, from every corner of the globe, agreed with each other in minute detail; and, using these traditions as his guide, presented a theory of the mechanism behind the event. According to Velikovsky, in the fifteenth century BC the earth had had a close encounter with an enormous comet, described by the ancients as a blood-red ball of fire, which had caused devastation throughout the planet. In *Worlds in Collision*, Velikovsky argued that our planet had passed through the tail of the comet, showering the earth with meteors, and that, even worse, the gravitational pull of the nearby body caused disruption in the earth's rotation, leading to vast seismic activity, as well as the raising of great ocean tides.

To describe *Worlds in Collision* as controversial would almost be to commit an under-statement. In fact, the book — a popular best-seller — ignited a controversy as bitter as anything ever witnessed in the halls of academia. The reaction of the establishment (with one or two notable exceptions, such as Albert Einstein and Claude Schaeffer), was almost universally hostile, and within a very short time a concerted campaign of suppression was launched. This campaign, headed by Professor Harlow Shapley, the Dean of Astronomy at Harvard, more or less closed the debate before it had properly begun. Through their influence in the publishing world, and especially through their control of scientific organs such as *Nature* and *Scientific American*, Shapley and his associates were able to put forward the notion that Velikovsky had been disproved, and that, in addition, his ideas were not even worthy of serious consideration. But though Velikovsky was consigned to the fringes and his work excluded from the pages of mainstream scientific journals, the controversy he ignited refused to die: and in fact, by the late 1970s, scientific catastrophism began to make a major comeback with the work of Nobel Prize-winner Luis Alvarez and his son Walter. These two had found a layer of the heavy metal iridium at the termination of the Cretaceous period throughout North America. Since virtually all of the earth's iridium is at the core, this material must have been spewed out from their by massive volcanism, or fallen on the earth from space. In either event, this was evidence of some terrible catastrophe. Alvarez's ideas, published first in 1979 in the *Geological Society of America: Abstracts with Program* (Vol. 11) and then in 1980 in *Science*, Vol. 208, met with stiff resistance at the start, though this weakened in time; and it is now generally accepted that the dinosaurs were destroyed by some form of natural catastrophe — either an outbreak of "super-volcanism" or the effects of an asteroid impact on the earth.

Yet this represented only a limited victory for catastrophism: after all, it was not too difficult to talk about a cosmic catastrophe so long as it could be placed in the distant past — 65 million years, according to conventional ideas. What

Donnelly and (especially) Velikovsky had proposed was much more unsettling: a cataclysmic upheaval just a few thousand years ago, and one within the memory of human beings. Indeed, although both Velikovsky and Donnelly had deployed much evidence from the "hard" sciences, such as geology and astrophysics, they also used human tradition as a valid and important kind of evidence. Such evidence only becomes important of course if the last catastrophes occurred after the appearance of *homo sapiens* — a proposition which the academic establishment still doggedly resists. Still, the evidence for these upheavals is also to be found in the earth, in the rocks and under the sea. Indeed, though catastrophes as recent as those claimed by Velikovsky are still denied by most academics, the evidence of all kinds that something did happen is rapidly becoming difficult to ignore.

THE EVIDENCE OF ANCIENT LEGEND

One of the most important accusations leveled at Velikovsky was that his conclusions were based solely upon material gleaned from ancient myths and legends. A proper scientific theory, it was said, should not need to depend upon such data. It was grudgingly admitted that all ancient peoples seemed to speak of immense upheavals of nature, yet these were, after all, only myths, and could not be a solid foundation upon which to build a scholarly hypothesis. With such criticisms in mind, Velikovsky produced, in 1955, his third book, *Earth in Upheaval*, where he ignored completely the evidence of tradition and looked at hard science. Here, in the disciplines of geology, paleontology, and archaeology, he found an abundance of material to support the thesis of *Worlds in Collision*.

It is true, of course, that ancient tradition alone could not be used to prove that catastrophes happened. Were the legends and myths not supported by geology and archaeology, they would need to be disregarded. Whether such support is forthcoming shall be demonstrated presently. For the moment however we need to say something else about legend and tradition *per se* as scientific evidence.

It was pointed out, both by Velikovsky and his supporters, that data gathered from historical records is regularly used in science and that gathering data and searching for earlier data is a normal part of the scientific method. The movements of the tides, for example, are calculated according to observations made over the past few centuries. Weather forecasting is likewise heavily dependent upon the interpretation of data gathered in the past; often over long periods of time. Velikovsky claimed that his use of ancient tradition was the same. If there was any difference it was only in the fact that he looked further into the past than most other scientists.

Anyone who has made a thorough study of myth, as compiled for example by Velikovsky in *Worlds in Collision*, will be left in no doubt that many, if not all, ancient peoples spoke of world-shaking cataclysms involving titanic earthquakes, volcanic eruptions, tidal waves, and extra-terrestrial phenomena, such as meteorite showers. The skeptics never denied this. What they did and do say is that whilst ancient man spoke of these things, he exaggerated. Knowing nothing of the earth and its size, small, local catastrophes were exaggerated out of all proportion, and made to appear universal and world-shaking.

Velikovsky countered this by pointing to the striking parallels between these stories, from civilizations and continents far removed from each other. All seemed to speak of comets or a great comet as the harbinger of destruction; they all identified the same heavenly bodies as involved; and, most importantly, they all spoke of phenomena which, we now know, would really occur if the earth were involved in a close encounter with another heavenly body. A close encounter between our world and another planet-sized body would indeed shake the earth off its axis. Vast tides would be raised, volcanoes would erupt, and the earth's tectonic plates would convulse. We need only picture the likely consequences of the moon, for example, moving on an orbit just a few thousand miles closer to our world than at present.[1] During its journey round the earth, the moon, which keeps a fairly constant distance from the earth of about a quarter of a million miles, raises the ocean's tides about three to six meters, depending on location. It is not difficult to imagine what would happen were the earth's satellite to move even thirty or forty thousand miles closer to us. Tides would be raised not three to six meters, but hundreds of meters. And they would not rise gradually; they would rise in great walls of water which would sweep over the continents, annihilating everything in their paths.

The effect upon the earth's crust would be scarcely less devastating: The planet's tectonic plates would go into convulsions; in some places, they would crash together, raising mountains hundreds of meters in a few hours; elsewhere, they would move apart, consigning land to the depths of the sea. In addition, every volcano on the globe would erupt, very quickly shrouding our world in a pall of darkness.

In *Worlds in Collision*, Velikovsky collected evidence from the traditions of numerous ancient peoples which strongly suggested that just such a collision of worlds had taken place in the geologically recent past. Everywhere, he found reports of a comet, variously described as a ball of fire, a fiery serpent, or a feathered serpent, which had given the earth a near-miss and brought devastation in

---

1 Were the moon as large as the earth, even at its present distance, it would raise tides around 240 meters (roughly 750 feet) high.

its wake. Often, the ancients had connected unusual events in the cosmos with giant tidal waves, a pall of darkness, volcanic disturbances, and rapid mountain-building. How, Velikovsky, asked, could the ancients, who knew nothing of either gravitation or plate tectonics, have described such interconnected phenomena unless they had actually witnessed them? In the manuscripts of the Spanish chroniclers Avila and Molina, for example, who collected the traditions of the Native Americans, it is related that the sun was darkened for five days; a cosmic collision of stars preceded the cataclysm; people and animals tried to escape to mountain caves. "Scarcely had they reached there when the sea, breaking out of bounds following a terrific shock, began to rise on the Pacific coast. But as the sea rose, filling the valleys and the plains around, the mountain of Ancasmarca rose, too, like a ship on the waves. During the five days that this cataclysm lasted, the sun did not show its face and the earth remained in darkness."[1]

Another tradition referred to by Velikovsky was that of Phaeton. The Greeks told how Phaeton, son of the sun-god Helios, begged his father's permission to drive the solar chariot across the sky for one day. Finally receiving permission to take charge of the solar disc, the young god found himself unable to control the wild steeds, who pulled the celestial body off course. Ovid, the Roman poet, provides one of the most celebrated retellings of the tale. The chariot of the sun, he said, driven by Phaeton, moved "no longer in the same course as before." The horses "break loose from their course" and "rush aimlessly, knocking against the stars set deep in the sky and snatching the chariot long through uncharted ways." The northern constellations tried to plunge into the forbidden sea, and the solar chariot roamed through unknown regions of the air. It was "borne along just as a ship driven before the headlong blast, whose pilot has let the useless rudder go and abandoned the ship to the gods and prayers."[2]

Now the carnage began: "The earth burst into flame, the highest parts first, and split into deep cracks, and its moisture is all dried up. The meadows are burned to white ashes; the trees are consumed, green leaves and all, and the ripe grain furnished fuel for its own destruction ... Great cities perish with their walls, and the vast conflagration reduces whole nations to ashes."

Volcanoes erupt everywhere. "The woods are ablaze and the mountains.... Aetna is blazing boundlessly ... and twin-peaked Parnassus.... Nor does its chilling clime save Scythia; Caucasus burns ... and the heaven-piercing Alps and cloud-capped Apennines." In the smoke and ash a great darkness comes over the earth. Phaeton sees the earth aflame. "He can no longer bear the ashes and whirl-

---

1 C. E. Brasseur de Bourbourg, *S'il existe des Sources de l'histoire primitive du Mexique dans les monuments égyptiens, etc.* (Paris, 1864) p. 40.
2 Ovid, *Metamorphoses*, ii, 1-329.

ing sparks, and is completely shrouded in the dense, hot smoke. In this pitchy darkness he cannot tell where he is or whither he is going."

"It was then, as men think, that the peoples of Aethiopia became black-skinned, since the blood was drawn to the surface of their bodies by the heat."

It was then too that the Sahara became a dry wasteland. "Then also Libya became a desert, for the heat dried up her moisture.... The Don's waters steam; Babylonian Euphrates burns; the Ganges, Phasis, Danube, Alpheus boil; Sperchoes' banks are aflame. The golden sands of the Tagus melt in the immense heat, and the swans ... are scorched.... The Nile fled in terror to the ends of the earth ... the seven mouths lie empty, filled with dust; seven broad channels, all without a stream. The same mischance dries up the Thracian rivers, Hebrus and Strymon; also the rivers of the west, the Rhine, Rhone, Po and Tiber.... Great cracks yawn everywhere.... Even the sea shrinks up, and what was but now a great watery expanse is a dry plain of sand. The mountains, which the deep sea had covered before, spring forth, and increase the numbers of the scattered Cyclades."

As Velikovsky rightly comments:

> How could the poets have known that a change in the movement of the sun across the firmament must cause a world conflagration, blazing of volcanoes, boiling of rivers, disappearance of seas, birth of deserts, emergence of islands, if the sun never changed its harmonious journey from sunrise to sunset?[1]

The story of Phaeton is particularly important to us, for it is mentioned by none other than the priest who recounted to Solon the story of Atlantis; and it is perfectly evident from this that the celestial body (evidently not the real sun, but some kind of fiery body that resembled the sun in brightness) was in some way crucial to the Atlantis legend. We recall that the priest told Solon how there had been, and would again be "many and diverse destruction of mankind, of which the greatest are by fire and water." These were not normal forest-fires or river-floods, as the next sentence makes perfectly clear: "The story that is told in your country as well as ours, how once upon a time Phaethon, son of Helios, yoked his father's chariot and, because he was unable to drive it along the course taken by his father, burnt up all that was on the earth — that story, as it is told, has the fashion of a legend, but the truth of it lies in the occurrence of a shift in the bodies in the heavens which move around the earth and a destruction of the things on the earth by fierce fire, which recurs at long intervals."

Here is a cosmology worthy of a modern scientist. We know now, of course, that should there be a "shift of the bodies in the heavens that move round the earth" there would indeed be a destruction of the things on the earth both by fire

---

1 Immanuel Velikovsky, *Worlds in Collision*, (New York, 1950) p. 147.

and water — both agents being also mentioned by the priest. How, we might ask, could an Egyptian priest of the sixth century BC have known such a thing? Whence was the knowledge derived? The only possible answer is from actual experience of such events.

Were such tales confined to the western hemisphere, we might be justified in skepticism; yet, as Velikovsky illustrated at great length in *Worlds in Collision*, they are to be found throughout the globe. Some of the most telling of these accounts come from the Americas, where Spanish chroniclers of the sixteenth century were struck by the parallels they found with biblical and Greek tradition. It seemed that every people of the New World told of world catastrophes which decimated mankind and changed the face of the earth. Among the peoples of Mexico, in particular, there was a tradition that the earth's history had been punctuated by terrible cataclysms which destroyed or darkened the sun, after which there appeared a new sun in the sky. The Mayas of Yucatan counted their historical ages by the names of their consecutive suns. These were named Water Sun, Earthquake Sun, Hurricane Sun, Fire Sun. "These suns mark the epochs to which are attributed the various catastrophes the world has suffered."[1]

A native Indian scholar named Ixtlilxochitl (1568–1648) described these world ages. The Water Sun (or Sun of Waters) was the first age, terminated by a deluge in which almost all men and beasts perished; the Earthquake Sun or age perished in a terrific earthquake when the earth split apart and mountains fell. The age of the Hurricane Sun came to its end in a cosmic hurricane, whilst the Fire Sun was the world age that went down in a rain of fire.[2]

According to Gómara, the Spanish writer of the sixteenth century, "The nations of Culhua or Mexico believe according to their hieroglyphic paintings, that, previous to the sun which now enlightens them, four had already been successively extinguished. These four suns are as many ages, in which our species has been annihilated by inundations, by earthquakes, by a general conflagration, and by the effect of destroying tempests."[3]

It would be quite fruitless to simply retell the myriad similar stories collected by Velikovsky from the literature of the Chinese, Indians, Persians, Babylonians, Greeks, Vikings, Africans, Polynesians, etc. He did not, of course, mention the traditions of all of the ancient nations: that would have been virtually impossible, since such an undertaking would fill many volumes. What he did collect however is meticulous and far-reaching, and if the reader wishes to see more, *Worlds in Collision* is the best place to go.

---

1 Brasseur de Bourbourg, op. cit. p. 25.
2 H. B. Alexander, *Latin American Mythology* (1920), p. 91.
3 Quoted by Humbolt, *Researches*, II, 16.

Before moving on, it should be noted that the sequence of four cataclysms mentioned by the Mexicans matches very precisely the archaeological evidence from Mesopotamia, where well-stratified ancient settlements reveal a sequence of four catastrophes, one on top of the other. We shall have more to say on this evidence presently. We should also note that there is striking agreement between the number and nature of the catastrophes mentioned by the Mexicans and those recorded in the Old Testament. Thus for example in the Book of Genesis we are told that ten generations after the Flood of Noah, men attempted to raise a great tower (Tower of Babel) to the heavens, but gave up when God confused their languages. This story is linked to that of Abraham (who is mentioned immediately after the Tower), in whose time there was a great catastrophe — the destruction of Sodom and Gomorrah — which also involved a tower: Lot's wife, we are told, was transformed into a crystal pillar when she looked at the destruction of Sodom.

How peculiar then, and how strange, that Mexican legend should describe events during the great catastrophe which ended the second age of Ehecatonatiuh, the sun of wind, in almost identical terms. After narrating the story of the Flood which brought to a close the first world age, the native historian Ixtlilxochitl went on to describe the catastrophic end to the second age:

> ... and as men were thereafter multiplying they constructed a very high and strong Zacualli, which means a very high tower; in order to protect themselves when again the second world should be destroyed. At the crucial moment their languages were changed, and as they did not understand one another, they went into different parts of the world.[1]

The striking similarity to the biblical story of Babel has of course led some to regard this as proof of ancient cultural diffusion, and see the Mexican story as inspired by early seafarers from the eastern Mediterranean. As we shall see, there is evidence aplenty of early transatlantic cultural links; but this was not one of them. The story of the Tower, or World Tree, or Tree of Life, is a universal myth and refers to events of natural not human history. As I have shown in great detail elsewhere, after the first Flood catastrophe, there appeared at the polar region a pillar of crystal appearance, apparently an electro-magnetic phenomenon of some sort. This "Pillar" or "Tower" was the focus of events during a second great catastrophe, after which the Tower disappeared.

Two other great upheavals of nature, the great famine in the time of Joseph, which seems to have involved seven celestial cows, and the Exodus, coming

---

1 Don Fernando de Alvara, "Ixtlilxochitl," *Obras Historicas* (Mexico, 1891), Vol. 1, p. 12.

several generations later, offer precise equivalents to the final two catastrophic events described in Mexican tradition.

THE CATASTROPHIC END OF THE PLEISTOCENE EPOCH

As mentioned above, in response to the criticisms leveled at *Worlds in Collision*, Velikovsky produced, in 1955, *Earth in Upheaval*, a volume which examined the evidence of geology and paleontology as well as, to some degree, archaeology. Here Velikovsky revisited much of the territory already covered by Donnelly. He also invoked the work of earlier catastrophists, such as Cuvier, and brought forth a great deal of new data, collected in the first half of the 20th century, highlighting the recent and cataclysmic termination of the Pleistocene. Since Velikovsky's death in 1979 even more evidence has accumulated, and the material is now so extensive that there really can be little doubt as to the cause of the extinction of the Pleistocene mega fauna; the mammoths, mastodons, cave-bears, saber-toothed cats etc. Some of the more important recent contributions to the debate are the following: D. S. Allan and J. B. Delair, *When the Earth Nearly Died* (1994); Vine Deloria, *Red Earth, White Lies* (1997); and, above all, Richard Firestone, Allen West and Simon Warwick-Smith, *The Cycle of Cosmic Catastrophes: How a Stone-Age Comet Changed the Course of World History* (2006). These, and other works, leave the reader in little doubt that the extinct Pleistocene creatures did not simply lie down and die; they were destroyed by a catastrophe of almost unimaginable dimensions.

The new research is welcome and long overdue. As we have seen, since the 1980s geologists and paleontologists have been happy to admit that the dinosaurs died in catastrophic circumstances at the end of the Cretaceous; yet study of the Pleistocene extinctions have been caught in something of a time-warp, with specialists continuing until recently to insist that it was climate-change, or disease, or (ludicrously) over-hunting by humans, that led to the demise of the mammoth and their contemporaries. But the situation has at last begun to change. The existence of an iridium-rich layer at the termination of the Pleistocene (very similar to the one which marked the close of the Cretaceous) has caused particular comment. As recently as August 2007 an article posted on the National Science Foundation's website remarked on the discovery of the iridium spike in "a dozen archaeological sites in North America," noting that this element "is rare on earth and is almost exclusively associated with extra-terrestrial objects such as comets and meteorites."[1] Furthermore, it is now evident that, whilst a major upheaval terminated the Pleistocene, this catastrophe marked the beginning of a veritable age of catastrophes, a period of time reaching into the Holocene, or geologically

---

1 Cheryl Dybas, "Comet may have exploded over North America 13,000 years ago," in National Science Foundation website, August 14, 2007.

modern age, during which the earth was visited by further disturbances in the natural order, though these were not as severe as the initial event which terminated the Pleistocene.

Since the amount of material dealing with these catastrophes is truly enormous, I shall confine myself here to looking at a small portion of the more salient features.

In *Earth in Upheaval* Velikovsky noted the skeletons of a number of whales, found in bog land of a post-Glacial date — i.e.., very recent — in various parts of North America. These whales, it should be noted, were of a still-surviving species and were discovered at considerable elevations above sea level, and often very many miles distant from the ocean. Thus for example in Michigan, skeletons of two whales were found over 190 meters above the present sea level, whilst just to the north of Lake Ontario bones of a whale were found roughly 140 meters above present sea level. Again, a skeleton of a whale was discovered in Vermont, over 160 meters above sea level.[1]

There can be no doubt that these creatures were deposited where they were found by enormous tidal waves, yet it is equally certain that these waves were an event of the recent past, for the bones were located in post-Glacial deposits.

Evidence of these vast waves is found in abundance throughout the globe, yet this material is now rarely, if ever, mentioned in official academic literature. In Antarctica, for example, the frozen bodies of whales, of species still living, are found sometimes hundreds of kilometers from the seashore and hundreds of meters above sea level. The bodies of these animals, often dismembered, as well as of seals and other marine life such as fish, are found perfectly preserved by the cold, and often look as if they might have died only a matter of weeks earlier. Now, these animals cannot have been deposited where they are found by glaciers flowing from the ice-cap, since these flow downwards and outwards towards the sea. Neither can a sudden rise in the continental landmass of Antarctica be called upon as a solution, for such a rise would itself have been of cataclysmic proportions, involving immense seismic activity. And some of the animals are found frozen within an already existing ice-cap, whilst others occur under the ice and in regions where no ice accumulates (owing to high-velocity winds). For the whales to have found their way to such high altitudes without tidal waves, they would presumably have died of natural causes, their bodies then sinking to the sea bed, and then being raised above sea level by earthquake activity. And during all this process, little or no decomposition had time to take place!

---

1 Ibid. p. 43.

Yet for two reasons such a "solution" is utterly impossible. To begin with, the bodies of whales and other marine life do not, in any case, sink to the sea bed when they die. They float to the surface, where they are immediately consumed by scavengers and microscopic life. Secondly, a major upsurge of the Antarctic continent, as envisaged by the above hypothesis, is entirely absurd, given the fact that the Antarctic landmass is actually *compressed* by the weight of thousands of meters of ice. Were this ice to be removed, the continent would presumably rise and achieve a far greater altitude than at present. In short, the growth of the ice-cap on Antarctica saw the land *sink*, not rise.

Which leaves us with a single possible solution: The frozen creatures of Antarctica were placed there by tidal waves, tidal waves, of immense proportions. And, since all such creatures are of species still alive today, these waves must have washed the continent in very recent times.

In their 1994 book, *When the Earth Nearly Died*, D. S. Allan and J. B. Delair highlighted evidence of this type and in general revisited much of the ground first covered by Donnelly and Velikovsky, though adding fascinating insights of their own. In particular, they examined the question of "the Drift," the vast deposit of clay, sand, gravel, and boulders (much of the latter rounded by the action of waves) that covers a great portion of the surface of the earth. They were able to show that this material, which is now explained away as the debris left behind by glaciers during one or more phases of the Ice Age, could only have been deposited where it is, in the condition it is found, by the action of onrushing waves. These waves, of apparently titanic dimensions, not only lifted forests and herds of animals wholesale, but even enormous boulders, some weighing thousands of tons, and tossed them around like pebbles. As well as uprooting forests, the waves also, in places, buried them under billions of tons of Drift material, where they are found to this day, often in a remarkably good state of preservation. This is the case, for example, over much of North America. "For example," say Allan and Delair, "at Scarborough Heights and elsewhere near Ontario, clays yielded remains of cedar and pine trees, portions of rushes, leaves, a variety of seeds, specimens of *Chara*, *Bryum*, *Fontinalis* and two species of *Hypnum*. Then, near the River Don, Toronto, leaves and wood fragments were discovered in dark hued clays 70ft (22m) below ground level, where, also, a Maple leaf occurred in overlying reddish ferruginous sand, itself overlain by boulder-clay. Boulder-clay also overlies a bed at Rolling River, Manitoba, containing shell and fish debris mixed with a great variety of plant remains."[1] Such remains were encountered throughout vast swathes of North America, taking in much of Canada and the United States. In Canada,

---

1 D. S. Allan and J. B. Delair, *When the Earth Nearly Died* (London, 1994) p. 91.

the buried trees were often of species, such as oak and plane, which can no longer grow in the latitudes where they occur. Indeed, the evidence shows clearly that even into the Arctic, great deciduous forests flourished at a very recent age. Thus,

> The peaty and woody accumulations in the Bow and Belly river valleys of Alberta are ... examples from western Canada, where pressure has sometimes hardened them to the consistency of lignite. Further north, just below the top soil at certain places in the valley of the Mackenzie River, shales forming the river banks are covered with the largely undecayed leaves of very ancient deciduous forest trees such as maple, oak and poplar, none of which can now thrive at that latitude.[1]

Early geologists were astonished by this evidence and reported it as they found it. They also drew the only conclusion that was possible from it: Namely that at some time in the recent past the climate of North America, including the Arctic reaches of Canada, had been much milder than now, and this mild epoch had been terminated by some cataclysm which had buried the forests under billions of tons of clay and gravel.

It should be noted that even in the Arctic there was discovered trees of the temperate regions, some of them still rooted in the original earth in which they grew. These trees were of species characteristic of the Miocene and Pliocene ages. Yet the territory in which they were found is believed to have been scoured by giant ice caps during the Pleistocene, during which such trees would have been obliterated. Evidently, as Allan and Delair observed, no ice caps ever covered these regions, and the whole concept of an Ice Age is open to question.[2] Glaciers, as opposed to large ice caps, were indeed formerly more extensive than now, and there is no question, for example, that even regions such as the highlands of Scotland supported glaciers in an age not too far distant. Allan and Delair however came to the conclusion that this "Ice Age" was of much shorter duration than is generally realized, and that it followed rather than preceded the extinction of the Pleistocene fauna. Indeed, for Allan and Delair it was the very catastrophe which brought about the extinction of these creatures, with its accompanying outbreak of massive volcanism, which (coating the planet with a dense cloud of volcanic ash and temporarily blotting out the sun) caused the cold spell and the growth of glaciers. But this "Ice Age" did not last millennia; it probably endured no more than a few centuries.

Allan and Delair also drew special attention to the hecatombs of animals, of the same epoch as the buried forests, found in caves throughout the world. The bones of these creatures, typically of the Pliocene and Pleistocene epochs, are found in great quantities all over the earth. The remains of hippopotamus, rhi-

---

1 Ibid., pp. 91-2.
2 Ibid.

noceros, lion, bear, deer, and occasionally mammoth and even man, lie smashed and mixed with a hardened mud known as "breccia." Such remains first came to the attention of the scholarly world in the early nineteenth century. Explorers, first in Europe and then in other regions, such as North and South America, were astonished to find vast quantities of "normally incompatible kinds of animals lying in unnaturally close juxtaposition."[1] Debris of every kind is found together: "Often accompanying these organic masses are both rounded and angular stones of dissimilar composition and, less frequently, sizable boulders." These sites, say Allan and Delair, "amount to underground charnelhouses."[2] One of the earliest reports, from Kent's Cavern in Torquay, England, the remains of the animals "suffered considerably from pressure, after having first undergone violence from the force which impelled and congregated them in this narrow creek. They were found driven into the interstices of the opposite wall, or piled in the greatest confusion against its side."[3]

Other British bone-caves and fissures of note occur on the Isle of Portland in Dorset; Durdham Down near Bristol; in the Mendip Hills, Somerset; at Cresswell Crags and Windy Knoll, both in Derbyshire; at the south end of Kirkdale, Yorkshire; on the Gower peninsula, Caldy Island and around Tenby in south Wales, where great accumulations of red clay invaded the cave at Cefn so forcefully that it ploughed up its original floor. "The bones in this cave belonged to mixed 'northern' and 'southern' animals — the 'northern' forms being represented by the bison, reindeer, and woolly rhinoceros and the 'southern' species by the ancient straight-tusked elephant (*Palaeoloxodon antiquus*), the round-nosed rhinoceros (*Dicerorhinus hemitoechus*), and *Hippotamus major*."[4]

As geologists and paleontologists began to explore more of the world, it became apparent that such cave-burials were by no means confined to Europe and North America. In time, they were found in every corner of the globe. Thus all over Asia caves packed with these remains were encountered. "Immense quantities of 'Pleistocene' animals bones closely resembling those from aforementioned European caverns and fissures have been excavated from numerous bone-caves in the Altai mountains of central Asia. They include such interesting forms as mastodon, giant camel, gazelle, saiga antelope, giant beaver and ostrich, and are reminiscent of others from parts of inland China and Korea, which are riddled with fissures and caverns closely packed with shell and animal remains closely

1 Ibid., p. 111.
2 Ibid.
3 J. McEnery, *Cavern Researches, or discoveries of Organic remains and of British and Roman Relics, in the caves of Kent's Hole, Anstis Cove, Chudleigh and Barry Head* (London, 1859).
4 Allan and Delair, op. cit., p. 112.

analogous to those we have just discussed."[1] Australia and New Zealand too revealed the same phenomenon: "Evidence clearly echoing all this has come to light in various Australian caves. Ice-sheets like those advocated by orthodox glaciologists were, of course, conspicuously absent from Australia, so this evidence is especially significant. It occurs, for example ... in caverns ... at Wellington; at Boree; near the head of the Colo river; at Yesseba, on the Macleay river; at the head of the Coodradigbee; not far from the head of the Bogan, and in other places."[2]

These caverns and similar ones in New Zealand contained the shattered bones of the local fauna of the Pliocene/Pleistocene epoch. These included various extinct marsupials and flightless birds, as well as specimens of those species still extant.

What, asked the explorers, could have caused such a phenomenon? What could have deposited the bodies of countless creatures, of diverse species and frequently of species not even from the same climate-zone or continent, into caves and fissures all over the world? What also could have shattered the bodies of these animals, mixed them with mud, gravel and other debris, and deposited them in the deepest and most inaccessible regions of the caves? The answer of the explorers, and the one agreed upon by Allan and Delair, was that the animals were washed into these caverns by onrushing waters and their bodies shattered and dismembered by the same force. It should be noted that the entrance to many of these caves is hundreds of meters above sea level. Yet it would appear that not all of the creatures — and occasionally men — were washed into the caves. Many, think Allan and Delair, may have gone there of their own volition. Sensing some oncoming calamity, they appear to have huddled into the underground retreats in hope of escaping. In the scenario outlined by Allan and Delair, as well as by Donnelly and Velikovsky before them, the tidal waves would have been preceded by a terrible wind, a hurricane of terrifying strength, with winds of hundreds of miles per hour; winds capable of lifting entire forests and even large rocks and sending them hurtling through the air. To escape this tempest, beasts of every species — and also human beings — retreated to the underground shelters, where they were, at least for the time being, safe. Yet the hurricane was followed by the great waves; and from these, caves offered little protection — unless of course the topography of the grotto led to the formation of air pockets which the waves could not penetrate, or alternately the great wind had blocked the cave entrance with debris prior to the arrival of the waves. Both these alternatives appear to have, on occasion, saved the lives of the fugitives, and Allan and Delair

---

1 Ibid., p. 114.

2 W. B. Clarke, "Remarks on the Sedimentary Foundations of New South Wales," *Annual Report of the Department of Mines, New South Wales* (3rd ed. 1875) p. 163.

drew attention to the fact that in legends from many lands, men had sought ref-uge from the Flood in caves. Often it is told how they had to dig themselves out of their underground retreat.

Before moving on, we should note that Allan and Delair highlighted much evidence to suggest that the so-called Pliocene epoch — the epoch during which the mastodon and other European mega fauna reached America — was contem-porary with the Pleistocene, and that the catastrophic destruction which left its signature throughout the globe ended the existence of the Pliocene mega fauna simultaneously with the destruction of the Pleistocene creatures. They noted that many of the "Pliocene" species, which had earlier been viewed as becom-ing extinct by the Pleistocene, are now known to have lived well into the latter epoch; and that, in general, the fauna identified as Pliocene were those of warmer climes, whereas those seen as "Pleistocene" tended to be characteristic of north-ern (or "glaciated") regions. In short, these were not two different epochs, but two different climate-areas.

EVIDENCE FROM THE ARCTIC

The most striking, and perhaps most talked-about, evidence for this recent cataclysm comes not from the Antarctic but from the Arctic, more specifically from the permafrost regions of Siberia and Alaska. The evidence from these areas was discussed in some detail in *Earth in Upheaval*, but, again, invariably ignored in modern textbooks.

In the Fairbanks district of Alaska, where the Tanana River joins the Yukon, gold is mined out of gravel and "muck." This muck is a frozen mass of animals and trees. Velikovsky quotes F. Rainey, of the University of Alaska, where he describes the scene:

> Wide cuts, often several miles in length and sometimes as much as 140 feet in depth, are now being sluiced out along stream valleys tributary to the Tanana in the Fairbanks District. In order to reach the gold-bearing gravel-beds an over-burden of frozen silt or 'muck' is removed with hy-draulic giants. This "muck" contains enormous numbers of frozen bones of extinct animals such as mammoth, mastodon, super-bison and horse.[1]

It is freely admitted that these animals perished in comparatively recent times. Along with extinct species were found enormous quantities of ani-mals of species still surviving. Mixed with the bodies of the animals, most of whom were dismembered and whose bones were smashed — although their flesh and skin are often well preserved — were found millions upon millions of uprooted and smashed trees, along with other types of debris, such as sand and gravel. The whole mass of animals, trees and gravel was found thoroughly mixed in a promiscuous mass, as though thrown to-

1 F. Rainey, "Archaeological Investigation in Central Alaska," *American Antiquity*, V (1940), 305.

gether by some immense and virtually random force. According to F. C. Hibben of the University of New Mexico; "Although the formation of the deposits of muck is not clear, there is ample evidence that at least parts of this material were deposited under catastrophic conditions. Mammal remains are for the most part dismembered and disarticulated, even though some fragments yet retain, in their frozen state, portions of ligaments, skin, hair, and flesh. Twisted and torn trees are piled in splintered masses.... At least four considerable layers of volcanic ash may be traced in these deposits, although they are extremely warped and distorted.[1]

We have encountered these four destruction episodes already, in ancient human tradition; and we shall encounter them again, in archaeological records, in regions far removed from Alaska.

It seems apparent that when these deposits were laid down the area was subjected to repeated and violent volcanic activity; yet the scale and nature of the devastation goes well beyond anything attributable to volcanoes alone. Evidently great waves from the ocean had repeatedly, on four separate occasions, uprooted entire forests and lifted herds of animals, of every kind and variety, and thrown them together, twisted, smashed and dismembered, along with billions of tons of sand and gravel, into the Polar regions.

In various levels of the icy muck, stone implements were found "frozen *in situ* at great depths and in apparent association" with the Ice Age fauna, implying that "men were contemporary with extinct animals in Alaska."[2] In Velikovsky's words, "Worked flints, characteristically shaped, called Yuma points, were repeatedly found in the Alaskan muck, one hundred and more feet [about thirty meters] below the surface. One spear point was found there between a lion's jaw and a mammoth's tusk."[3] Yet similar weapons were used only a few generations ago by the Athapascan Indians, who camped in the Upper Tanana Valley.[4] According to Hibben, "It has been suggested that even modern Eskimo points are remarkably Yuma-like," all of which, as Velikovsky noted, "indicates that the multitudes of torn animals and splintered forests date from a time not many thousand years ago."

Such discoveries recall the opinion of a number of American geologists in the latter part of the nineteenth and the first part of the twentieth centuries, among them George Frederick Wright (1838–1921), Newton Horace Winchell (1839–1914) and Warren Upham (1850–1934). Wright came to the conclusion that the Ice Age "did not close until about the time that the civilization of Egypt, Babylo-

---

1 F. C. Hibben, "Evidence of Early Man in Alaska," *American Antiquity*, VIII (1943), 256.
2 Rainey, loc cit., p. 307.
3 "Earth in Upheaval," p.5. Cf. Hibben, *American Antiquity*, VIII, 257.
4 Ibid. Cf. Rainey, loc cit., p. 301.

nia and Western Turkestan had attained a high degree of development," a view opposed to the "greatly exaggerated ideas of the antiquity of the glacial epoch."[1]

The permafrost regions of the Russian north revealed a situation precisely paralleling that in Alaska. From the sixteenth and seventeenth centuries, when Russian explorers and trappers began to penetrate the frozen wastelands of Siberia, there came reports of elephants, of a type no longer in existence, found in great quantities in the icy ground. A lucrative trade in mammoth ivory quickly developed. By the middle of the nineteenth century so much of this material was reaching Europe that people began to talk about the "ivory mines" of the region, and soon Northern Siberia was to provide more than half the world's supply of the material.

One remarkable feature of these creatures was the state of preservation of the soft tissue. Flesh, skin and hair are often seen, and the flesh so well-preserved by the cold, that it can, on occasion, be safely eaten.

It soon became clear that many areas of the Russian east, but most especially north-eastern Siberia, held vast quantities of these creatures just beneath the surface. They are found, as a rule, in conditions very similar to those of the "muck" deposits in Alaska, where, as we saw, the bodies of mammoths are found intermingled with those of other species, both extinct and extant, mixed along with other kinds of debris, but most especially sand and gravel, as well as smashed and uprooted trees.

In the Arctic Ocean, just to the north of Siberia, lie various groups of islands. The earliest of these to be explored, the Liakhov Islands, were found to be full of the bones of mammoths and other creatures. "Such was the enormous quantity of mammoths' remains that it seemed ... that the island was actually composed of the bones and tusks of elephants, cemented together by icy sand."[2] The New Siberian Islands, discovered in 1806 and 1806, present the same picture. "The soil of these desolate islands is absolutely packed full of the bones of elephants and rhinoceroses in astonishing numbers."[3] Again, "These islands were full of mammoth bones, and the quantity of tusks and teeth of elephants and rhinoceroses, found in the nearby island of New Siberia, was perfectly amazing, and surpassed anything which had as yet been discovered."[4]

It would appear that these islands were formed, at least in part, by billions of tons of animal and vegetable matter, as well as sand and gravel, which was swept

---

1 G. F. Wright, *The Ice Age in North America* (1891), p. 683.
2 D. Garth Whitley, "The Ivory Islands of the Arctic Ocean," *Journal of the Philosophical Society of Great Britain*, XII (1910), 35.
3 Ibid. p. 36.
4 Ibid. p. 42.

into the polar regions by enormous waves, waves which were, by the nineteenth century, termed "waves of translation." These waves, it appears, were accompanied by a sudden and dramatic climate change. Temperatures dropped catastrophically. J. D. Dana, the leading American geologist of the second half of the nineteenth century, wrote: "The encasing in ice of huge elephants, and the perfect preservation of the flesh, shows that the cold finally became *suddenly* extreme, as of a single winter's night, and knew no relenting afterward."[1]

It has often been emphasized, rightly, that the mammoth, as well as the woolly rhinoceros, so many of whose bodies are found in Siberia, are *not*, in spite of their hairy coats, creatures of the Arctic. Elephants in particular, whose daily calorie intake is enormous, could never survive on the sparse mosses and lichens which now cover the barren wastelands of northern Siberia. These were animals of the temperate zones, a fact confirmed by the contents of their mouths and stomachs. Here were found plants and grasses that do not now grow in northern Siberia. "The contents of the stomachs have been carefully examined; they showed the undigested food, leaves of trees now found in Southern Siberia, but a long way from the existing deposits of ivory. Microscopic examination of the skin showed red blood corpuscles, which was proof not only of a sudden death, but that the death was due to suffocation either by gases or water, evidently the latter in this case. But the puzzle remained to account for the sudden freezing up of this large mass of flesh so as to preserve it for future ages."[2]

On the islands of the Arctic Ocean "neither trees, nor shrubs, no bushes, exist ... and yet the bones of elephants, rhinoceroses, buffaloes, and horses are found in this icy wilderness in numbers which defy all calculation."[3] Clearly, either the climate of the region was much warmer when the above creatures lived, or they were swept into these latitudes by some titanic force, almost certainly tidal waves. Or, alternatively, both these options might be correct: The cataclysm which threw together the animals and extinguished their lives, may also have changed the climate suddenly and dramatically; a freezing so rapid that flesh and hair was preserved intact.

The contents of the mammoths' mouths and stomachs revealed another astonishing fact. Some had been eating, as well as grass and other herbs, flowering plants, such as buttercups *in full bloom*. The comments of American zoologist Ivan T. Sanderson say it all: "Not one trace of pine needles or of the leaves of any other trees were in the stomach of the Berezovka mammoth; little flowering buttercups, tender sedges and grasses were found exclusively. Buttercups will not even

1 J. D. Dana, *Manual of Geology* (4th ed., 1894), p. 1007.
2 Whitley, loc cit., p. 56.
3 Ibid. p. 50.

grow at forty degrees (4.4°C), and they cannot flower in the absence of sunlight. A detailed analysis of the contents of the Berezovka mammoth's stomach brought to light a long list of plants, some of which still grow in the arctic, but are actually much more typical of Southern Siberia today. Therefore, the mammoths either made annual migrations north for the short summer, or the part of the earth where their corpses are found today was somewhere else in warmer latitudes at the time of their death, or both."[1]

The circumstances surrounding the deaths of these creatures constitute, in Sanderson's testimony, a profound mystery: "Here is a really shocking — to our previous way of thinking — picture. Vast herds of enormous, well-fed beasts not especially designed for extreme cold, placidly feeding in sunny pastures, delicately plucking flowering buttercups at a temperature in which we would probably not even have needed a coat. Suddenly they were all killed without any visible sign of violence and before they could so much as swallow a last mouthful of food, and then were quick-frozen so rapidly that every cell of their bodies is perfectly preserved, despite their great bulk and their high temperature. What, we may well ask, could possibly do this?"

What indeed.

One notable aspect of the cataclysm which terminated the Pleistocene, and which was stressed by Velikovsky, was the universal signature left by giant tectonic disturbances. Everywhere, even in areas of the planet now tectonically inactive, vast earthquakes erupted. In some places, it seems, mountain-ranges rose overnight to prodigious heights. In others, the land sank, consigning whole regions into the depths of the sea. During these events, rivers changed their courses and lakes overflowed. In some places, earth movements dammed rivers, forming new lakes. Velikovsky stressed that in many localities, geologists found to their astonishment that lakes, river-valleys, deltas and cataracts were often no more than three to four thousand years old. Often it was possible to be much more precise, and it was discovered that a great many of these features were between 3,000 and 3,500 years old.

GEOLOGY OF THE ATLANTIC

With the development of new technologies over the past century, our knowledge of the ocean-bed has changed dramatically. It is now known, for example, that an enormous submarine mountain range, with numerous active volcanoes, runs from the farthest reaches of the North Atlantic down to the Antarctic Ocean. In places, this range reaches the surface, where we find islands such as Iceland,

---

1 Ivan T. Sanderson, "Riddle of the Frozen Giants," *Saturday Evening Post*, No. 39, (January, 1960).

and archipelagoes such as the Azores. This mountain-range marks a vast fault-line where the earth's plates are subjected to upward pressure, one result of which has been the pushing-apart of the African and South American plates. The west-ward movement of the South American plate, crashing against the Pacific Plate, caused the rise of the Andes Mountains. As we shall see, there is evidence that in very recent times the Andes rose by thousands of feet, indicating a correspond-ingly recent and powerful outburst of activity in the Mid-Atlantic Ridge. North America and Europe have also been pushed apart by this pressure, though the direction of movement is not here so clear. Certainly Europe and North America do not "fit" together the way Africa and South America do.

In 1948 and again in 1949, two new surveys of the Atlantic, employing the latest techniques, were launched. The results of the latter expedition, ironically enough aboard a ship named *Atlantis*, were astonishing. In an article published in the *National Geographic*, the expedition's leader, Professor M. Ewing of Colum-bia University, admitted that what they had found amounted to a series of "new scientific puzzles."[1] These "puzzles" all pointed to the fact that extensive areas of the Atlantic, now under hundreds and even thousands of meters of water, had once — in the apparently not-too-distant past — been dry land. First on the list of these was the discovery, adjacent to the Mid-Atlantic Ridge, in the region of the Azores, "of prehistoric beach-sand ... brought up in one case from a depth of two and the other nearly three and one half miles, far from any place where beaches are today." One of these sand deposits was found twelve hundred miles from land.

Sand forms along shore-lines, where the action of waves, together with wind and rain and changes in temperature gradually breaks down the rocks into small particles. Sand cannot form under the sea, which is a still and virtually weather-free environment. If it is found under seas and oceans it must have formed on dry land, and in this case, on an ancient beach. The deposits were found to be well-sorted by surf action into the usual pattern of shoreline beaches familiar to geolo-gists. Ewing's conclusion was that "Sometime in the distant past this sand found deep beneath the ocean must have been located on a beach, at or near the surface of the sea." These considerations presented Professor Ewing with a dilemma: "Ei-ther the land must have sunk two to three miles, or the sea once must have been two or three miles lower than now. Either conclusion is startling. If the sea was once two miles lower, where could all the extra water have gone?"

There were other surprises in store. One of the greatest of these concerned ocean-bed sediment. This sediment consists of silt so fine that its particles can

---

1   M. Ewing, "New Discoveries on the Mid-Atlantic Ridge," *National Geographic Magazine,* Vol. XCVI, No. 5 (November, 1949)

be carried in ocean water for a long time before sinking to the bottom, as well as the skeletons of minute animals, foraminifera, which live in the upper waters of the ocean in vast numbers. Judging by the supposed age of the oceans, it was believed that this oozy sediment would be of great depth. The foothills of the Mid-Atlantic Ridge, not surprisingly, did have thousands of feet of sediment, yet the ocean-bed was almost devoid of it. In Ewing's words, the expedition's measurements "clearly indicate thousands of feet of sediments on the foothills of the Ridge. Surprisingly, however, we have found that in the great flat basins on either side of the Ridge, this sediment appears to be less than 100 feet thick," a fact, Ewing went on to describe as "startling." Actually, it was admitted that the sound echoes, used to measure the depth of the silt, arrived almost simultaneously, and the most that could be attributed in such circumstances to the sediment was less than hundred feet of thickness, or the margin of error. In short, the silt was almost undetectable and maybe much less even than 100 feet thick.

What all this meant, though it was never openly admitted, was that the ocean-bed was not millions of years old. It can only have formed in comparatively recent times.

The sediment that they did find, according to Ewing, consisted of "the shells and skeletons of countless small creatures" as well as from "volcanic dust and wind-blown soil drifting out over the sea; and from the ashes of burned out meteorites and cosmic dust from outer space sifting constantly down upon the earth."

It was however the Mid-Atlantic Ridge itself which provided some of the greatest surprises. Some of what they found, they expected: "We dredged up rocks of igneous, or 'fire-made,' type from the sides and tops of peaks on the Mid-Atlantic Ridge, which indicated that submarine volcanoes and lava flows have been active there." In the area of the Azores the expedition found an uncharted submarine mountain, 8,000 feet high, with "many layers of volcanic ash," and farther on, a great chasm dropping down 1,809 fathoms (10,854 feet), "as if a volcano had caved in there at some time in the past." Although this speaks of a vast volcanic explosion, it was not entirely unexpected. But not everything made sense. "In a depth of 3,600 feet (600 fathoms) we found rocks that tell an interesting story about the past history of the Atlantic Ocean ... granite and sedimentary rocks of types which originally must have been part of a continent."

This last statement is astonishing, given the dogma, routinely and frequently asserted, that the Azores represent a recent *uplifting* of the Mid-Atlantic Ridge, and that no rock formations of a continental type could ever have existed there. A little explanation is here called for. Granite is classed by geologists as *sial* (rocks rich in silicates and aluminum), the basic building-blocks of continents, and it is lighter than the rock of the ocean-floor, known as *sima*, which is composed of basalt. Geologists see the lighter granite sial as sitting, or even floating, upon the heavier sima, much like ice bergs floating upon the ocean. And just like ice bergs, the granite continents protrude only a little above the oceans, with over 90% of their volume rooted deep in the basalt of the earth's mantle. Thus finding granite on the Mid-Atlantic Ridge was a sure sign that continental land had once existed there.

Ewing goes on to state that "Most of the rocks that we dredge here were rounded and marked with deep scratches, or striations." Markings like this are routinely ascribed to the actions of glaciers. "But we also found some loosely con-solidated mud stones, so soft and weak they would not have held together in the iron grasp of a glacier. How they got here is another riddle to be solved by further research."

At various points along the Mid-Atlantic Ridge the expedition dredged up large amounts of coral, deep under the ocean and far removed from any modern coastlines.[1] Since coral only grows in shallow water near coastlines (no species can survive at a depth exceeding 40 meters), this constituted first class evidence of the prior existence of islands in or near the regions where the coral was located.

The expedition did not confine itself to the Mid-Atlantic Ridge and the ocean bed. The continental shelf of North America was also examined. Here they found evidence scarcely less startling. The entrance to New York Harbor, the Hudson River, was found to have a canyon running into the ocean, not only as far as the edge of the continental shelf, a hundred and twenty miles offshore, but also for another hundred miles in deeper water. "If all this valley was originally carved out by the river on dry land, as seems probable, it means either that the ocean floor of the Eastern seaboard of North America once must have stood about two miles above its present level and has since subsided, or else that the level of the sea was once about two miles lower than now."[2]

Taken all together, the results of the 1949 expedition indicate that, at some time in the comparatively recent past, the Atlantic Ocean was smaller, and that in many areas now covered by water, there was dry land. Some paroxysm of nature had dramatically altered the shapes and sizes of the continents, turning areas that had been dry land into sea many thousands of feet deep. Ewing avoided terms like "catastrophe" and "paroxysm" and instead, fearful perhaps of being seen as the proponent of a heresy, made only a negative statement: "There is no reason to believe that this mighty underwater mass of mountains [of the Mid Atlantic Ridge] is connected in any way with the legendary lost Atlantis which Plato described as having sunk beneath the waves."

---

1   Ibid. p. 286.
2   Ibid.

MORE EVIDENCE FROM THE ATLANTIC

Professor Ewing's expedition was only one of a series, from many countries, which around the same time reported anomalous and frankly astonishing discoveries in the Atlantic. One of these, from Sweden, was headed by Dr. Otto Mellis. The expedition, during the years 1947-1948, yielded core samples containing sand from the Romache Deep along the Mid-Atlantic Ridge. Perhaps wary of the controversial nature of his discoveries, Mellis did not publish these findings until ten years later.[1] So compelling was the nature of the findings however, that geologists have gradually come round to the idea that the Azores are composed chiefly of continental material, some even conceding that there might be enough such material (*sial*) in the mid-Atlantic to make up a landmass the size of Spain. Such, for example, was the opinion of geologist (and noted Atlantis skeptic) L. Sprague de Camp.[2] In line with this, it is now admitted that a separate continental plate, called a microplate, underlies the Azores, and that the islands, moreover, mark one of the most volcanically-active regions of the earth. Nevertheless, the area encompassed by the microplate is a good deal smaller than Spain, and much closer to Ireland in terms of size; so it unlikely that the any prior existing island could have been very much bigger than this.

Commenting on a still earlier oceanographic study, headed by American geophysicist Charles S. Piggot, which produced core samples containing two zones rich in volcanic ash,[3] Swedish oceanographer Hans Pettersson wrote: "The topmost of the two volcanic strata is found above the topmost glacial stratum, which indicates that this volcanic catastrophe or catastrophes occurred in postglacial times.... It can therefore not be entirely ruled out that the Mid-Atlantic Ridge, where the sample originated, was above sea level up to about ten thousand years ago and did not subside to its present depth until later."[4] This was a truly sensational admission to make, and more or less constitutes an official scientific seal of approval on the whole Atlantis story.

In 1957, Dr. Rene Malaise of the Riks Museum in Stockholm announced that a colleague, Dr. R. W. Kolbe, had found definitive proof of the geologically recent subsidence of the Mid-Atlantic Ridge. Dr. Kolbe of the Swedish Museum of Natural History had been commissioned to investigate diatoms (small freshwater lake animals) found in deep-sea cores obtained during the above men-

---

1 Otto Mellis, "Zur Sedimentation in Der Romache-Tiefe (Ein Beitrag zur Erklärung der Enstellung des Tiefseesandes in Atlantischen Ozean)," *Geologischen Rundschau*, (Goteborg, 1958).

2 L. Sprague de Camp, *Lost Continents*, (New York, 1970).

3 Charles S. Piggot, "Core samples of the ocean bottom," *Carnegie Institution of Washington News Service Bulletin* Staff Edition, 4 (no. 9), 6 (December 1936).

4 Hans Pettersson, *Atlantis och Atlanten* (Stockholm, 1944).

tioned Swedish Deep-Sea Expedition. Although the expedition included a globe-encircling study, only those cores taken from the Mid-Atlantic Ridge yielded the following: Multitudinous shells of fresh-water diatoms and fossilized remains of terrestrial plants.[1] So compelling was the evidence that by 1975, the British journal *New Scientist* could produce a headline which asked, "Concrete Evidence of Atlantis?" Commenting upon a recent oceanographic expedition, the magazine noted that, "Although they make no such fanciful claim from their results as to have discovered the mythical mid-Atlantic landmass, an international group of oceanographers has now convincingly confirmed preliminary findings that a sunken block of continent lies in the middle of the Atlantic Ocean. The discovery comes from analyzing dredge samples taken along the line of the Verma offset fault, a long east-west fracture zone lying between Africa and South America close to latitude 11 degrees N."[2]

Taking into account both geological and biological evidence, Malaise came to the conclusion that parts of the Ridge must have existed as large islands up to the end of the last Ice Age or later. He also theorized that these landmasses must have had fresh-water lakes in order to account for the existence of fresh-water animals.[3] Commenting on Malaise's theory, Kolbe wrote; "it provides a natural explanation of the layer consisting exclusively of fresh-water *diatoms*, which is otherwise difficult to comprehend."[4]

Notwithstanding all these sensational revelations, the academic establishment, especially in America and Britain, continued to produce articles which completely ignored them, pronouncing the mantra again and again that no sizeable landmass ever existed in the middle of the Atlantic. The Mid-Atlantic sandbanks, for example, which should have provided definitive proof for a recent and catastrophic subsidence of coastline, was "explained" by Ewing himself as the result of deep-ocean currents washing the sand from continental coastlines into the middle of the Atlantic. Yet no evidence for the existence of such currents, known as "turbidity currents," has even been found in the relevant regions. Likewise the continental rock of the Azores region was explained as something of the distant past. A geologist (Richard Cifelli) who, twenty years after Ewing's 1948 and 1949 expeditions, reviewed the latter's findings, failed completely to

---

1   R. W. Kolbe, "Fresh-Water Diatoms from Atlantic Deep-Sea Sediments," *Science*, Vol. 126, No. 3282, 22 (November, 1957).
2   "Concrete Evidence of Atlantis?" *New Scientist* (1975).
3   Rene Malaise, Sjunket l and i Atlanten, (Stockholm, 1956). See also his *Atlantis en Geologisk Verklighet*, (Stockholm, 1951).
4   Kolbe, loc cit.

mention the discovery of continental material in the Mid-Atlantic Ridge.[1] Ewing was puzzled, even dismayed, by these discoveries; yet he was honest enough to report them. However, in attempting to explain away such discoveries he helped solidify the consensus that nothing catastrophic had ever happened, and paved the way for reviews of his work like those of Cifelli.[2]

The academic outlook was not so bleak in Russia, where the facts were at least noted and given honest consideration. Thus in 1963 Russian chemist Nikolai Zhirov collated all the evidence up to that point, in a publication aimed at putting the Atlantis debate on a scientific footing.[3] He quoted not five or ten but quite literally scores of geologists, oceanographers, paleontologists and biologists, many of them from the then Soviet Union, who were of the opinion that the Mid-Atlantic Ridge had stood above the water as recently as the end of the Ice Age and even later. Thus for example in Chapter 9 he quotes A. V. Zhivago, and G. B. Udintsev, who noted that although the "narrow, elongated submarine" mountains of the Mid-Atlantic Ridge cannot have formed a submerged continent, nevertheless, "in the past the summits of these ranges were evidently in a subaerial [above sea level] position; this fits in excellently with paleozoological and paleobotanical data. Quite recently many of these ranges were bridges linking up continents and the route for the migration of fauna and flora."[4] Thus also V. E. Khain wrote: "The rugged topography of the slopes of the submarine ranges was evidently formed under subaerial conditions, by river erosion. This is indicated by the finding of fresh-water fauna on the slopes of the Mid-Atlantic Ridge. It must be pointed out that even today some sections of the ridge jut out above the surface of the ocean in the shape of islands.... It is quite possible that there were many more such sections in the relatively recent past."[5] Similar opinions were expressed by geologist D. I. Mushketov,[6] geologist A. N. Mazarovich,[7] marine geologist Professor M. V. Klenova,[8] world-famous geologist and geographer and

1 Richard Cifelli, "Age relationships of Mid-Atlantic Ridge sediments," *Special Paper* No. 124, *Geological Society of America*, (1970).

2 For another example of an enormous genre of such material, see John Speicher, "Plate Tectonics — A Startling New View of Our Turbulent Earth," *Popular Science*, Vol. 200, No. 6, (June, 1972).

3 Nikolai Zhirov, *Atlantis: Atlantology, Basic Problems* (English ed. 1968).

4 A. V. Zhivago and G. B. Udintsev, "Sovremenniye problemy geomorphologni dna morei i okeanov ("Modern Problems of the Geomorphology of the Floor of the Seas and Oceans"), *Herald of the USSR Academy of Sciences*, Geography Series, No. 1, (1960) p. 28.

5 V. E. Khain, *Proiskhozhdeniye materikov i okeanov (Origin of Continents and Oceans)* (Moscow, 1961) pp. 5-7.

6 D. I. Mushketov, *Regionalnaya geotektonika (Regional Geotectonics)* (Moscow, 1935) p. 117.

7 A. I. Mazarovich, *Osnovy regionalnoi geologii materikov (Fundamentals of the Regional Geology of Continents)*, Part 2 (Moscow, 1952) p. 105.

8 M. V. Klenova, *Geologiya morya (Geology of the Sea)* (Moscow, 1948) p. 411.

Fellow of the Moscow Academy Vladimir Obruchev,[1] as well as scores of other specialists from both the Soviet Union and elsewhere.

What made these and so many other Soviet and Scandinavian scientists certain that much of the Ridge was above water in such a recent age? There were many indicators in that direction, some of the most significant of which was the distribution on the sea bed of erratic boulders and gravel, supposedly carried south by icebergs during the last Ice Age. This material was invariably found only to the east of the Ridge, indicating that the now submerged mountain-range had once formed a barrier to the icebergs which had brought the Polar debris to the region. Furthermore, it was found that the sediments on either side of the Ridge differed radically in composition: Those to the east were composed chiefly of the skeletal remains of cold-dwelling plankton and foraminifera; those to the west of warmth-loving varieties: Again proof that a barrier had existed against the movement of the Gulf Stream. In Zhirov's words: "One of the first serious attempts to obtain a cross-section of the sediments on the North Atlantic Ridge was made by C. S. Piggott, who studied a series of 13 cores taken along the line Halifax-Falmouth. One of these cores was obtained near the summit of the North Atlantic Ridge, and the others from each of its sides. On the western side, about 30 kilometers from the summit, the sediments contained the remains of warmth-loving foraminifera of the species now inhabiting the Gulf Stream. This indicates that here sedimentation was slow and more or less homogeneous. A completely different picture is given by the sediments from the eastern side of the ridge, likewise taken at a distance of about 30 kilometers from the summit. They contained thick layers of sand and gravel along with remains of cold-loving foraminifera. Here sedimentation obviously took place during a period when the climate was colder than today — in the period of the last glaciation."[2] The point is that nowadays the warm Gulf Stream flows right over the submerged Mid-Atlantic Ridge and deposits warm water foraminifera right across the Atlantic. The only possible conclusion, according to Zhirov and a whole host of scientists, is that during the last Ice Age the Mid-Atlantic Ridge formed a mountain range above sea level and divided the Atlantic in two. The ocean to the west of the Ridge was kept mild by the Gulf Stream, whereas to the east a cold current flowing south from the glaciers and ice-caps of Britain and Scandinavia brought icebergs to the region which deposited debris in the sea bed.

It is generally held that during the Ice Age the Bay of Biscay was full of icebergs, and a cold current flowed from northern Scandinavia down along the coast

1 In a paper titled, "The Riddle of the Siberian Polar Region," quoted by Zhirov, op. cit., p. 317.

2 N. Zhirov, op. cit., p. 276.

of Spain towards North Africa. However, since Allan and Delair have proved that the "Ice Age" was a relatively short period of cooling that followed (rather than preceded) the end of the Pleistocene, we have to assume that the cold northern current flowed during the early part of the Holocene; and that the Mid-Atlantic barrier still existed during the Mesolithic period.

Continuing in the same mode, Zhirov quotes scientist J. Bourcart: "Evidently the cores did not reach the base of ancient Quaternary [Pleistocene and Holocene] layers. The tube went through four thick layers of glacial (terrigenous sediments of icebergs) and inter-glacial sediments (globigerina ooze interspersed with substrata of volcanic ash). The upper glacial layer was covered with globigerina ooze. It should be noted that these layers are very thin along the American and European continental platforms, as well as on the ridges themselves (for example, Core No. 8 was only 1.20 meters long). This thinness of the sediments is evidently due to erosion by fast-flowing currents, which could not have existed at the present water depth of 1,300 meters over the ridge; it is testimony of a great uplift of the ridge in the Quaternary period. One must assume that the ridge was above the water level during the glacial phases. On the other hand, in the European-African Basin the sediment layer is so thick that instead of four glacial layers only one was discovered. The polar currents, deflected by the Earth's rotation towards the Newfoundland Banks, ended in those days evidently more to the east, where they were stopped by the then subaerial [above sea level] Atlantic Ridge."[1]

Incidentally, the attempt to explain this away by suggesting that during the Ice Age the Gulf Stream was simply not as strong as now and just faded away in the middle of the Atlantic founders on the evidence. If this were correct, then we would expect the warm-water foraminifera of the western Atlantic to be gradually replaced by the cold-water varieties of the east. But this is not the case. On the contrary, the boundary between the two varieties is defined *precisely* by the barrier of the Mid Atlantic Ridge — proof positive that it then stood above the waves.

PLANTS AND ANIMALS OF THE ATLANTIC SHORES

The evidence of the ocean itself thus points to a Mid-Atlantic Ridge above the water just a few thousand years ago, in the epoch during which human beings had entered the Middle and New Stone Ages. The land tells a similar tale. A great many species of both plants and animals living today are found on either side of the Atlantic Ocean, and only in those regions. Some occur in Western Europe and eastern North America; others in West Africa and Brazil; still others in south-west Europe and north-west Africa and the Caribbean. Many of these also

1 J. Bourcart, *Géographie du fond des mers* (Paris, 1949) p. 266.

occur in the Atlantic islands, in the Azores, Canaries, Madeira, and elsewhere. The existence of this "Atlantic" biota has long been known and, by the early years of the twentieth century, had begun to make such an impact that many mainstream scientists began to openly support the notion of a land-bridge between the Old and New Worlds; a land-bridge surviving into very recent times. Many of the plants and animals — animals in particular — it was pointed out, could not have survived a long sea passage; and indeed several of them, such as land mollusks and earthworms, die very quickly on being exposed to sea water.

It would be impossible, in the pages of a book such as this, to provide a comprehensive overview of this Atlantic flora and fauna: such an endeavor would require an enormous volume of its own. Here we shall confine ourselves to a brief overview.

Of plants found only in Western Europe and North America we might mention *Calluna, Leerzia*, the sedge *Carex extensia, Lobelia dortmanna, Eriocaulon septangulare*, and the water-weeds *Alisma, Lemna, Potamogeton* and *Myriophyllum*. The freshwater genus *Naias flexilis*, present in most North American streams and ponds, occurs in Europe only in south-west Ireland, Galway, the Isle of Skye, Perthshire and Esthwaite Water in Cumbria. To these may be added the American strand-plant *Spartina stricta*, which still thrives in south-western Europe and *Scheucheria palustris* which, although common in Canadian bogs, has only a tenuous foothold in western-most Europe. As might be expected, more than one writer has seen these links as proof of a former and recent land-link. Thus H. E. Forrest comments: "In particular, it is difficult to believe that water-weeds such as *Potamogeton, Lemna, Alisma* and *Myriophyllum* could have reached their present habitats by an Arctic route. If, however, they were denizens of the lakes and marshes of an Atlantean continent in Miocene and Pliocene times, their distribution is accounted for quite naturally."[1] Similar conclusions were drawn by botanist R. F. Scharff, who concentrated on the flora of southern Europe and the Atlantic islands of Madeira and the Azores. The evidence, he believed, showed that the Azores and Madeira were united to mainland Europe at least until "glacial" times.[2]

One of the plants studied by Scharff was the orchid *Spiranthes*, which flourishes today only in North America and Ireland. We hear that "*Spiranthes* is apparently a relict member of what has been called the North Atlantic Arctic flora, the present disjointed distribution of which suggests original dissemination via

---

1 H. E. Forrest, *The Atlantean Continent: its bearing on the Great Ice Age and the distribution of species* (2nd ed. London, 1935) p. 297.
2 R. F. Scharff, "Some remarks on the Atlantis Problem," *Proceedings of the Royal Irish Academy*, sect. B, (1902) Vol. XXIV, pp. 268-303.

islands or land-routes now far below Atlantic waters."[1] Similar clear links are found further south, and the western extremity of the transatlantic land-route passing through Madeira and the Azores seems to have lain in what is today the Caribbean region. Thus, "A connection between the flora of Madeira and that of the West Indies and tropical America has been inferred by the presence in the former of six ferns found nowhere in Europe or North Africa, but existing on the islands of the east coast of America or on the Isthmus of Panama. A further relationship to that continent can be traced by the presence in Madeira of the beautiful erinaceous tree *Clethra arborea*, belonging to a genus which is otherwise wholly American; and of a *Persea*, a tree laurel, also an American genus."[2]

The distribution of animals, almost exclusively tiny animals such as insects and mollusks, tells a similar tale. Numerous species of land snails and freshwater mollusks, for example, occur in Western Europe and North America, and in no other regions. Thus a type of freshwater mollusk inhabiting a bog in County Down, Northern Ireland, is a stunted form allied to some still living in Greenland and North America. The same affinities are found in the Atlantic islands, particularly the Canaries and Azores. On this topic D. S. Merezhkovsky noted, "The geographical distribution of the molluscs *Oleacinidae*, existing only in Central America, in the Antilles, the Canaries, the Azores, on the island of Madeira and in the Mediterranean basin, presupposes the existence ... of a continent embracing all these regions. Fifteen varieties of molluscs live only in the Antilles and on the Senegal coast of Africa, and it is impossible to explain their presence by the transportation of the embryos; while the coral fauna of the islands of St Thomas includes six varieties, one of which, apart from the island, breeds on the submarine rocks of Florida; while four are on the Bermuda isles, which again can scarcely be explained by the transportation of the embryos, as their watery life is too short to allow for their being transported by ocean currents."[3]

As with mollusks, so with annelids (earth worms) and insects: The French writer L. Germain highlighted the fact that certain insects, such as the Canary Islands butterfly *Setomorpha discipunctella*, also occur in West Africa and tropical America.[4] On the same topic, Lewis Spence notes that: "Sixty percent of the butterflies and moths found in the Canaries are of Mediterranean origin, and twenty per cent of these are to be found in America.... The (crustacean) *Platyarthus* is represented by three species in Western Europe and North Africa, one in the

1 Allen and Delair, op. cit. p. 87.
2 H. E. Forrest, op. cit. p. 249.
3 D. S. Merezhovsky, *The Secret of the West* (trans. J. Cournos, London, 1933) p. 118.
4 L. Germain, "Le problème de l'Atlantide de la Zoologie," *Annales de Géographie, Paris*, Vol. xxii (1913) No. 123 p. 216.

Canaries, and one in Venezuela."[1] Of the insects of the Azores, Wallace said: "The butterflies, moths and *Hymenoptera* are few in number.... Beetles are more numerous.... The total number of species is 212, of which 175 are European.... 23 of these are not found in any of the other Atlantic islands.... Besides these are 36 species not found in Europe, of which 19 are natives of Madeira or the Canaries, 3 are American, and 14 are altogether peculiar to the Azores. These latter are mostly allied to species found in Europe, or in the other Atlantic islands, while one is allied to an American species.... Many of these small insects have, no doubt, survived the glacial epoch, and may, in that case, represent very ancient forms which have become extinct in their native country."[2]

The same phenomenon is found among European and North American ants and beetles. Among the *Lepidoptera* 243 species are common to these continents, while: "A great number of North American ants are identical with European ones.... Northern Europe possesses one peculiar genus of Ant — *Anergetes*. This is closely allied to *Epoccus*, another genus confined to North America....487 species of *Coleoptera* are common to North America, Northern Asia and Europe."[3] As Allen and Delair note, the restriction of the water-mite *Hydrachna geographica*, a creature, which they stress, "with limited powers of flight," to Europe and eastern North America provides yet another example, and also parallels the distribution of the freshwater sponge *Hetermeyenia ryderi*, which thrives today only along the North American Atlantic coast and western Scotland and Ireland.[4] "Such distribution is inexplicable," assert Allen and Delair, "unless continuous land with freshwater lakes and ponds once existed between Europe and North America." They go on to note that the distribution of the pearl mussel (*Margaritana margaritifer*) suggests it as another relic species, since, "The European freshwater pearl mussel is found in the United States, where other allied species exist. In Eastern Europe and Western Asia the genus is unknown. It is widely spread in Western Europe from Northern Scandinavia to Spain — without, however, entering a single river communicating directly with the Mediterranean or crossing directly the coastline of that ancient Central European ocean which extended along the northern border of the European Alps eastward to Asia in Miocene times. Its very discontinuous range, coupled with its peculiar European distribution, and its absence from Western Asia, seem to imply that the freshwater pearl mussel found its way across the Atlantic with the sponges just referred to, at a very remote time."[5]

1 Spence, op. cit. p. 63.
2 A. R. Wallace, *Island Life* (3rd ed. London, 1911) p. 244.
3 C. Emery, "On the Origin of European and North American Ants," *Nature*, Vol. LIII, (1895) pp. 399-400.
4 Allen and Delair, op. cit. p. 97.
5 R. F. Scharff, *European Animals* (London, 1907) p. 34.

It needs to be stressed that most of the above plant and animal species are young in evolutionary terms, many of them appearing first during Miocene times, though several are even younger, appearing only in Pliocene times (and we recall that much evidence suggests the Pliocene was identical to the Pleistocene). This means that the land connection across the Atlantic must have been severed in very recent times indeed, a view expressed by no less an authority than Professor L. S. Berg, Fellow of the Moscow Academy, in 1947: "The recent, Quaternary [Pleistocene or Holocene], existence of the Atlantic Ridge explains many features of the geographical distribution of plants and land animals as a bipolar [on both shores of the Atlantic] distribution."[1] He concluded: "There are all sorts of considerations regarding the biogeography of the Atlantic countries, but sight must not be lost of the sinking of the Atlantic Ridge, part of which subsided in Quaternary times. The exchange of flora and fauna took place here not across some hypothetical bridges but across the spurs of the Atlantic Ridge or the chains of islands that stretched from the Atlantic Ridge to the east or west towards the continents."

Yet a question now arises: If the evidence points so overwhelmingly to a Mid-Atlantic Ridge above water at such a recent time, how is it that scientists turned their backs on it and on the contrary promulgated the idea that there has been no land-bridge across the Atlantic for many millions of years? How have they been able to disseminate the notion that no land ever existed in the region and that, far from sinking, the Ridge and the Azores are actually *rising* from the Ocean?

The answer lies not so much in other evidence as in *a priori* assumptions about what some evidence means. Above all, the discovery of granite erratic boulders on the Azores was crucial in formulating opinions. These, on Santa Maria and Terceira islands, are found up to 200 meters above the present shoreline.[2] It was assumed that these fragments were transported to the Azores by drift ice during the last glaciation, when they would have been deposited on the beaches or just offshore. Since some are now 200 meters above present sea level, this was seen as definitive proof that the Azores are actually *rising*, and that during the Ice Age the islands must have been at least 200 meters lower and ever tinier than they are today. *Ergo*, no Atlantis!

---

1 L. S. Berg, "Nekotoriye soobrazheniya o teorii peredvizheniya materikov" ("Some Considerations Regarding the Theory of the Movement of Continents"), *News of the USSR Geographical Society*, 74 (1947).
2 See e.g., F. Machatscheck, *Das Relief der Erde* (2nd. ed. Berlin, 1955).

Significantly, not even Zhirov could answer this problem, contenting himself with reporting the facts and lamely pointing out that, notwithstanding the position of the erratics, the Azores are actually sinking — around 5.3 mm per year.[1]

Zhirov could not answer the question of the erratics because he, like the great majority of Soviet and American scientists, had long ruled-out the possibility of world-wide cataclysms of the type envisaged by Donnelly and Velikovsky. The latter two, as well as more modern authors such as Allen and Delair, have demonstrated in great detail how erratics have little or nothing to do with glaciers or ice, but are the result of the actions of titanic tidal waves which washed over the continents. (See Allen and Delair, *When the Earth Nearly Died.*) If these writers are correct, and the present writer is convinced that they are, then the erratics on the Azores were deposited there by waves (being themselves material from the granite base of the Azores microplate), and they tell us precisely nothing about the past elevation of the archipelago.

It should be noted that plants and very small animals such as mollusks and insects are the forms of life best placed to survive tidal waves. Plants can survive in various ways, and tiny animals can survive either in ovular form, or by seeking refuge in rock crevices, caves etc. It is worth pointing out also that those scientists who now maintain that the Azores and Canaries were never connected to the European/African or American continents cannot explain the existence of these land-dwelling creatures. The problem is simply ignored.

It would thus appear that during the Pleistocene and well into the Holocene, into the period of the Middle and New Stone Ages, the mountainous chain of the Mid-Atlantic Ridge stood at a much higher elevation than at present. Much, if not all of it, reached above sea level. Around the Azores there was located a substantial landmass, perhaps just a little smaller than Spain, which formed a major link in a chain stretching down the middle of the Atlantic, in the direction of South America. It is certain, also, that the archipelago of Atlantic islands comprising the Canaries and Madeira (known as Makaronesia) was larger than at present and that many underwater peaks which now come near to the surface at that time reached above. Thus between the main "Atlantis" landmass at the Azores and the Straits of Gibraltar, there lay another archipelago of smallish islands whose appearance and density would have produced an impression similar to the Cyclades in the Aegean.

The Atlantic then was home to a great array of islands, stretching from the Canaries all the way down to within a couple of hundred kilometers of the Brazilian coast. As such, the region would have been very navigable by ancient sailors,

---

1 Zhirov, op. cit., p. 207.

and we cannot doubt that there existed a lively commerce between the African and European continents on the one hand and the American continents on the other.

CONTINENTAL DRIFT AND THE AZORES MICROPLATE

It is evident that any search for Atlantis must focus its attention closely upon the Azores. The evidence that these islands form but the mountain-peaks of a recently-submerged landmass becomes more extensive with every passing year. It is now freely admitted that the archipelago sits upon a continental plate composed largely of granite and sedimentary rock, described as the Azores Microplate.[1] The Microplate, of triangular shape, encompasses an area roughly the size of Ireland, and it is obvious that this mini-continent must at one time have been conjoined to the African and Iberian plates. A glance at a map reveals that the Microplate forms a rather neat "fit" into the triangular Atlantic indent between Spain and Morocco.

The existence of this mini-continent has now attracted a substantial literature. Thus in 1997 geologist Christian O'Brien revealed evidence for the existence of an extensive system of sunken river-valleys in the seas around the Azores:

> During underwater explorations off the island of São Miguel, the largest island in the Azores group, in 1971.... O'Brien found clear evidence of an underwater river bed filled with water-worn boulders. By applying detailed contouring methods to hydrographic charts, the O'Briens discerned that rivers draining off the southern slopes of São Miguel once converged together in a huge valley, now situated some 64 kilometres out from the present coastline. Other islands in the Azores group have yielded similar hydrographic anomalies, and in one case the O'Briens even traced a series of river valleys which extended for a distance of 288 kilometres before converging together in a much larger river basin.

> With a knowledge of ancient river systems, the O'Briens were able to reconstruct a land profile which revealed an Azorean landmass "about the size and shape of Spain," with high mountain ranges rising over 3655 metres above sea level, as well as impressive rivers that run 'in curving valley systems'. Furthermore, they have pointed out that: "In the southeast, a feature which we have called 'The Great Plain' covered an area in excess of 3500 square miles [9065 square kilometres], and was watered by a river comparable in size to the River Thames in England. It has, as we shall see, points in common with a great plain described by Plato in his Critias, as being a feature of the island of Atlantis."

> The conclusion drawn from these findings is that the Azores once formed part of a much greater landmass which sank beneath the waves and is now situated 'many thousands of feet' below the current sea level.

---

1 See e.g., www.ovga-azores.org/pdf/NVIslands.pdf. Also, www.ewpnet.com/azores/geology.htm.

> To obtain a more substantial insight into this fascinating subject, the O'Briens propose that a scientific team take a series of core samples from the proposed sites of their river channels. They confidently predict that these will show not only evidence of ancient river beds, but also of the freshwater flora and fauna which once thrived on the former Azorean landmass.[1]

That the Azores rest on continental material dislodged from North-West Africa brings to our attention the whole question of the Atlantic Ocean's age. The discovery by Ewing of an extremely thin sediment layer on the ocean bed proved beyond question that as a geological feature it was extremely young. We recall that, working upon the hypothesis that the Atlantic had formed many millions of years ago during the Mesozoic Era, perhaps in the Cretaceous or perhaps even the Jurassic Period (both had many supporters), the expedition expected to find an enormous thickness of sediment. That such a layer did not exist, at least in the abyssal plains, proved the youth of the ocean. But what does "young" mean in a geological sense? The fact that certain types of land-dwelling mammals, which could not have crossed any substantial expanse of open water, are found in both the Old World and the New, is a crucial clue. In particular, the occurrence of monkeys — creatures of African origin — in South America, tells us that the final separation of the two continents occurred quite late in the age of the mammals. The occurrence of other warmth-loving mammals, such as tapirs, in both the Old World and the New, points in the same direction. Both tapirs and monkeys appear first in the fossil record during the most recent of the great geological eras, the Cenozoic. In fact, they evolved in either the Eocene or the Oligocene phase of the Tertiary period, the last of the pre-human epochs.

The Oligocene immediately preceded the Miocene, and there exists a whole host of evidence to suggest that the final break between the Old World continents and those of the New occurred during the latter time, probably at its close. Thus, as we have seen, scientists have long noted the similarity of the Miocene insects and land snails of Western Europe with those of Central America. Identical species of Miocene corals also occur in Central America and Europe. According to V. V. Bogachov, "The North American animals (particularly land mollusks) differ sharply from their European brethren, and the animals common to both areas are Miocene types. Hence the conclusion that the land communication between Europe and North America was cut off during the early Pliocene [immediate post-Miocene epoch] at the latest."[2] Because the Atlantic is still believed to have formed in the Mesozoic Era, in the age of the great reptiles, the appear-

---

1 www.andrewcollins.com/page/interactive/midatlan.htm.
2 V. V. Bogachov, *Atlantida* (Yuryev, 1912).

ance of identical mammals of a much later epoch on both sides of the ocean has compelled scientists repeatedly to return to the idea of "land bridges" across the water. Thus as far back as 1904-1910 Argentinean scientist F. Amerigo showed that the migration of some Argentinean mammals could be explained solely by accepting the theory that there was a bridge between Guadalupe in the Antilles and Senegal in Africa, a bridge that must have existed in the Miocene.[1]

The Miocene is normally reckoned to have ended around 10 million years ago.

It is customary to view the megafauna of the Ice Age, or more precisely of the Pleistocene Age, as having migrated to America via the Bering Strait, which we are told formed a land-bridge during one of the glaciations of the Pleistocene. Thus it is held that the mammoth, mastodon, camel, and African-type lion etc. reached America over this land-bridge. However, as K. N. Nesis points out, these animals first appear in America during the Pliocene (which immediately followed the Miocene), and at that time the Bering Strait was open and a powerful current flowed through it into the Arctic.[2] According to T. Arldt, the mastodon, an animal of European origin, migrated to America on two occasions. A palaeomastodon of the *Tetrabelodon* species inhabited America already in the mid-Tertiary (Oligocene/Miocene) period. The real mastodon appeared in America only in the Pliocene — i.e., just after the close of the Miocene. According to Zhirov, "there could not have been a second migration of the mastodon from America to Asia. This animal reached America not by an eastern [Bering Strait] but by a western [Atlantic] route."[3]

It is worth recalling at this point that Allan and Delair pointed to strong evidence that the Pleistocene and Pliocene epochs were contemporary, and that the designation "Pleistocene" is an artificial one, introduced to give credence to the belief in a separate and lengthy "Ice Age," during which many animals had to be adapted for extremely cold conditions. In fact, the massive deposits of animal and vegetable material from this epoch invariably shows Pleistocene and Pliocene species coexisting side by side, with the types designated as "Pliocene" generally deriving from more southerly, warmer climates. If this is correct, it means that the land-bridge connecting the Old and New Worlds was broken at an even more recent date: For even if we assign this to the Miocene, it follows that it *directly* preceded the end of the most recent geological epoch, the Pliocene/Pleistocene.

---

1 J. Imbelloni and A. Vivante, *La livre des Atlantides* (Paris, 1942) p. 80.
2 K. N. Nesis, "Puti i vremya formirovaniya razorvannogo areala u amfiborealnykh vidov morskikh donnykh zhivotnykh," ("The Ways and Time of the Formation of the Ruptured Areal of Amphiboreal Species of Sea Bottom Fauna") *Okeanologiya*, 2 (1962) pp. 893-903.
3 Zhirov, op. cit., p. 315.

The evolution and migration of the horse points us to the same epoch, the border between the Miocene and Pliocene. The horse actually evolved in the New World and migrated from there to Africa and Eurasia. But how did it get there? While protohippos were widespread in North America during the Upper Miocene, the *Hipparion* and the *Hippodactilus* appeared, according to Arldt, in Eurasia only during the Lower Pliocene. There are many arguments in favor of the North American origin of the Hipparion, the first true horse. In order to explain its migration from eastern America to Europe, L. Joleaud, writing in 1922, returned

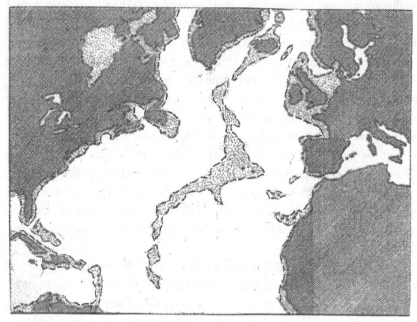

Fig. 2. Suggested Atlantic totpography during the Pleistocene/Paleolithic epoch.

to the idea of some form of land-bridge between Morocco and the West Indies.[1] And he invoked the same expedient to explain the migration of some species of pigs (*Hystracidae*) from South America to Africa. In the opposite direction, he says, there was a migration of the African antelope (*Hippotraginidae*) to the pastures of North America. He assumed that this bridge existed during the Sarmatian and Pontian stages of the Upper Miocene and the Astian stage of the Pliocene.

Joleaud of course wrote before Wegener's theory of continental drift was accepted, and it is now understood that no "bridge" of dry land could have existed between the Old and New Worlds over the distance of the present Atlantic Ocean. Even during the Miocene and Pliocene epochs, it is assumed, the Atlantic

---

1 Ibid., p. 316.

was already very wide — almost as wide as at present. However, the evidence from the ocean-bottom garnered by Ewing's and various other expeditions tell a different story. The astonishingly thin layer of sediment on the abyssal plains speak of a young ocean — much younger, by an enormous degree, than is presently accepted. Indeed, combining this with the zoological data, we may be justified in seeing the Atlantic as a much narrower body of water during the Miocene — so narrow, in fact, that parts of the Old World still touched on parts of the New. It may even be that the volcanic fault-line which now runs down the middle of the Ocean, and which was itself responsible for the creation of that

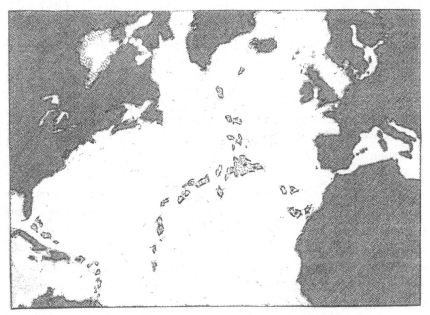

Fig. 3. Suggested Atlantic topography during the Holocene/Neolithic epoch.

Ocean, formed, by way of the mountain chain of the Mid-Atlantic Ridge, the link, or "bridge," which still connected the continents at the time.

If all this is correct, we may at last arrive at a satisfactory solution to the problem of how monkeys and other forms of warmth-loving creatures made it from the Old World to the New. There was no need to navigate the icy wastes of the Bering Strait, or to float across the Atlantic on "rafts" of mangrove-swamp material (as has been seriously suggested). The Miocene mammals made it across because then the continents had not fully separated.

This of course raises the problem of catastrophes and catastrophism. According to the Uniformitarian ideas which are now taught as dogma, no cataclysms of the type envisaged by Donnelly or Velikovsky ever occurred. Thus the Atlantic is believed to have grown at the rate observed at the present day along the Mid-Atlantic Ridge — no more than a few inches per year. Now, even if we accept the conventional date of 25 million years to 1.5 million years from the commencement of the Miocene till the close of the Pliocene (which the present writer does not), this rate of continental drift is still not nearly enough to produce the Atlantic Ocean which we now see. Had the landmasses finally parted company at the end of the Miocene, supposedly ten million years ago, this would have produced an Atlantic Ocean less than 200 miles wide! If they had separated at the beginning of the Miocene, the Atlantic would still be little more than 400 miles wide. We can thus say with certainty that if the Old and New World continents drifted apart during the Miocene or Pliocene, as the biological evidence indicates, then there must have been catastrophic episodes during which the plates moved rapidly, perhaps dozens of miles in a single day!

The question of catastrophes and catastrophism is of course central to the whole Atlantis problem. The very existence of Atlantis presupposes the existence in the past of cataclysms of nature unlike anything witnessed in modern times.

How then might we reconstruct the history of the Atlantic from the final separation of the continents till the present day?

From what we have said this far, it will be apparent that no "land bridge" could have existed between the Old and New Worlds after the end of the Miocene, which was the last geological epoch before the appearance of modern man (if, as we believe, the following epoch, the Pliocene, was identical to the Pleistocene). It was in this latter epoch that modern man arrived in the Americas, a period during which the Atlantic must have been a little narrower than today and must have been divided, right down the middle, by the mountain chain of the Mid-Atlantic Ridge, which then stood above the water. This chain widened around the region of the Azores, where a portion of continental material torn away from North-West Africa, formed a substantial land-mass; and from the chain there extended mountainous "spurs" which almost joined the Ridge to the Old World and the New. One of these spurs probably existed between the Azores region and Spain; another seems to have extended from the Ridge to the north-east coast of Brazil. According to the reconstruction of Rene Malaise, the landmass around the Azores would have been covered an area comparable to modern Spain, though we suspect it was somewhat smaller. Was it inhabited? The Atlantic land, we recall, was then not far distant from the shores of the Old World and the New; and the striking parallels observed in the Old Stone Age cultures of the Old Worlds and the New (which will be examined below) indicates that the Azores/Mid-Atlantic land was occupied, and was used by human beings as a pathway between the Old and New Worlds. This adequately explains the striking parallels between Old Stone Age cultures of Western Europe and North America. It seems that even as early as the Paleolithic, the highly gifted folk of the Solutrean and Magdalenian cultures had devised ways to cross water; and we possess several illustrations of boats from the main Upper Paleolithic centers in Western Europe — as well as from the contemporary centers in America. Although none of these craft have survived, they were evidently canoes of some sort; and these must surely have been of such design as could take travelers over

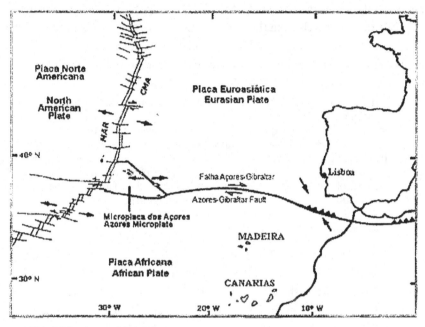

Fig. 4. The Azores Microplate.

substantial stretches of open sea. We recall that the Polynesians crossed much greater distances of the Pacific in large canoes.

The end of the Pleistocene, we have seen, witnessed a terrible catastrophe throughout the planet, and the extinction of a great many species. The Mid-Atlantic fault-line, one of the most volcanically-active regions on the earth, was affected; and the terraced shore-lines observed by countless expeditions in the submerged slopes of the Mid-Atlantic Range speak of a series of dramatic subsidences.[1] Indeed, it would appear that the Atlantic islands were constantly changing shape — as well as being reduced in size — before finally disappearing sometime

---

1 Zhirov notes that "scientists of the American school and their supporters do their best to ignore the existence of terraces, particularly stepped terraces, on the ridge. These terraces are direct evidence of the prolonged subsidence of the ridge, a subsidence that took place sporadically." Zhirov, op. cit., p. 235.

in the Holocene (geologically modern) Age. Taking the number of terraces into account, Rene Malaise came to the conclusion that the submergence of the Ridge took place in four stages — a conclusion dramatically in concordance with a whole raft of evidence pointing to four great natural cataclysms between the end of the Paleolithic and the Early Bronze Age. Nikolai Zhirov and very many of the scientists whom he quotes agreed that the island of continental material underlying the Azores was the last to sink, and that this event occurred very recently. But just what do we mean by recent? Towards the end of his volume, Zhirov noted the occurrence of corals from the Azores region encrusted with manganese, the thickness of which indicated to him, a trained chemist, that the coral had died between four and five thousand years ago. This, together with other evidences of various kinds, brought him to the following conclusion:

> It seems to us that there are grounds for assuming that in the sinking of Atlantis there were two stages, the first between the 13th and 10th millennia BC. Generally speaking, the main subsidence of Atlantis took at least 5,000 years, but the final subsidence was in the nature of a cataclysm. It is quite probable that the main subsidence left small remnants of the destroyed continent which, perhaps, finally sank in the north along the latitude of the Azores (to the north and south of them), in about the year 1300–1200 BC. Evidently, the southernmost remnants, in the equatorial region, finally sank later, in the 6th century BC. However, all these latest dates require further confirmation.[1]

On page 384, Zhirov provides a map of the Atlantis archipelago in its various stages of decline. The Pleistocene territory formed a considerable landmass linking the Azores plate with the long mountain range of the Mid-Atlantic Ridge. At some stage, possibly in the Mesolithic (between Old and New Stone Ages) this shrank considerably, leaving a roughly triangular island just a little smaller than Spain; and still later, there was left only one substantial island (with several smaller isles to the north of Madeira), about the size of Ireland. This existed, apparently, into the Bronze Ages.

The cataclysm or rather cataclysms which sank most of the Atlantic archipelago must have been of a violence scarcely imaginable to moderns. If we assume that the main "Atlantis" landmass near the Azores was, until the late Neolithic and Early Bronze Age, about the size of Ireland, then the sinking of such an area within a few days can only have caused devastation throughout the region.[2] We may imagine tsunamis of truly apocalyptic size sweeping the Atlantic coasts of

---

1 Ibid., p. 385.
2 Whilst this final subsidence, in the Early Bronze Age, would have submerged the Atlantis island, we must not imagine that the subsidence ended at that stage. On the contrary, the entire microplate upon which the Azores rests has been sinking steady for several thousand of years, and the seas around the Azores must now be much deeper than they were immediately after the final cataclysmic submergence of the island.

the Americas as well as of Europe and Africa. Tidal waves of five or six hundred meters are not to be discounted. The Mediterranean world would have been more protected, especially insofar as the channel leading to the Atlantic was possibly even narrower then than now. (Ancient legend, we should remember, tells of Hercules actually pushing the two pillars apart). Nevertheless, the final destruction of Atlantis — the remnant Atlantis — was clearly part of a world-wide cataclysmic event, and the Mediterranean would not have escaped unscathed. As we shall see in the following chapter, the violence of these events left very evident markers in the Neolithic and Bronze Age settlements of that region.

CHAPTER 3. CATASTROPHE AND CIVILIZATION

THE CATASTROPHES UNCOVERED BY ARCHAEOLOGY

A central thesis of Velikovsky's, and certainly among the most controversial aspects of his overall hypothesis, is that the last of the cosmic catastrophes of which he wrote occurred within the period of recorded human history. In other words, the earth suffered near-collisions with comets and other cosmic bodies in a time when men had already settled in cities, practiced agriculture, and kept written records. In *Worlds in Collision* he was very specific in placing the last of these catastrophes in the eighth and seventh centuries BC.

The evidence Velikovsky cited in support of this date was chiefly literary and historical. He looked mainly at the written documents of ancient Near Eastern lands, most especially at Assyria and Babylonia, and at the Bible. Yet it was not only the Near Eastern cultures which spoke of violent catastrophes during the historical age. Traditions from many lands, as demonstrated in *Worlds in Collision*, pointed in the same direction.

In his *Earth in Upheaval*, published in 1955, Velikovsky introduced his readers to the enormous body of geological and archaeological material which corroborated the literary traditions. And indeed an honest examination of the evidence presented here, as well as in a multitude of other publications, leaves one in no doubt that from the end of the Old Stone Age (Paleolithic), right through to the New Stone Age and the Early Bronze Age, the earth suffered a series of calamities unlike anything in the experience of modern man. The most terrible of these events was without question the first; that which brought the Old Stone Age, (and the Pleistocene geological epoch) to an end. It is now admitted, for example, that the end of the Paleolithic witnessed massive land subsidence throughout the globe. This is nowhere more obvious than in Europe where the region now occupied by the North Sea was dry land, from which to this day the bones of Pleistocene creatures such as mammoth and woolly rhino, as well as the implements of Paleolithic man, are regularly dredged. But later catastrophes, during the Middle and New Stone Ages, and in the Early Bronze Age, were also terrible in their destructiveness, and cannot fail to have impressed the peoples who lived through them. These events too were characterized by seismic and volcanic activity of monumental dimensions — activity which in some places raised shorelines hundreds of feet above their previous positions and which in others consigned dry land to the depths of the sea. Evidence of such topographic dislocation has been found throughout the Mediterranean and on the Atlantic coasts of Europe. Along the coasts of Britain and Denmark, for example, archaeologists have found abundant remains of sunken settlements of the Neolithic Age. This was the case, for example, near the Scilly Isles[1] and just off Heligoland in Denmark.[2] Massive changes in shorelines are evident too in the Mediterranean, where Neolithic temples and other structures now lie under the sea near the island of Malta.[3]

Apparently acting in concordance with earthquakes, geologists and archaeologists also found evidence of vast and terrible conflagrations, as well as tidal waves of enormous destructive power.

All in all, it would seem, the earth was struck by a total of four separate catastrophes, each of which terminated the main epochs of the Stone Age, namely the Paleolithic, Mesolithic, and Neolithic, and a final one which terminated the Early Bronze Age. Some archaeological sites, as we shall see, actually record these events in well-defined stratigraphies; and we cannot fail to be struck by the fact that these events, revealed by the evidence in the ground, correspond so strikingly with the traditions of many ancient peoples which speak of precisely four catastrophes and four World Ages.

Whilst it would be possible to fill many volumes with a detailed examination of this material, we shall confine ourselves here to looking at some of the better-known cases. Of these, the Mediterranean island of Crete stands out.

---

1 See e.g., T. A. Rickard, *Man and Metals* (2nd ed., New York and London, 1932) pp. 322-3; also C. Reid, *Submerged Forests* (London, 1913).

2 See e.g., C. Vallaux, *La géographie générale des mers* (Paris, 1933); also V. G. Childe, who spoke of a great transgression of the sea between 1900-1800 BC, called forth by massive subsidences of the shores around the British Isles and Scandinavia.

3 A very good description of the sunken Maltese remains, including photographs, are given by Graham Hancock in his *Underworld: The Mysterious Origins of Civilization* (Three Rivers Press, 2003).

In the 1920s, Arthur Evans, the excavator of the ancient settlement of Knossos in Crete, spoke of the island having been laid waste by a "great catastrophe" on more than one occasion.[1] All the important ages of this Cretan or "Minoan" civilization, from the Early Minoan, through Middle to Late Minoan (corresponding to the Near Eastern Early, Middle and Late Bronze Ages), were terminated by some form of natural catastrophe. At the end of Middle Minoan II, for example, he noted how, "A great destruction befell Knossos on the northern shore of the island and Phaestos on its southern shore."[2] The destruction of Late Minoan II also appears to have had a natural cause. At Knossos Evans found evidence of "another of those dread shocks that again and again caused a break in the Palace history." The earthquake damage was aggravated by a "widespread conflagration," and the catastrophe attained "special disastrous dimensions owing to a furious wind then blowing."[3] After this final catastrophe the palace at Knossos was never again rebuilt.

Lying just to the north of Crete is the volcanic island of Santorini, anciently known as Thera or Kalliste. In ancient times the volcano which forms the island erupted in an explosion the likes of which modern man has no experience. Volcanologists have estimated that the blast threw out six times as much material as the eruption of Krakatoa in 1883. Yet the explosive force of Krakatoa was equivalent to 10,000 Hiroshima bombs, and the bang was heard 4,500 kilometers away. What kind of cataclysm then destroyed Santorini? Visitors today can readily see a sea-filled crater or caldera of enormous dimensions, the precipitous walls of which rise 300 meters (984 feet) above the bay. The water-filled crater itself is 400 meters (1,300 feet) deep and stretches roughly 12 km by 7 km. Yet this vast caldera was not formed during the Late Bronze Age; it is the result of an older eruption apparently at the end of the Pleistocene. By the Bronze Age, the northern part of the caldera had been refilled by the volcano, only to collapse again during the final eruption.

Nevertheless, the Bronze Age blast was truly enormous. Excavations starting in 1967 at the site called Akrotiri ("Upper Thira") under the guidance of late Professor Spyridon Marinatos have uncovered a very large and complex settlement buried under hundreds of feet of volcanic ash and pumice. Only the southern tip of a large town has been cleared, yet it has revealed complexes of multi-level buildings, streets and squares, with remains of walls standing as high as 8 meters, all entombed in the solidified ash of the famous eruption.

---

1 Sir Arthur Evans, *The Palace of Minos at Knossos* (1921-35), Vol. 3, p. 14.

2 Ibid. Vol. 2, p. 287; Vol. 3, p. 347.

3 Ibid. Vol. 4, Pt. 2, p. 942.

The dating of this final Bronze Age destruction remains controversial. The general consensus is that it be placed sometime in the Late Bronze Age, with estimates varying anywhere between the seventeenth and fifteenth centuries BC. Whatever the time, it is agreed that the explosion caused a terrible catastrophe throughout the Aegean, and the eruption is seen as an important factor in the final disappearance of the Minoan civilization.

Yet Crete and Santorini were not the only areas to be violently overthrown during the Bronze Age. On the contrary, the progress of archaeology has revealed the Bronze Age to be an epoch far more seismically and volcanically active than the present. Everywhere, throughout the Near East and far beyond, excavators have found the tell-tale signature of earthquakes, conflagrations and devastating floods.

In 1873 German adventurer Heinrich Schliemann uncovered the ruins of Troy at the hill of Hissarlik, near the Dardanelles. Schliemann was immediately struck by the extensive evidence of catastrophic destruction in almost all of the six or seven cities which lay one on top of the other. The most terrible of these, it appears, destroyed Troy II and Troy III, near the end of the Early Bronze Age. Wilhelm Dörpfeld, the renowned archaeologist who worked with Schliemann at the site, spoke of "a most terrible fire" which obliterated Troy III, and wondered how a comparatively small city like this could have left, as a result of the fire, an ash layer of great thickness.[1] Subsequent expeditions to the site only confirmed the findings of Schliemann and Dörpfeld. Thus during the 1930s, the Cincinnati University expedition led by Carl Blegen was struck by the frequency and violence of these destructions. Blegen found that Troy IV, built on top of the ashes of Troy III, had been overthrown by a new and unexpected conflagration. Once again the ground was covered "with a thick bed of ashes and carbonized substance indicating clearly that the buildings fell during a fire."[2] Troy VI, which followed the fifth city and is usually recognized as the capital of King Priam, was destroyed by an earthquake. A violent shaking of the ground, far more powerful that the army of Agamemnon, brought about the city's end.[3]

Blegen's report attracted the attention of French archaeologist Claude Schaeffer, who had found similar indications at Ras Shamra, the ancient port of Ugarit, in Syria. Schaeffer came to Troy to compare Blegen's discoveries with his own and became convinced that the earthquakes and conflagrations he had noted at Ras Shamra were synchronical with the earthquakes and conflagrations of Troy,

---

1 W. Dörpfeld, *Troja and Ilion* (1902).
2 C. W. Blegen, "Excavations at Troy, 1936," *American Journal of Archaeology*, XLI (1937), pp. 570ff.
3 Ibid.

six hundred miles away. He then proceeded to compare the evidence from these two sites with numerous other localities of the ancient East and came to the conclusion that more than once in historical times the entire region had been shaken by prodigious earthquakes, an area impossibly large when compared with the largest areas affected by earthquakes in modern times. His findings were finally published in his seminal *Stratigraphie comparée et chronologie de l'Asie Occidentale (IIIe et IIe millénaires)* (Oxford, 1948) He wrote: "There is not for us the slightest doubt that the conflagration of Troy II corresponds to the catastrophe that made an end to the habitations of the Old Bronze Age at Alaca Huyuk, of Alisar, of Tarsus, of Tepe Hissar [all in Asia Minor], and to the catastrophe that burned ancient Ugarit (II) in Syria, the city of Byblos that flourished under the Old Kingdom of Egypt, the contemporaneous cities of Palestine, and that was among the causes which terminated the Old Kingdom of Egypt."[1]

Altogether, Schaeffer discerned six separate upheavals which, simultaneously, destroyed settlements as far apart as Egypt and Persia, the Aegean and Arabia. In *Stratigraphie comparée* he looked at sites in Asia Minor, Mesopotamia, the Caucasus, Iran, Syria, Palestine, Cyprus and Egypt, and these regions were the focus of detailed enquiry. However, recognizing the magnitude of the catastrophes that have no parallels in modern annals or concepts of seismology, he became convinced that these countries, which he had studied, represented only a fraction of the area that was gripped by the shocks. Could it be, he wondered, that in earlier times earthquakes were of much greater force and wider spread than they are now because geological strata, originally out of equilibrium, were settling with the passing of time?[2] But this explanation could not be valid since geology tells us the world is three or four billion years old, and three or four thousand years is only a millionth of this period. The planet would have adjusted its strata in its youth, and no major disturbances could now be expected. However, if the earth was thrown out of equilibrium only a few thousand years ago, the recent readjustments are to be expected.

THE RUINS OF SOUTH AMERICA

Schaeffer suspected that the upheavals of nature he observed in the Near East were part of a series of cataclysms which afflicted the entire globe. Had he extended his investigations to the Americas, he would have found, particularly in South America, ample evidence to confirm this.

---

1 Claude F. A. Schaeffer, *Stratigraphie comparée et chronologie de l'Asie Occidentale (IIIe et IIe millénaires)* (Oxford, 1948) p. 225.
2 Ibid., Avant-propos, p. xii.

In the Bolivian Andes, near to Lake Titicaca, at an elevation of 12,500 feet, lie the remains of Tiahuanaco, one of the perennial mysteries of archaeology. The walls of the ancient city, some of which are fashioned of gigantic blocks of stone, are carved with precision and decorated with rich reliefs. It is clear that the site was once a metropolis of some importance. Yet herein lies the mystery: for the plain upon which the city stands is now a barren wasteland, high above the regions where corn will ripen or most crops grow. According to Sir Clemens Markham, "There is a mystery still unsolved on the plateau of Lake Titicaca, which, if stones could speak, would reveal a story of deepest interest. Much of the difficulty in the solution of this mystery is caused by the nature of the region, in the present day, where the enigma defies explanation."[1] The problem lies in the climate. "Such a region is only capable of sustaining a scanty population of hardy mountaineers and labourers. The mystery consists in the existence of ruins of a great city at the southern side of the lake, the builders being entirely unknown. The city covered a large area, built by highly skilled masons, and with the use of enormous stones."[2]

When Markham posed this question to the scholarly world, Leonard Darwin, then president of the Royal Geographical Society, suggested that the plateau had risen considerably after the city had been built. Markham wondered whether such an idea was "beyond the bonds of possibility," but came to the conclusion that, were it to be upheld, were the Andes two to three thousand feet lower than they are now, "maize would then ripen in the basin of Lake Titicaca, and the site of the ruins of Tiahuanaco could support the necessary population. If the megalithic builders were living under these conditions, the problem is solved. If this is geologically impossible, the mystery remains unexplained."[3]

In the hills around Tiahuanaco the traveler observes the remains of endless agricultural terraces, some of which rise to a height of 18,000 feet and more, terraces now abandoned and useless. Some of them rise as far as the permanent snowline on Illimani. Conventional geological theory suggests that mountain-building is a slow process, taking millennia and even hundreds of millennia to raise a range just a few feet. Yet Tiahuanaco proves the opposite. In the words of A. Posnansky: "At the present time, the plateau of the Andes is inhospitable and almost sterile. With the present climate, it would not have been suitable in any period as the asylum for great human masses" of the "most important prehistoric centre of the world."[4] Noting the "Endless agricultural terraces" of the ancient

1 Clemens Markham, *The Incas of Peru* (1910), p. 21.
2 Ibid. p. 23.
3 Ibid.
4 A. Posnansky, *Tiahuanaco, the Cradle of the American Man* (1945), p. 15.

inhabitants, Posnansky observes that, "Today this region is at a very great height above sea level. In remote periods it was lower."

At one time Tiahuanaco was a port: Lake Titicaca was ninety feet higher. Yet it was not just climate change and desiccation that removed the lake from the city. The old shore line, still clearly visible, is tilted dramatically, obviously as a result of massive earthquake activity. In some places, it is actually 350 feet *above* the present level of the lake. There are numerous raised beaches, and geologists stressed the "freshness of many of the strandlines and the modern character of such fossils as occur."[1]

Other ancient structures scattered throughout the Andes pose similar questions.

The ancient fortress of Ollantaytambo, in Peru, constructed of blocks of stone twelve to eighteen feet high, sits on top of a high elevation. "These Cyclopean stones were hewn from the quarry seven miles away ... How the stones were carried down to the river in the valley, shipped on rafts, and carried up to the site of the fortress remains a mystery archaeologists cannot solve."[2] Another stronghold, Ollantayparubo, in the Urubamba Valley in Peru, northwest of Lake Titicaca, "perches upon a tiny plateau some 13,000 feet above sea level, in an uninhabitable region of precipices, chasms, and gorges." It is built of large blocks of red porphyry. These must have been brought "from a considerable distance ... down steep slopes, across swift and turbulent rivers, and up precipitous rock-faces across swift and turbulent rivers, and up precipitous rock-faces which hardly allow a foothold."[3] It has been suggested, with good reason, that the transportation of the building-blocks was feasible only if the topography of these localities was very different at the time of construction. That such changes occurred is evident enough from the abandoned terraces reaching above the snow-line and from tilted shorelines.

On his travels to South America in 1834–35, Charles Darwin was impressed by the raised beaches at Valparaiso, Chile. The former surf line was at an altitude of 1300 feet. He found that the sea shells which littered these ancient beaches were undecayed, to him a clear indication that the land had risen 1300 feet from the Pacific Ocean in a very recent period, "within the period during which upraised shells remained undecayed on the surface."[4]

1 H. P. Moon, "The Geology and Physiography of the Altiplano of Peru and Bolivia," *The Transactions of the Linnean Society of London*, 3rd Series, Vol. 1. Pt. 1 (1939), p. 32.

2 Don Ternel, in *Travel*, April, 1945.

3 Hans Schindler Bellamy, *Built before the Flood* (1953) p. 63.

4 Charles Darwin, *Geological Observations on the Volcanic Islands and Parts of South America*, Part II, Chapter 15.

Reading through the histories of many lands, one is left with the unmistakable impression that seismic activity, both with regard to earthquakes and volcanoes, was much greater in olden times. But this is more than just an impression. It is, if records over the past couple of thousands years are anywhere nearly correct, a simple fact.

In his *Earth in Upheaval*, Velikovsky took a general look at the world's volcanoes and earthquake-prone zones; and everywhere he found the same thing: volcanoes that had until recently been active were now dormant and regions that had been subject just a few centuries ago to massive earthquakes were now quiescent. Such, for example, was the case in both South and Central America, two areas that "abound in volcanoes." In Central America these are mostly extinct or dormant and the highest of them, Orizaba in Mexico, was active for the last time three centuries ago.[1] Further to the north, in the United States, Velikovsky notes, "few volcanoes are active, though many became extinct very recently, in the geological sense."[2] The Japanese islands "contain volcanoes by the score; most of them are extinct, some recently so." In the east Asian ring of fire, comprising "Formosa [Taiwan], the Philippines, the so-called Volcano Islands — one of which is Iwo Jima — the Moluccas, northern New Zealand, the Suna Archipelago — all are crowded with volcanoes, most of them only recently extinct."[3] The Indian Ocean is circled with volcanoes and along the coast of the Red Sea stretches a long chain of volcanoes, "the numerous craters [of which] are all extinct, but it is not so long ago that they became inactive, the last eruptions having taken place in the year 1222 at Killis in northern Syria and in 1253 at Aden." All in all, Velikovsky says, "only about four or five hundred volcanoes on earth are considered active or dormant, against a multiplicity of extinct ones. Yet only five or six hundred years ago many of the presently inactive volcanoes were still alive. This points to very great activity in a time only a few thousand years ago. At the rate of extinction witnessed by modern man, the greater part of the still active volcanoes will become inactive in a matter of several centuries."[4]

Earthquake activity displays precisely the same pattern, with Roman and Greek records, for example, speaking of huge numbers of tremors in classical times; whilst traditions from places like Britain and Ireland, now almost completely earthquake-free, speak of vast tremors in antiquity. I leave the last word on this topic to surveyor and legendary explorer Percy Fawcett, who remarked that in South America, "Devastating earthquakes seem to take place only once

1 Velikovsky, *Earth in Upheaval*, p. 130.
2 Ibid.
3 Ibid.
4 Ibid. pp. 131-2.

or twice in a century.... The whole of South America trembles periodically in the recurrent but diminishing waves of a vast eruptive age, the history of which can only be found in Indian legend."[1]

We need to know exactly when this eruptive age occurred.

THE STRATIGRAPHY OF ARMAGEDDON

As we have seen, in *Stratigraphie comparée*, Claude Schaeffer enumerated six upheavals of nature which afflicted the entire ancient East. His calculations, as the title of his book suggests, were based on a comparison of the excavated sites, with the culture found determining the epoch in which the settlement belonged.

Schaeffer's approach was admirable and his method cannot be faulted. Nevertheless, the French scholar was working within the constraints of his own discipline, and the terminologies and dating-systems which he employed were not his. What he did not understand, and perhaps could not have been expected to understand, is that there exists a profound confusion with regard to the meanings scholars working in different areas attach to terms like "Mesolithic," "Neolithic" and "Early Bronze." If he had fully understood this, he would have realized that in fact only four universal catastrophes afflicted the ancient world. These, as we have already indicated, terminated the epochs generally known among archaeologists as the Old, Middle and New Stone Ages, as well as the Early Bronze Age. The catastrophes noted by Schaeffer after the Early Bronze Age were essentially local disasters — though disasters indubitably more violent than those generally experienced by modern man. Yet, as evidence we shall examine presently indicates, it is beyond question that the epoch of universal world-wide cataclysms came to an end at the termination of the Early Bronze Age. This is most clearly illustrated at sites where there was continuous occupation from the Paleolithic through to the Bronze Age, and among such sites the best preserved is perhaps that of Ur in Mesopotamia — widely regarded as the "Queen of Stratigraphies."

Much ink has been spilt on discussion of the archaeology of Ur, reputedly the home of the biblical patriarch Abraham, where in the 1920s Englishman Leonard Woolley uncovered evidence of a series of catastrophic floods. The first, and by far the most violent of these, was located immediately under the earliest levels showing evidence of literate culture. This deluge, widely known as the Flood of Ur, left a layer of water-borne silt three meters in depth, above which lay another four meters' deep stratum, loosely described as "debris." All the indications are that this "debris" layer was a stratified deposit of lighter waste thrown by flood waters on top of the heavier silt. Altogether then the Flood of Ur left a stratum about eight meters in depth. Underneath this vast deposit Woolley found much

---

1 *Exploration Fawcett* (1953) p. 174.

evidence of human occupation in the form of pottery and other artifacts. These belonged to a pre-literate culture which was immediately recognized: 'Ubaid. In the decades before Woolley had commenced his work, archaeologists had uncovered much 'Ubaid pottery throughout Mesopotamia and, since it occurred in pre-literate strata, was designated either as "Neolithic" or, more commonly, "Chalcolithic" (Copper Age). This was because the 'Ubaid folk already displayed some knowledge of metals (copper and gold) and their properties. In line with the accepted dating of Mesopotamian history, the 'Ubaid culture was believed to have ended sometime between 3400 and 3300 BC.

In the strata above the Flood layer, Woolley found a culture named Jamdat Nasr which showed the first signs of literacy. This culture too was terminated by a flood, though a much less violent one than that which had ended the 'Ubaid epoch. Two further flood events, which terminated the first and second phases of the Early Bronze Age, were located above the Jamdat Nasr destruction layer, thus:

Early Bronze 3b

FLOOD LAYER

Early Bronze 3a

FLOOD LAYER

Early Bronze 1 and 2

FLOOD LAYER

Jamdat Nasr (First writing and wheel-made pottery)

GREAT FLOOD

'Ubaid (Chalcolithic)

Woolley therefore found that in Mesopotamia the latest catastrophic event of which there was clear evidence occurred in the Early Bronze Age.

Woolley's discovery caused much excitement at the time, and it was even mooted that definitive evidence of the biblical Flood had now been unearthed. Yet in time it was claimed that no evidence of the disaster could be found outside Lower Mesopotamia, and so it was claimed that what he had discovered was merely a local flood caused by heavy rainfall in the upper reaches of the Tigris and Euphrates rivers. This soon became the accepted view, and is one that we now find repeated in publication after publication.

Elsewhere I have dealt with this question in some detail, and have shown how the apparent non-existence of Woolley's Flood outside Lower Mesopotamia is an illusion caused by inconsistent and contradictory naming and dating techniques. Thus the vast catastrophes discovered beyond Mesopotamia, which were actually contemporary with the Flood of Ur, were dated differently; and so appeared to be the signatures of different events. In fact, as I shall now argue, the Flood of Ur, which apparently destroyed a "Neolithic" or "Chalcolithic" culture in the Land of the Two Rivers, was actually identical to the Flood catastrophe which elsewhere simultaneously destroyed the Paleolithic or Old Stone Age culture and the Pleistocene eco-system.

This can be shown in great detail in a whole host of ways. And it should in any case be obvious that the great catastrophe of Mesopotamia, which everyone agrees was the origin of the biblical Flood story, must (if one accepts world-wide catastrophes at all) be identical to the catastrophe which in other parts of the world, such as the Americas, was the origin of *their* Flood stories. And the identity of the two is put beyond question when we note the parallel mythology attached to all Flood legends, not matter where they are found. So, for example, the Flood of Mesopotamia is associated with the goddess and planet Ishtar (Venus), whilst the Flood of North America is also associated with the Morning Star, or Venus. Yet for all that, modern catastrophist writers such as Allen and Delair, as well as Hancock and a host of others, still insist in placing the catastrophic end of the Pleistocene — and the Flood traditions associated with it — in the tenth millennium BC; and the catastrophe of Mesopotamia — and the Flood traditions associated with it — in the fourth millennium BC! How they can justify this dissociation is never fully explained.

Yet leaving aside the obvious and the general, and going into the particulars of archaeology and cultural development, the contemporaneity of the Mesopotamian Flood with the end of the Pleistocene can be demonstrated in great detail.

To begin with, let us recall that American geologist George Frederick Wright had, on the evidence of very modern-looking Native American artifacts found alongside the bones of mammoth, mastodon, etc., placed the great Pleistocene extinction (and therefore the Flood cataclysm) at an epoch during which the civilizations of Egypt and Babylonia had already attained a "high degree of development." The evidence from the Old World fully confirms Wright's hypothesis. Thus we note that the 'Ubaid culture of Lower Mesopotamia, the one destroyed by Woolley's Flood, was clearly (notwithstanding its normal designation as "Neolithic") contemporary with the Paleolithic cultures of Western Europe. This is demonstrated most convincingly by the fact that in Egypt, where the culture contemporary with 'Ubaid is named Badarian, Paleolithic artifacts occur alongside this Badarian material — even in the same graves. This was noted first by Flinders Petrie, who remarked, with evident puzzlement, that "the finest ripple-flaked flint knives [of the Badarian Age] are in the same grave, side by side with long typical Magdalenian flakes. These might seem centuries apart, but they witness instead to two contemporaneous civilizations."[1] The striking parallels between Badarian and Solutrean (Paleolithic) cultures was also discussed by M. C. Burkitt in the journal *Man* (1926) and by E. W. Gardner and G. Caton-Thompson in the same year.[2]

It is true that these Middle Eastern cultures (Badarian and 'Ubaid) seem more advanced than the Solutrean and Magdalenian of Western Europe, at least in some regards. They were, for example, already using pottery, whilst there is little evidence of this in Europe. Nonetheless, it cannot be emphasized too strongly that we should not expect all technical and cultural innovations to appear simultaneously in all regions. It cannot be forgotten that, until the European Age of Discovery in the fifteenth and sixteenth centuries, large parts of the world remained in the Neolithic Age, and some parts — such as Australia — in the Paleolithic. That new technologies or techniques were not taken up immediately in some parts of the world is not necessarily proof of their belonging to a different epoch. Yet it must be stressed that the most telling innovations of the post-Deluge (Mesolithic) age in Western Europe — namely the axe and the bow, only occur in Mesopotamia during the post-Flood epoch, the Jamdat Nasr.

The actual depth of the Flood layer at Ur — altogether over eight meters — also speaks strongly of it being one and the same as the Flood which devastated Europe and North America at the end of the Pleistocene, where, as we saw, vast regions of forest lie buried under debris deposits variously eight to twenty meters in depth.

That this was the same Flood as that recalled in legend and tradition all over the earth is made abundantly clear when we look at the art and literature of the Jamdat Nasr culture — the early literate civilization that appeared immediately above the Flood. Everything about Jamdat Nasr civilization shows it to have been profoundly influenced by the Deluge cataclysm which stratigraphy tells us occurred shortly before. This is a topic to which we shall return in the next section, but it should be noted here that the appearance of star and dragon worship, as well as temple building and blood sacrifice, are all typical expressions of post-Flood cultures worldwide — and this goes too for the Americas. Even more striking is the fact that the Jamdat Nasr period, as well as the Early Bronze period which came immediately after, seemed to be obsessed with the idea of the

1 Flinders Petrie, *The Making of Egypt* (London, 1939) p. 6.
2 E. W. Gardner and G. Caton-Thompson, "The Recent Geology and Neolithic Industry of the Northern Fayum Desert," *The Journal of the Royal Anthropological Institute of Great Britain and Ireland*, (1926).

Celestial Tower or Cosmic Pillar or World Tree. Elsewhere I have dealt with this myth in great detail.[1] Suffice for the present to note that in all parts of the world legend held that immediately after the Flood men (or demigods or giants) sought to reopen communication with heaven by the construction of a Tower or Pillar. This project however inevitably brings down upon the builders the wrath of the gods, who destroy the Tower and thereby definitively end the link between mankind and heaven.

It is striking that this myth is found in both the Old and New Worlds, and that in virtually all cases the Tower destruction is believed to have immediately followed the Great Flood. This is the case, for example, in the biblical story of the Tower of Babel and also in the Mexican legend as recounted (as we saw in the previous chapter) by Ixtlilxochitl. We note too that in both the biblical and Mexican stories this event marked the second world catastrophe or second World Age.

And this brings us to the remarkable fact that the four catastrophes revealed by the flood-layers in Ur, the last of which more or less terminated the Early Dynastic Age, agree precisely in number with the four catastrophes spoken of in Native American legend — and in the legends of peoples throughout the globe. We note too that, just as in the Old World, the peoples of the New World spoke of the rise of the first civilizations in the immediate aftermath of the first and greatest Flood. All this indicates that the civilizations of the Old World are not thousands of years older than those of the New, and that the two sets of civilizations arose more or less simultaneously. There is thus evidently an enormous error in the chronology of the ancient civilizations; and I leave it to the final chapter to go into more detail on this question.

We cannot leave this topic without a brief explanation of the Tower or Pillar. That it was not a human construction is obvious: Many traditions describe it as made of crystal, or shining like gold or silver, and it is normally, in the legends of both Old and New Worlds, placed at the North Pole (the latter term itself deriving from the myth). The best explanation, in the opinion of the present writer, is that it was some form of enhanced aurora borealis effect, which appeared at the North Pole in the wake of the violent electromagnetic disturbances of the Flood event.[2] Quite possibly it was some form of plasma funnel or tube, which shimmered and frequently changed appearance. Plasma filaments seem at times to

---

1 Especially in my *Genesis of Israel and Egypt* (2008).

2 The most detailed and authoritative discussion of the Tower Legend to date is contained in David Talbott and Wallace Thornhill, *Thunderbolts of the Gods* (Mikamar Publishing, 2005). See also an article by plasma physicist Anthony L. Peratt, "Characteristics for the Occurrence of a High-Current, Z-Pinch Aurora as recorded in Antiquity," *Transactions on Plasma Science*, (December, 2003). Perratt concludes that ancient petroglyphs represent

have emanated from the top of the Pillar, looking to all intents and purposes like branches of a great tree. Hence the World Tree, or Tree of Life, also located at the North Pole. On occasion, spiraling electrical sparks may have flickered up and down the pillar, looking remarkably like fiery serpents entwining the column. This was almost certainly the origin of the magic wand of Hermes (Thoth), the caduceus, with its entwined serpents.

The "branches" emanating from the Pillar seem at times to have appeared like the limbs of a human being, and the Tower was often imagined in anthropomorphic terms, as a giant or titan holding up the heavens. In at least one tradition from Greece, Atlas, who held up the sky, was said to have been positioned at the North Pole;[1] and this is strikingly reminiscent of a Viking legend, which recounts how the Frost Giants sought to storm Asgard by constructing an enormous man made of clay.

Much of the religious art of the Jamdat Nasr and Early Dynastic periods of Mesopotamia (and the Early Dynastic period of Egypt) portrays this pillar and its intertwined serpents. This is also the case with the very early art of South and Central America. It should be noted also that the myth of the Pillar is widely connected with the custom of human sacrifice. Either a maiden was locked in the Tower by her evil demigod father, or a child was buried beneath it. This story is found even in Britain, where is it an integral part of the Merlin story. It is significant also that, though the Tower was not a human construction, it was often identified as such in both the Old and New Worlds, thus indicating that in both these regions man had taken the first steps towards architecture. And the earliest structures in both hemispheres were indeed man-made towers — the first pyramids and ziggurats.

We should note too that the Tower was often connected in legend with the hammer or the axe, the symbols of lightning and the thunderbolt, which were introduced after the Flood and which enabled men to begin reshaping the landscape and constructing permanent settlements. This is seen most obviously in the Norse legend, where Thor strikes the Pillar, or clay giant, with his mighty hammer, destroying it.

---

a plasma "instability" which he sees in his laboratory, and must have been observed by ancient man over the Polar skies.

1 Apollodorus (ii, v, 11) noted that "Atlas [stands] among the Hyperboreans [i.e., in the far north]," whilst other writers described the North Pole as the "Atlantic pole" or the "pole held up by Atlas. See e.g., E. Tiede, "Atlas als Personifikation der Weltasche," ("Atlas as the Personification of the World Axis") *Museum Helveticum*, 2 (1945) pp. 65-86. The peoples of the New World also had this concept of the World Axis as a titan supporting the heavens, portrayals of which are common in the art of Mexico, where such figures are actually called "Atlanteans."

As regards the catastrophes identified by Schaeffer and others in the ruins of ancient settlements of the Late Bronze and Iron Ages, we should note that after the definitive end of the period of great cosmic catastrophes, at the close of the Early Dynastic Age, our world continued to be afflicted by massive earth-tremors and seismic disturbances for some period of time. The reason for this has already been explained. After the last of the great "cosmic earthquakes," our planet's tectonic plates were seriously disturbed, and it took several centuries for them to readjust and achieve some form of equilibrium. Thus even into the Iron Age, indeed into the time of the Roman Republic and beyond, earth-tremors and volcanic disturbances of considerably greater magnitude than present-day experience, continued to be reported. We need only, in this context, think of the fifty-seven earthquakes reported in Rome during the Second Punic War (217 BC),[1] plus the fate of Pompeii and Herculaneum in AD 79.

BLOOD SACRIFICE AND THE RISE OF THE FIRST CIVILIZATIONS

In 1992, Gunnar Heinsohn published a paper in the journal *Religion* entitled "The Rise of Blood Sacrifice and Priest Kingship in Mesopotamia: A Cosmic Decree?,"[2] in which he argued that a comet-induced catastrophe had directly influenced the rise of the first high civilizations. Building strictly on the stratigraphic evidence, Heinsohn noted that the earliest literate civilization in Mesopotamia (Jamdat Nasr) had commenced directly after the Flood disaster uncovered by Woolley. The oldest texts from the region confirm that the Flood, usually attributed to the goddess Ishtar/Innana, but also to the dragon-monster Tiamat, occupied a central position in religious ritual at the time. Indeed, various prayers and poems make it clear that the construction of shrines or temples was in direct response to the recent catastrophe.[3] A central feature of these shrines, which were in fact the first pyramid-like ziggurats, was a high place, or altar (Latin, *altus*, "high"), known to the Mesopotamians as the House of the God. On this raised platform human and animals were offered to the celestial deities.

The progress of historical research over the past century, as Heinsohn noted, has begun to make it abundantly clear that the earliest phases of all civilizations were marked by a period during which blood sacrifices were offered atop raised platforms or mounds to the celestial deities, often to the Queen of Heaven, or to the Celestial or Cosmic Serpent — the Dragon.

---

1 Pliny, *Natural History*, ii, 86.
2 G. Heinsohn, "The Rise of Blood Sacrifice and Priest Kingship in Mesopotamia: A Cosmic Decree?," *Religion*, Vol. 22 (1992) pp. 309-334.
3 Thus after Marduk destroys the monster Tiamat, who had threatened to overwhelm the whole of creation, the gods, in thanksgiving, build a shrine to him at Babylon.

Working on the insights provided by Velikovsky, as well as earlier catastrophists like Donnelly, Heinsohn came to realize that the comet-induced Flood catastrophe, which he placed near the middle of the second millennium BC, had itself been directly involved in the appearance of the first literate cultures. We need to imagine a world overwhelmed by the unleashed elements. A planet plunged in a terrifying darkness, blasted by hurricane-force winds and shaken by terrible seismic disturbances. A planet, finally, bombarded by showers of meteors and deluged by mountainous tidal-waves. The survivors of this event, as we might well imagine, were utterly traumatized. Completely unable to comprehend what had happened, they could only imagine themselves the victims of some vengeful and violent deity. This deity, indeed, was clearly visible: It was an enormous fiery or winged serpent which flew through the skies, whence it breathed periodically fire and brimstone upon hapless humans. How to respond to such a threat?

A feature fundamental to people everywhere, as Heinsohn noted, is the tendency to see meaning in all things; to somehow view the events of life as either a reward or punishment for our own behavior. Clearly the Deluge had been a punishment visited upon a deserving humanity. Clearly too, the god inflicting this punishment delighted in his or her work. What, then, if this deity were voluntarily offered the blood which it so evidently delighted in? Perhaps it might leave the world in peace! And so, simultaneously throughout the world, men sought out high places, usually mountaintops, upon which to offer the sky gods the blood they seemed to require. High places were chosen, of course, because it was to such places that men had fled to escape the onrushing tides. But high places were also symbolic in that they were closer to the sky, to the heavens, where the celestial beings dwelt.

After some time, as the seismic and tidal wave activity abated, people settled again in the lower-lying regions. But now they began to construct artificial hills — to begin with merely small mounds — upon which to perform their bloody rituals.

And so, ironically enough, was literate civilization born. The raising of such structures required organization and, eventually, accounting. The obsessive watch kept upon the skies was instrumental in the development of both mathematics and geometry, whilst the use of stone and brick in the mounds gave birth to architecture.

But along with the first organized urban societies there came another phenomenon: the appearance of organized priesthoods and aristocracies. In Heinsohn's words:

> The first priestly counselors provided healing power to their infantile, regressed fellow-men through a similar kind of play. The play had to do

with sacrifice. These redeemers, by inventing the sacrificial drama and its deities, were capable of actively overcoming the paralyzing and agitating effects of catastrophes. They helped bring their fellow-men back to their senses. The cult founders- rising above their kin because of superior psychic stability — restore the power of action to their terrorized communities by becoming sacred executioners.

The early priests, by performing the ritual of blood sacrifice, became intermediaries with the gods and the saviors of their communities. In addition, they were seen as taking upon themselves the blood-guilt of the whole community:

The lion's share of guilt for the sacred execution ... falls on the priest. He has nobody to resort to for redeeming the guilt which weighs heavily on him. Self-flagellation and ascetic, penitential renunciation which went as far as self-mutilation, were therefore techniques used by priests as a means of expiation. The latter found its extreme expression in self-castration which is not only known for priests of the Syrian Great Goddess Cybele, but also for the sacred executioners in the Aztec cult of Quetzalcoatl.

The first priests able to provide release from collective frenzy were considered heroic not only for their innovative mind, but also because initially the sacrificial act was dangerous. The victim did not necessarily co-operate. It was no easy matter to dispatch a representative of raging cosmic forces. The victim virtually had to be defeated in the sacred ritual. The cult founders — presumably at a later date sacrificial victims received training and status or entered the arena in shackles — had to kill unwilling partners. Even where the natural forces were represented by a wild beast, whose capture supplied a wealth of material for myths, the outstanding courage of the cult founders was unquestionable.

Above all, the early heroic priests' acceptance of guilt feelings for the act of killing elevated them above the community. The community which had been relieved from emotional confusion — had truly been healed — was in debt to them. In this author's view, the payment of this debt was decisive in bringing about feudal, i.e., full-time, priestship which became the core of Bronze Age civilization: the Mesopotamian En or Lugal was a priest king who sacrificed, as was the Mycenaean Basileus. Early priesthood did not succeed by fooling the people with tricks. It had a legitimate basis: the priesthood provided healing power through rituals for terror-stricken communities. The priests' second great service — oracles — was no less in demand. When will it happen again?, was the question frightened people would have asked throughout the Bronze Age.

The first priests therefore were identical to the first kings. Thus the establishment of priesthoods brought with it the establishment of aristocracy and social stratification — another prerequisite of the organized literate civilization.

If what Heinsohn said is correct, it means that all high civilizations arose simultaneously as a response to the cataclysm witnessed by human beings in every corner of the globe. Thus the fact that early humans erected pyramids or mound-structures all over the planet — which, it is now obvious, they did — does not mean that cultural diffusion is indicated. This was a universal response to identical events that affected the entire human race.

What bearing then does this have on the Atlantis question?

To begin with, it means that many of the cultural parallels observed by Donnelly and others between the Old World and the New, such as, especially, pyramid-building, dragon-worship, priest-kingship and human sacrifice, do not need ancient transatlantic contacts to explain them. If we seek proof of cultural communication between the Old and New Worlds, we need to look beyond such religious/mythological and cult ideas. It may of course be that Old World and New World ideas about the dragon-cult, human sacrifice and priest-kingship did influence each other, but such influence may be impossible to prove in light of the virtual certainty that these concepts were developed independently.

Yet ironically enough, whilst removing one body of support for cultural diffusion, the Heinsohnian idea produces a new one. One of the most important criticisms leveled against those who saw evidence of ancient contact between Egyptians, for example, and Peruvians, was the insistence that the New World civilizations were much younger than the Old. Thus the similarities between Egyptian culture and Peruvian were declared to be insignificant because Egypt had long left the Bronze Age by the time the early Peruvians were entering it. The new chronology of civilization removes that problem. It is evident that, if Heinsohn is correct, the Old World had no two thousand year head-start over the New, and that both hemispheres entered the Bronze Ages simultaneously. Thus some parallels, such as, for example, mummification, found both in Egypt and Peru, may well be regarded as proof of early cultural contact.

As we shall now see, there is not only rich but definitive proof that (leaving aside pyramids, priest-kings, dragons etc.) the Old and New Worlds interacted with great frequency in Bronze Age times and even before.

CHAPTER 4. LINKS ACROSS AN OCEAN

STONE AGE CONTACTS

When Ignatius Donnelly wrote his *Atlantis* book, he expended much energy in describing cultural and artistic parallels between the ancient inhabitants of the New World and of the Old. Donnelly concentrated upon the high civilizations of the two regions, where he found numerous and remarkable similarities. He did not however, though he believed Atlantis to have perished over eleven thousand years ago, say a great deal about epochs prior to the Neolithic or New Stone Age. This was in part due to the very incomplete knowledge of Stone Age archaeology, particularly American Stone Age archaeology, in his time. Yet even as he wrote, archaeologists such as C. C. Abbott were making remarkable discoveries; discoveries which led him to propose a close link between the Old Stone Age of America and that of western Europe.[1]

Although Abbott's arguments were generally overlooked by mainstream academics, the discoveries he made were real enough, and the questions did not go away. Thus W. H. Holmes, although rejecting Abbott's theory of European settlers in America, included Europeans in his 1912 multiple waves theory to account for numerous shared cultural traits.[2] N. C. Nelson, curator of Prehistoric Archaeology at the American Museum of Natural History, specifically linked the European Solutrean culture the American Old Stone Age in 1919. By 1920s archae-

---

[1] See e.g., C. C. Abbott, H. W. Haynes and G. F. Wright, *The Paleolithic Implements of the Valley of the Delaware* (1881).

[2] See W. H. Holmes, B. Willis, F. E. Wright and C. N. Fenner, "Early Man in South America," *Bulletin of the Bureau of American Ethnology*, 52 (1912), 1–405

ologists had discovered another Paleolithic culture in North America which they named Folsom. This too bore striking parallels with the European Paleolithic, and in 1937 Nelson suggested that all such European influences had reached North America via Mongolia. Étienne Bernardeau Renaud, of the University of Denver, emphasized the relationship between Folsom and Solutrean points in 1931. This he elaborated in his native French 1933 for *Revue Anthropologique*, and reiterated in English 1934.

During the late 1930s Frank Hibben found a series of spear-points of Paleolithic age in a celebrated cave north-east of Albuquerque, and recognized their striking relationship to Solutrean points the collection of Grant MacCurdy published 1932 and 1937, but he could not "bridge Asiatic gaps of awe-inspiring magnitude," accepting European influence but rejecting the idea that it could have crossed the Atlantic. In 1952 John Witthoft saw chert fluted points excavated from eleven hunting camps from western New York dotting the 20-acre Shoop Site in eastern Pennsylvania as representatives of Old World Upper Paleolithic blade industry.

Thus the archeologists and anthropologists found clear proof of transatlantic contact in the days of the mammoth and mastodon, whilst textbook dogma insisted that no contact between the Old World and the New (save via the Bering Strait) existed before Columbus.

In 1963, British anthropologist E. F. Greenman took the debate as stage further in an article for *Current Anthropology*, where he proposed a route by which the European influences could have reached North America. During the Pleistocene, he theorized, the North Atlantic may have been largely frozen, and European hunters could have "hopped" across the ocean from ice-floe to ice-floe in kayak-like canoes. The tone of his introduction was pedestrian, merely reiterating what archeologists had noted again and again over the previous century: "There are many trait-parallels," he said, "between the Upper Paleolithic of southwestern Europe and North America. They are present in the latter in four main areas: that of the Eskimo culture, Newfoundland, the St. Lawrence drainage and the Greater Southwest. Among the more important North American parallels are certain boats and house-types, bone pendants, design motifs, and representations of animals. These resemble paintings in Upper Paleolithic caves or actual objects from Upper Paleolithic sites in the Biscayan area and farther north, as well as in two caves on the southeast coast of Spain.

> There is also a close correspondence between the points of the Sandia culture of New Mexico and those of a Solutrean [Paleolithic] site at Montaut, southwest France; at least one heavily stylized pictograph in Lower California is directly descended from one specific painting at Castillo Cave, northwest Spain. Several other specific Southwestern traits are

present in the St. Lawrence drainage, Newfoundland, and in the Upper Paleolithic of the Biscayan region.[1]

Because the existence of a land-bridge such as Atlantis was not even considered, Greenman was compelled to postulate "A crossing of the North Atlantic in skin boats during the last glacial period" which "was made possible by the presence of floating ice in the form of bergs, ice islands, and ice floes." He went on to state that,

> The Bering Strait hypothesis is not discarded as a possible route of entry concurrently with that across the North Atlantic, but [the] Bering Strait need not be considered until there is better evidence than the close proximity of Asia and North America, especially in the absence of bifacial blades from Siberia of an early enough time to be the source of those of the Early Man cultures in North America. The practice of giving a Siberian origin to any Alaskan feature that is duplicated in Siberia is faulty. The Direction of diffusion may usually have been from east to west. The Upper Paleolithic cultures represented in North America appear to be the Solutrean and the Magdalenian [European Paleolithic] minus its flint component. But certain animal petroglyphs in the upper St. Lawrence drainage show similarities to Aurignacian styles. The petroglyphs of all of North America show many correspondences to figures in Upper Paleolithic caves. Fragments of French and Spanish animal figures seem to have been brought to the New World and carved or painted on rock surfaces. The petroglyphs of the New World represent a long tradition in which the most ancient figures were obliterated as others were carved or painted over them.

Greenman's idea of Paleolithic influences crossing an ice berg strewn North Atlantic did not convince, and though his work caused some comment during the 1960s, it was largely ignored thereafter. It was not until the late 1990s that the debate was reignited.

A CONTROVERSY RENEWED

In 1997, American archaeologist Dennis Stanford, perhaps influenced by Greenman and his predecessors, reasserted the belief that some of America's earliest human inhabitants, maybe the earliest of all, had come from Europe. Convinced by establishment academics in America (ignoring of course the evidence garnered by Russian and Scandinavian geologists) that no land-bridge or island-bridge could have existed to facilitate transatlantic travel, Stanford was compelled to fall back upon Greenman's idea of iceberg-hopping hunters.

It is important to emphasize that Dr. Stanford, like his predecessors in this field, is no maverick. His mentors were luminaries in Stone Age American archaeology, people like Marie Wormington, Curator of Archaeology at the Den-

---

1 E. F. Greenman, "The Upper Paleolithic and the New World," *Current Anthropology*, Vol. 4, (1963) p. 41.

ver Museum of Natural History for 31 years and author of classic texts on early Americans, and C. Vance Haynes Jr., of the University of Arizona, an expert on the Clovis culture. What then could have made such a pillar of the establishment turn away from the Bering Strait route and look elsewhere for the first migration?

> His [Stanford's] thinking evolved over three decades. In the '60s Stan-
> ford, like most of his colleagues, believed that Clovis came from Asia. It
> wasn't until the '70s that he began to believe that Clovis was a New World
> development and that evidence of pre-Clovis would be found in the Arc-
> tic. "But I wasn't seeing evidence," he recalls, "and after a while it started
> not to make sense. Everything I found in Alaska that was fluted was post-
> Clovis in age." There was no technology he considered pre-Clovis. He
> hoped at the time that once Siberia was opened up to Western scientists
> we would find the missing evidence. But the end of the Cold War didn't
> provide the solution for Stanford and his co-theorist, lithics expert Bruce
> Bradley. Stanford and Dr. Bradley independently looked at the evidence
> and arrived at the same conclusion. They inspected late-Pleistocene sites
> and scoured museum collections in Siberia, Russia, and northern China,
> seeking pre-Clovis technology. Instead, what they found was a totally dif-
> ferent method of making tools and weapons.[1]

Put simply, Clovis blades, the earliest tools created by men in the Americas, were bifacial, i.e., they had a sharp cutting edge at both sides, rather like a Me-dieval European sword, whereas contemporary Stone Age artifacts from Siberia were microblades inserted into rods of bone or ivory. Totally different to Clovis blades:

> The Clovis fluted point is knapped from stone, flaked on both sides (bi-
> facial) and shaped into a beautiful thin, flat killing instrument; the base is
> thinned and relieved into a concave recess so that the point can be secure-
> ly hafted onto a foreshaft or shaft. (See "Lithic Caches" in this issue for
> a photo of spectacular examples of Clovis points.) The Asian upper-Pa-
> leolithic weapons that Stanford and Bradley found, however, were made
> using a microblade technology, where tiny blades struck from wedge-
> shaped cores of stone were inset into long, narrow rods of bone, antler,
> or ivory. When Far East craftsmen tried to make bifacial tools, the result
> was relatively crude implements (quite thick in cross section, compared
> with exquisitely thin Clovis points) and frequently bi-pointed. Stanford
> and Bradley suspect the Asian bifaces were knives instead of projectile
> points.

> True, they found assemblages containing bifaces and large blade cores.
> But those sites are in the Trans-Baikal region of central Asia — about
> 6,000 miles from Alaska — and date to 10,000 years before Clovis. To
> Bradley they appear to belong to the Streletskayan technology of the Eur-
> asian Plain and not to the Far East.

> Nowhere in Asia did Stanford and Bradley find the ancestor of the Clo-
> vis point. They reasoned that if the first immigrants were Asian, they must

---

1 www.freerepublic.com/focus/f-news/1013315/posts.

have brought with them their inset-microblade manufacturing process, in which case there must exist evidence of a transition to Clovis technology. So far, however, nothing resembling an intermediate form between inset microblades and a knapped biface has been found in North America.

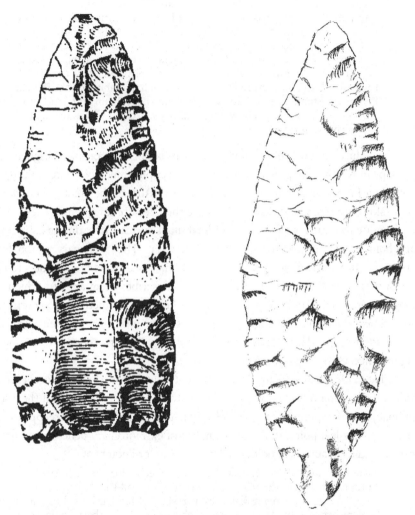

Fig. 5. Left: Clovis blade. Right: Solutrean blade. The Clovis blade has a fluted groove to facilitate affixation of spear shaft. Solutrean blades normally lack this groove, but a few have been found with it. (See eg Philip E. Smith, "A Fluted Point from the Old World," American Antiquity, Vol. 28, No. 3 (January, 1963) pp. 397-399).

But if Clovis technology did not come from Asia, where did it come from? The answer would prove astonishing:

> Stuck at a dead end, Stanford and Bradley took up a fresh trail. The roots of Clovis, they reasoned, must lie in the Paleolithic Old World outside of

Asia. They took up the search for a parent technology that specialized in making thin, flat bifacial projectile points, knives and other biface implements, and other artifacts of stone and bone similar to those of the Clovis culture. They didn't demand of the candidate that it precisely match Clovis technology, only that it exhibit features that could be reasonably interpreted as pre-Clovis. They found only one Paleolithic culture whose technology met their criteria, suggested by Nels Nelson of the American Museum of Natural History early in the 20th century and later by University of Arizona archaeologist Art Jelinek in an article published in 1971 in Arctic Anthropology: the Solutrean people. Named for the French town of Solutré, the culture spread across much of France and the Iberian Peninsula. Stanford and Bradley look to northern Spain and southwestern France for the people who might have carried pre-Clovis technology across the Atlantic.

The Solutreans, by all accounts, were an astonishing people. Originating perhaps in North Africa, at their height they occupied much of western Europe, including France and Spain — as well as North Africa. They technical and artistic skills are legendary: "Full bellies gave them leisure time, which they used to decorate the walls of their caves with fabulous surrealistic paintings of bison and horses and ibex that continue to awe us today. They were carvers, too, for art's sake. In Solutrean sites we find carved limestone tablets — at one site in Spain there are stacks of hundreds. Stanford describes them as '3 to 6 inches long, 3 inches wide, and half an inch thick. The design, sometimes zoomorphic, sometimes geomorphic, is engraved on one side or both.' They weren't drilled and made into pendants. They don't do anything. Perhaps they have religious significance. Or perhaps they just are.

What made the Solutreans deadly efficient hunters was their unprecedented skill at fashioning tools and weapons from stone. In the 4,000 years of their supremacy their knapping creations evolve from unifacial points (later reappearing as the willow-leaf point, unifacial again, but of extraordinary delicacy and fineness) to bifacial laurel-leaf points and blades. Stanford points out,

> They had the only upper-Paleolithic biface technology going in Western Europe. They were the first to heat-treat flint, and the first to use pressure flaking — removing flakes by pressing with a hardwood or antler tool, rather than by striking with another stone. 'In northern Spain, their technology produced biface projectile points with concave bases that are basally thinned,' he notes, not bothering to say he could just as well be describing Clovis points. The pressure flakes Solutrean knappers removed are so long it's almost a fluting technique — 'almost,' he's careful to say, but not quite.

Stanford and his associates found that Clovis and Solutrean artifacts were so similar they could almost have been produced in the same workshops: "The parallels between Solutrean and Clovis flintknapping techniques seem endless. The core technology, 'the way they were knocking off big blades and setting up their core platforms,' he explains, 'is very similar to the Clovis technique, if not identical.' They perfected the outre passé — overshot — flaking technique later seen in Clovis, which removes a flake across the entire face of the tool from margin to margin. It's a complicated procedure, he emphasizes, that has to be set up and steps followed precisely in order to detach regular flakes predictably. When you see outre passé flaking in other cultures, you're looking at a knapper's mistake. The Solutreans, though, set up platforms and followed the technique through to the end, exactly as we see in Clovis. 'No one else in the world does that,' Stanford insists. 'There is very little in Clovis — in fact, nothing — that is not found in Solutrean technology,' he declares.

Archaeologist Kenneth Tankersley of Kent State University seconds Stanford and Bradley's opinion:

> There are only two places in the world and two times that this technology appears- Solutrean and Clovis.

> On and on the similarities pile up. We find carved tablets in Clovis sites remarkably similar to Solutrean specimens. Both cultures cached toolstone and finished implements. (See 'Lithic Caches' in this issue.) Stanford and Bradley know of about 20 instances of caches at Solutrean sites; in North America, by comparison, according to Stanford, 'we're up to about nine or ten.' Just like Clovis knappers, Solutreans used flakes detached by outre passé to make scrapers and knives. Clovis bone projectile points bear an uncanny resemblance to ones made by Solutreans. When French archaeologists saw the cast of a wrench used by Clovis craftsmen at the Murray Springs site in Arizona to straighten spear shafts, they declared it remarkably similar to one found at a Solutrean site.

> In 1997 Stanford was invited by French archaeologists to bring specimens of Clovis tools and weapons to an exhibit at the museum of Solutré, organized by Anta Montet-White and Jack Hofman of the University of Kansas. It was on that trip in the summer of 1997 that Stanford, able to compare Solutrean and Clovis tools side by side, became confident he was looking at products of technologies so similar there was a high probability they were in fact historically related technologies — one culture — separated only by time and distance.[1]

Only two serious objections were raised against Stanford: First, how could Europeans (and/or North Africans) of the Old Stone Age have crossed the Atlantic? And, how to explain the 4,000-year difference (according to radiocarbon dating} between the start of the Solutrean and the Clovis cultures? Neither of these objections, the present writer holds, offers a serious obstacle. Radiocarbon, as I have demonstrated in detail elsewhere, is highly suspect as a dating tool, whilst

1 See www.freerepublic.com/fous/f-news/1013315/posts.

the journey across the Atlantic becomes very possible if a large island, or group of islands, acted as stepping-stones.

A CONTINUING LINK

Over a century ago, Donnelly found evidence of striking parallels from the earliest high civilizations of the Old World and the New; yet it now seems that the transatlantic contacts began even earlier. It has never been proven that the Neolithic and Bronze Age parallels identified by Donnelly were not the result of transoceanic contact. Instead, his critics suggested that such parallels were simply coincidental. Several of them may indeed be put down to coincidence, but many of them, specific and astonishing in their detail, cannot be so dismissed.

Presently we shall have occasion to examine some of the more salient features of this material.

With Donnelly however there were a number of objections. To begin with, he held by the fantastic idea that Atlantis was a high civilization eleven thousand years ago, a civilization that, moreover, had ceased to exist nine thousand five hundred years before Christ. It was, of course, quickly pointed out that Atlantis could not be invoked as a connecting link between the Old World and the New if it had ceased to exist eleven millennia ago. In that remote age no one, on either side of the Atlantic, had ever imagined building pyramids or mummifying the dead. So, the proposed link was broken even before the cultural traits highlighted by Donnelly existed.

There was another chronological problem. Even if Atlantis were to be regarded as a Bronze Age civilization, of the type that constructed pyramids etc. in the Old World, this would not explain the link: For the first pyramid-building cultures of the New World, such as Olmecs of Mexico and Norte Chicos of Peru, are said to be much younger than those of the Old. By the time the earliest civilizations of the New World had begun building pyramids, the custom had long died out in the Old.

Therefore, on yet another count, the links and parallels were held to be illusory.

There was a third and somewhat decisive objection. Parallels might exist; yet some of the most important characteristics of Old World civilization, such as the wheel, wheel-made pottery, the arch, stringed musical instruments, etc., never made it to the New. Even worse, many of the most important agricultural products and techniques of the Old World were unknown in the New; whilst some very useful products of New World agriculture were unknown in the Old. The situation is summed up thus by Friedrich Katz, as he criticizes the ideas of Robert Heine-Geldern, a proponent of ancient contacts between the Americas and Asia: "If there were in fact such enduring and close links between ancient America and the Old World, how is it that hitherto not a single object of Asiatic [and European/African] provenance has been discovered in America and conversely not a single object of American origin has been found in Asia [or Europe/Africa]? How is it that no evidence is to be found in Chinese or Indian sources of such odysseys? How is it that all the elements typical of Old World cultures — the true arch, the wheel, the cart, the potter's wheel, bellows, glass, iron and stringed instruments — are missing in the New World, and that the most important domestic animals and cultivated plants, such as rice, known in the Old World, are not known there?"[1]

It is on this note that the debate has more or less rested since Donnelly's time. In vain do the various "Atlantean" theorists continue to point to the obvious similarities between the ancient cultures of the two worlds. The similarities are there, it is said, but they are there by accident, the result of separate invention rather than cultural diffusion.

It is evident, even from a very brief summary of the situation, that in this debate chronology is of paramount importance. If what establishment academics say is true, then the links and parallels identified by Donnelly and others cannot be significant. But if the textbooks and those who write them have got the chronology wrong, as we claim, then we are involved in a very different situation.

Before continuing, let me reiterate what was said in the previous chapter: The evidence suggests strongly that the Paleolithic or Old Stone Age more or less directly preceded the rise of the first civilizations, those of the Neolithic and Early Bronze Ages. There was no 6,000–year gap. In addition, the first civilizations of the Old World and the New arose simultaneously, in the immediate aftermath of a Deluge catastrophe, the event which brought the Paleolithic Age to an end. As such, there was no awkward gap between the pyramid-building civilizations of the two worlds: they were parallel and contemporary. And yet, it is true, as Katz says, that some of the most useful inventions of the Old World failed to make it across the Atlantic before Columbus. If a link did exist during the time of the first civilizations, then it must have been broken before these innovations were widespread, or at least before they had reached Western Europe and North-West Africa. In a word, the proposed Atlantean link must have disappeared just before the use of the wheel and wheel-made pottery in Western Europe. This is a crucial marker in our attempt to reconstruct the chronology of events.

In this context, it is important to note that many of the above-mentioned arts, crafts and technologies did not spread throughout the great Levantine civilizations until a comparatively late date. Thus for example the wheel was unknown

---

1 Friedrich Katz, *The Ancient American Civilisations* (English ed. George Weidenfeld and Nicolson, 1972) p. 15.

in Egypt until the time of the Hyksos (presumably sixteenth century BC), who introduced it, together with the horse and chariot, from Mesopotamia; and glass was developed at roughly the same time. Yet before we attempt to identify the precise point at which the Old World civilizations introduced technologies unknown in the New (and thus to pinpoint the moment when the transatlantic connection was terminated), we need to say something more about technological developments on either side of the Atlantic which are traceable between the end of the Old Stone Age and the beginning of the Early Bronze Age. For it is a striking fact, unremarked by previous commentators, that the development from Old Stone Age, through to Middle (Mesolithic), through to New (Neolithic) and finally onto Early Bronze, is precisely matched on either side of the Ocean, with each and every feature of these cultural epochs occurring, in the same order, on the eastern and western shores. Thus we find that, in the Old World, the Mesolithic culture saw the introduction of several revolutionary innovations, amongst which were the bow and arrow and the axe. The latter permitted, for the first time, the large-scale clearing of forests and construction in wood. The Mesolithic also saw the domestication of the dog.

Similarly, in the New World, the culture which replaced the Paleolithic (Clovis), saw the introduction of the bow, the axe and the domestic dog. The last of these is now known to have been virtually identical in genetic terms to the domestic dog of the Old World. More on this presently.

The Neolithic Age, both in the New World and the Old, was to bring its own dramatic changes. Large-scale construction in stone commenced, as did temple building, agriculture, and the beginnings of urban settlements. There were major improvements in pottery manufacture, and the sail revolutionized travel by water. In the Neolithic too men took the first steps towards literacy.

All the above features are found on both sides of the Atlantic.

By the Early Bronze Age, which in fact largely overlapped the Neolithic, all the essentials of high civilization were in place. Metallurgy (in the form, mainly, of copper-working) had reached a sophisticated level, as had the art of building in stone. There now appeared also the centralized state presided over by the priest-king.

Once again, all of these features are found on either side of the Ocean. The situation may be represented thus:

EPOCH	NEW WORLD	OLD WORLD
PALEOLITHIC	(CLOVIS and FOLSOM) Bifacial blades Spear-throwers Carving of bone/ivory First art	(SOLUTREAN and MAGDALENIAN) Bifacial blades Spear-throwers Carving of bone/ivory First art
MESOLITHIC	("ARCHAIC" CULTURES) Bow and arrow Axe Domestic dog	(CAPSIAN and AZILIAN) Bow and arrow Axe Domestic dog
NEOLITHIC	(PUEBLO and RELATED MEXICAN CULTURES) First agriculture Temple building Sailing vessels	(MOUND-BUILDERS of EUROPE) First agriculture Temple building Sailing vessels
EARLY BRONZE	(MEXICAN and SOUTH AMERICAN CULTURES) First writing Pyramid-building Metallurgy Centralized state presided over by Priest-king	(NEAR EASTERN and BALKAN CULTURES) First writing Pyramid-building Metallurgy Centralized state presided over by Priest-king

It goes without saying that not all of the above were introduced either in the Old or New Worlds at precisely the same point in time. There is good evidence, as we saw in the previous chapter, to suggest that in some parts of the world, such as Mesopotamia and Egypt (and possibly some parts of America), knowledge of the rudiments of pottery existed as early as the Paleolithic; whilst many areas, both in the Old World and the New, never reached the level designated above as "Early Bronze." Nonetheless, in general, the above sequence is what is found in large areas of the Old World and the New; and the parallels observed, as well as the order in which they occur, surely cannot fail to impress. Now, it is generally held that the above features, when they occur in the New World, were the result of separate invention by the Native Americans; and that the parallels with Old World development are purely coincidental. But is that an adequate explanation? No one of course denies the intelligence and inventiveness of the Native Americans; yet the above similarities seem just too precise to be solely the result of separate development. We note, for example, that the natives of Australia failed even to learn the use of the bow and the axe before the arrival of Europeans, and remained, essentially, at a Paleolithic cultural level. Thus it was not inevitable that even these simple technologies would be developed independently by all humans.

The parallels become even more significant when we realize, as we now do, that the Old Stone Age culture of the New World was in direct communication with that of the Old. And they become quite irresistible when we learn (as we shall presently) that people of the Old World left a genetic imprint upon the populations of the New, whilst plants (such as tobacco and cocaine) and other products of the New World were imported into the Old during the Bronze Age — a fact we shall also explore in due course.

Yet even admitting all of this, there remains the problem of chronology; the problem that has bedeviled every attempt to make sense of the Atlantis story for over a hundred years. We remind ourselves that, according to accepted ideas, the Early Bronze Age cultures of the New World, notwithstanding their striking similarities to those of the Old, only appeared two or three thousand years after their Old World counterparts. And so it needs to be stressed once again that a fundamental principle of the present work is that the chronologies of the early civilizations, as we find them in the textbooks, is utterly flawed, and that no gap at all exists between the commencement of the Early Bronze Age in the Americas and in Europe, Asia and Africa. They are, as all the evidence implies — some of which we looked at in the preceding chapter — contemporary cultures; and they were in contact with each other. As we saw too in the previous chapter, four great natural catastrophes struck our planet between the end of the Old Stone Age and the end of the Early Bronze period. The first of these, and also the most violent, terminated the Paleolithic. The second brought to an end the Mesolithic. The third ended the Neolithic and the fourth, and last, brought the Early Bronze period to a close. This last cataclysm was also the one which sank the Atlantis island and terminated once and for all the transatlantic cultural link. It left the civilizations of Mexico, Central and South America essentially fossilized in the Early Bronze Age — a condition that persisted until the arrival of the Spaniards in Mexico in 1519.

The question of chronology, so crucial to unraveling the Atlantis mystery, is further explored in the final chapter.

Our position is thus that contacts across the Atlantic, at that time a smaller body of water than at present, commenced in the Old Stone Age. This was the age of the Pleistocene mega fauna, the mammoth, mastodon, cave bear, saber-toothed tiger etc. These creatures were encountered by the "Solutrean" colonizers and hunted by them. Using the (at that time, above-water) mountain range of the Mid-Atlantic Ridge as a highway, these early adventurers and hunters, "hopped" from the ends of the spurs of the Ridge, which at that time must have almost touched the coast of South America, onto the latter continent. They were, these first Atlanteans, even then, seafarers. But we must not imagine ships, or anything approximating to them. We must think in terms of large canoes, similar perhaps to the vessels employed by Polynesians to this day.

Then came the Deluge. As we saw earlier, this event would have disrupted the transatlantic connection but not severed it. Some parts of the Mid-Atlantic Mountain range were no doubt lost, and the ocean may have become larger; but Atlantis remained, and an archipelago of smaller islands linking it to South-West Europe and North-West Africa also remained. After recovering from the initial devastation wrought by the unleashed forces of nature, the Atlanteans, by then at the "Mesolithic" stage of culture, introduced the bow and the axe to the Americas. Then came a further cataclysm, the second described in Mexican legend and encountered in tradition throughout the earth. Much of the Mid-Atlantic Mountain range sank, though a chain of large and precipitous islands must have remained, as well as a larger landmass around the region now occupied by the Azores. This was the true Atlantis, the Atlantis of popular history and legend. The Atlanteans, now at the "Neolithic" stage of development, began the construction of a genuine maritime civilization. True ships, with sails, were now constructed, and settlements built of stone, the precursors of real cities, sprang up. Temple-building and sacrifice began. Then came a third catastrophe. More of the Mid-Atlantic Ridge was submerged, and the main island of Atlantis was reduced in size. But the Atlanteans survived, and within a very short time there took shape the powerful and prosperous Early Bronze Age culture of tradition. Better and faster sailing ships were deployed, and the routes to the Americas re-opened. The Atlanteans, ethnically Berber, had strong and long-standing links with North Africa and the Iberian Peninsula; and these regions were heavily settled by them. Trade with peoples further to the east, in the Aegean and the Levant, was quickly established, and new ideas travelled along with the merchants and sailors. Thus there came into being a proto-civilization, at the very beginning of the Bronze Age (more properly described as the Copper Age, since true bronze was as yet unknown), with one foot in South America and the Caribbean and another in Libya and the Aegean. Its centre, however, apart from the mid-Atlantic "island of Atlas," was in Western Europe and North Africa, where vast numbers of temple-structures, fashioned from large "megalithic" stones, began to be raised.

As might be expected, a culture in contact with Egypt might be influenced by the Egyptians in many things, and might have carried those influences right to the other side of the ocean. And this is exactly what we do find. In fact, a myriad of traditions and practices from various parts of the Old World, from Egypt, through to Babylonia and various parts of Europe, found precise echoes in the traditions and practices of the peoples of North and South America. Importantly however, as we have stressed above, none of the advanced technical and agricultural developments which were later to characterize the Old World reached the Americas because, as we shall see, the link was finally and definitively broken in the Early Bronze Age.

THE CULT OF THE THUNDER-AXE

In the course of the present chapter we shall look at some of the detailed parallels between the cultures of the Old World and those of the New as observed by Donnelly and others. We shall also have occasion to examine the latest forensic evidence which takes ancient transatlantic contact out of the realm of theory and into that of scientific fact. Before doing so however I wish to examine a cultural feature which combines within itself evidence pointing towards the impact of ancient catastrophes, transatlantic exchange of ideas, and a clear and definitive chronological marker.

I refer to the cult of the axe or the thunderstone.

We noted above that the axe was an implement introduced in both New World and Old immediately after the end of the Paleolithic, and thus immediately after the Deluge cataclysm. Along with this iconic tool of civilization, a tool which allowed for the clearing of forests, construction in wood and general reshaping of the natural landscape, there came a whole mythology and system of beliefs. The axe, or pickaxe, or hammer, was to become a central symbol in the iconography of the natives on both sides of the Atlantic. This tool, as we saw, first appeared in the Mesolithic, and from the Neolithic onwards, "Axes are found in graves, under standing stones, in dwelling sites and hearths; in quantities and in positions which show clearly that they must be interpreted as ritual offerings. Often an axe is set in the earth upright, with the cutting edge in the air, and held in place by small stones."[1] Specific axe-finds mentioned by the writer just quoted were: "two unpolished, narrow-backed flint axes at the edge of a great stone near Lottorf in Schleswig; four identical ones under another great stone near Sorring Skov in the neighbourhood of Arhus; a polished, pointed axe found under the heart at a dwelling site in Troldebjerg, Langeland, and three flint axes set in a triangle near Bedsted on the Thy peninsula, Denmark."[2] Also noteworthy were the discoveries of G. de Mortillet in Brittany, where six of the seven Megalithic tombs he excavated contained stone axes stuck in the earth, cutting edge up. Five smaller stone axes, four of diorite and one of fibrolite, were found in the same position at the foot at the foot of a menhir in Mane-er-Hroek, whilst inside burial chamber no. 1 at St Michel near Carnac, "thirty-nine stone axes, ten made

1 Jurgen Spanuth, *Atlantis of the North* (London, 1980) p. 109.
2 Ibid.

of jadeite, were found, all buried edge-upwards.[1] Similar finds have been made throughout the British Isles, whilst in the Mediterranean the axe-cult is observed at various places, but most especially in Crete and the Aegean.

Frequently these votive axes were made of rare or valuable materials, and fashioned with the utmost care. Beside the three flint axes found near Bedsted in Denmark "lay some amber beads, which had clearly been placed on purpose near the votive axe."[2] Amber was sacred in antiquity because of its ability to generate static electricity; its name in Greek was *electron;* and the entire cult of the axe, as we shall see, was connected with thunder, lightning, and meteorites. The whole axe-cult was inseparably linked to the unleashed forces of nature.

Strikingly, the cult was as prevalent in the New World as in the Old, particularly in early times. This was the case, for example, among the Olmecs, Mexico's first civilized people, who left us the mysterious colossal stone heads carved with negro features.[3] And the cult had not entirely disappeared even into modern times. The use for example of specially-designed axes or tomahawks in tobacco-smoking rituals amongst the tribes of North America is well-known. We should note too that the early axes of the Americas, whether of stone or metal, were remarkably similar in design to those of Neolithic and Bronze Age Europe.

The first researcher, as far as I am aware, to understand the meaning of the axe or hammer motif and to identify its transatlantic occurrence was Lewis Spence. He noted that the axe or hammer was connected, on both sides of the Atlantic, with the "thunder-stone." "This symbol," he said, "is almost universal, and is regarded not only by primitive, but by many modern peoples as the source of tempests and seismic and volcanic phenomena, whether as the bolt of Vulcan, the lance of the Carib, or the arrow of the Mexican and Egyptian deities."[4]

We note that the axe was introduced in the years after the Deluge catastrophe, during which we have surmised the earth suffered very severe meteorite bombardment. The earliest axes, hammers and thunderstones were clearly meteorites. Since these tools permitted men for the first time to reshape the landscape it is only natural that the gods who were currently also reshaping the terrestrial topography should be portrayed as carrying an axe. We recall that the axe seemed to be connected also with the legend of the Celestial Tower, and it is worth mentioning that according to classicist Bernhard Schweitzer Poseidon, the "Earth-shaker," was originally worshipped at pillars and that in his most primitive form

---

1 Ibid. p. 110.
2 Ibid., pp. 109-110.
3 See e.g., Elizabeth Easby, "Seafarers and Sculptors of the Caribbean," *Expedition*, 14 (1972), 3.
4 Spence, op. cit., p. 234.

he carried an axe or double-axe.[1] This was later substituted for a trident. Spence noted that, "In another of its forms it [the axe] was undoubtedly regarded as an earth-shaking implement, by means of which the gods fashioned the contours of the earth."[2] Strikingly, Spence drew attention to the numerous American Indian legends which speak of the gods reshaping the landscape very much in the way Poseidon was said by Plato to have reshaped the island of Atlantis: "The hammer of the thunder-god or creative deity with which he carved and shaped the earth was indeed identical with the implement by which the early sculptor fashioned his work. Manibozho, the god of the Algonquin Indians, shaped the hills and valleys with his hammer, constructing great beaver dams and moles across the lakes. His myth says that 'he carved the land and sea to his liking,' precisely as Poseidon carved the island of Atlantis into alternative zones of land and water. Poseidon was notoriously a god of earthquake as well as a marine deity, and it is a fair inference that he undertook the task in question with the great primeval pick, a sharp flint beak set in a wooden haft, the mjolnir of Thor, the hammer of Ptah, by which the operation of land-moulding was undertaken in most mythologies."[3]

Spence also drew attention to the fact that the icon of the "Great Hand," the hand used by the gods to reshape the earth, was also connected to the axe and the thunder-hammer. "The mythology of Mexico holds many allusions to a certain Huemac or 'Great Hand,' who seems to be identical with Quetzalcoatl. This figure is also found in Maya mythology as Kab-ul, the 'Working Hand,' a deification of the hand which wields the great pick or hammer, as is obvious in its representations in the native manuscripts. Quetzalcoatl was the skilled craftsman, the mason, who came from an Atlantic region. In his Quiche form of Tohil he is represented by a flint stone. It seems then that we have here the culture-hero from a marine locality symbolized by what appears to be the central emblem of the Atlantean culture-complex. Quetzalcoatl is also the planet Venus, and this identification gives a double significance to the complex. This is by no means weakened, when we discover that this Great Hand is actually identified with Atlantis in medieval legends, for the map of Bianco, which dates from 1436, contains an island, the Italian name of which may be translated 'the Hand of Satan.' Formaleoni, an Italian writer, had observed the name, but did not appreciate its significance until he chanced to stumble on a reference to a similar name in an old Italian romance, which told how a great hand rose every day from the sea and carried off a number of the inhabitants into the ocean. The legend is undoubtedly

---

1 Bernhard Schweitzer, *Herakles, Aufsätze zur griechische Religion und Sagengeschichte* (1922) p. 93f.
2 Spence, op. cit. p. 235.
3 Ibid., p. 236.

associated with the idea of earthquake or cataclysm in a marine locality, and it seems obvious that the Great Hand was the god of this Atlantic island, who took tribute of human lives by earthquake."[1]

Importantly, Spence notes too that "thunder-stones" (evidently meteorites) were kept in certain parts of the world wrapped in cloths, evidently in imitation of mummy-wrapping. This was the case, for example, in Ireland, where "tempests were precipitated by unwinding the flannel bandages in which the sacred stones were wrapped, and in Mexico the god Hurakan, the hurricane, was the southern equivalent of the god Itzilacoliuhqui, who was merely the stone-knife of sacrifice, Quetzalcoatl, in his form of the planet Venus, wrapped up in mummy bandages."[2] In Spence's opinion, "the thunder-stone was regarded as the very germ and essence of the tempest, the magical thing that caused ebullitions of nature, winds, earthquakes or eruptions.... To wrap it in bandages, however, seems to have been to render it temporarily quiescent, to have made a 'mummy' of it."[3]

Mummification itself, as we shall see, was one of those cultural traits which made it across the Atlantic in ancient times.

OTHER TRANSATLANTIC CULTURAL PARALLELS

The aforementioned parallels are but the tip of a vast iceberg. I mentioned them first because in a sense they come first chronologically. The earliest implements and weapons employed by humanity, together with the myths and traditions relating to them, match each other precisely on both sides of the ocean. In addition to these however there exists a truly enormous number of other correspondences, many of them so precise that it is impossible to believe they could have developed separately. Many of these were mentioned by Donnelly, though even his list was by no means exhaustive; and the number has only increased in the hundred years since his time. So extensive is this material that it would be impossible to examine or even list all of it in a single book: such a project might fill many volumes. The parallels range from the examples quoted above to fine details of custom and tradition on both sides of the ocean. We find, for example, identical religious and spiritual ideas, similar burial customs and beliefs, architectural and metallurgical similarities, and numerous linguistic peculiarities — the presence of various words in Native American languages which seem to have a North African or European origin. In addition to these, we need to cite the extremely substantial (and rather conclusive) evidence of early transatlantic exchanges of flora and fauna. The latter is a relatively new topic of study, but it

---

1 Ibid., pp. 237-8.
2 Ibid., p. 234.
3 Ibid., p. 235.

has already yielded astonishing results. And we cannot, of course, fail to mention American legends of white and bearded men sailing across the ocean and communicating new ideas to the natives, as well as native American portrayals of bearded and apparently Caucasian individuals.

Fig. 6. Left: Neolithic stone axe from Illinois. Right: Neolithic stone axe from Germany. (after Donnelly)

Since the arrival of the first Spanish expeditions in the late fifteenth century, Europeans travelers were astonished by stories, traditions, and ideas they found among the natives which were strongly reminiscent of those from home. In particular, they remarked upon the myths and legends of the Mexicans and Peruvians, which seemed often to mimic exactly the stories and traditions familiar from the writings of the Greeks and Romans and the Bible. Such, for example, was the case with the various Flood and catastrophe legends which occupied such a prominent position in the religion and customs of the Mexicans and Peruvians.

As reported earlier, many of these cosmogonic myths can best be explained as human reactions to natural events witnessed by the whole of humanity. Yet other parallels cannot be so explained. In the pages to follow I shall present some of the evidence brought forth by Donnelly, shorn of most of the material which might be explained as cosmogonic or the result of coincidence. If this material were to be added, and there is good reason to believe that much of it should, then, as I said, many volumes would be needed to do it justice.

The Megalithic culture of Western Europe (which, we shall argue, was in its earliest phase the mainland expression of Atlantean culture), left vast numbers of monuments throughout the Atlantic seaboard, ranging from barrow-graves, to standing-stone circles, to dolmens. All of these found parallels in the Americas, parallels which included details of the interment rites often associated with them. In Donnelly's words: "The grave-cists made of stone of the American mounds are exactly like the stone chests, or *kistvaen* for the dead, found in the British mounds. (Fosters *Prehistoric Races*, p. 109.) Tumuli have been found in Yorkshire enclosing wooden coffins, precisely as in the mounds of the Mississippi Valley. (Ibid.,

p. 185.) The articles associated with the dead are the same in both continents: arms, trinkets, food, clothes, and funeral urns. In both the Mississippi Valley and among the Chaldeans vases were constructed around the bones, the neck of the vase being too small to permit the extraction of the skull. (Foster's *Prehistoric Races*, p. 200.)"[1]

 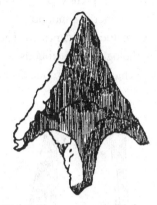

Fig. 7. Left: Stone arrow-heads from America. Right: Stone arrow-head from Switzerland. (after Donnelly)

Serpent-worship was a prominent feature of the Neolithic/Megalithic cultures of both Europe and the Americas. Now, as we have seen, serpent-worship is found throughout the world and has a cosmogonic origin. Nevertheless, the types of serpent-cult which appeared in the Megalithic cultures of both Old and New Worlds are so similar that they seem to demand a common cultural bedrock. As in the Old World so in the New, the Cosmic Serpent was honored atop pyramid or mound structures, which were effectively high platforms of sacrifice. Among the mound-builders of the Mississippi region, great earthworks in the shape of serpents were raised — the most famous of these being the Serpent Mound of Ohio. Among the megalith-builders of Western Europe, mounds and mound-like structures often took the shape of the serpent. In this context, Donnelly quotes the *Pall Mall Gazette*, which wrote an account of the explorations of John S. Phené at a serpentine mound at Glen Feechan in Argyleshire, Scotland. "The mound, says the *Scotsman*, is a most perfect one. The head is a large cairn, and the body of the earthen reptile 300 feet long; and in the centre of the head there were evidences, when Mr Phené first visited it, of an altar have been placed there. The position with regard to Ben Cruachan is most remarkable. The three peaks are seen over the length of the reptile when a person is standing on the head, or

---

1 Ibid., pp. 139-40.

cairn. The shape can only be seen so as to be understood when looked down upon from an elevation, as the outline cannot be understood unless the whole of it can be seen. This is most perfect when the spectator is on the head of the animal form, or on the lofty rocks to the west of it. The mound corresponds almost entirely with one 700 feet long in America, an account of which was lately published, after careful study, by Mr Squier. The altar toward the head in each case agrees. In the American mound three rivers (also objects of worship with the ancients) were evidently identified. The number three was a sacred number in all ancient mythologies. The sinuous winding and articulations of the vertebral spinal arrangement are anatomically perfect in the Argyleshire mound."[1]

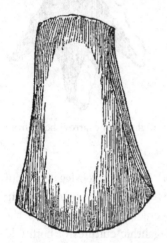 

Fig. 8. Left: Copper axe from mound near Laporte, Indiana. Right: Copper axe from Waterford, Ireland. (after Donnelly)

Like us, Donnelly, noted the striking parallels between the weaponry used by the Amerindians and Europeans of the Neolithic or early Megalithic epoch. "The weapons of the New World were identically the same as those of the Old World; they consisted of bows and arrows, spears, darts, short swords, battle-axes, and slings; and both peoples used shields or bucklers, and casques of wood or hide covered with metal."[2]

Religious beliefs common to both sides of the ocean abounded, as Donnelly observed: "Religious Beliefs. — The Guanches of the Canary Islands, who were probably a fragment of the old Atlantean population, believed in the immortality of the soul and the resurrection of the body, and preserved their dead as mummies. The Egyptians believed in the immortality of the soul and the resurrection

1 Ibid., pp. 205-6.
2 Ibid., p. 143.

of the body, and preserved the bodies of the dead by embalming them. The Peruvians believed in the immortality of the soul and the resurrection of the body, and they too preserved the bodies of their dead by embalming them. 'A few mummies in remarkable preservation have been found among the Chinooks and Flatheads.' (*Schoolcraft*, vol. v., p. 693.) The embalmment of the body was also practiced in Central America and among the Aztecs. The Aztecs, like the Egyptians, mummified their dead by taking out the bowels and replacing them with aromatic substances. (Dorman, *Origin Prim. Superst.*, p. 173.) The bodies of the kings of the Virginia Indians were preserved by embalming. (Beverly, p. 47.)"[1]

 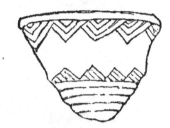

Fig. 9. Left: Fragment of pottery from San Jose, Mexico. Right: Fragment of pottery from Switzerland. (after Donnelly)

Yet more parallels involved, "The use of confession and penance ... in the religious ceremonies of some of the American nations. Baptism was a religious ceremony with them, and the bodies of the dead were sprinkled with water." Furthermore, "Vestal virgins were found in organized communities on both sides of the Atlantic; they were in each case pledged to celibacy, and devoted to death if they violated their vows. In both hemispheres the recreant were destroyed by being buried alive. The Peruvians, Mexicans, Central Americans, Egyptians, Phoenicians, and Hebrews each had a powerful hereditary priesthood."[2]

Strikingly similar rituals occur on both sides of the ocean: "The ancient Mexicans believed that the sun-god would destroy the world in the last night of the fifty-second year, and that he would never come back. They offered sacrifices to him at that time to propitiate him; they extinguished all the fires in the kingdom; they broke all their household furniture; they hung black masks before their faces; they prayed and fasted; and on the evening of the last night they formed a great procession to a neighboring mountain. A human being was sacrificed exactly at midnight; a block of wood was laid at once on the body, and fire was then produced by rapidly revolving another piece of wood upon it; a spark was carried

---

1 Ibid., pp. 143-4.
2 Ibid., p. 144.

Fig. 10. Top: Narrow-based vases from mountds in Mississippi Valley. Middle: Narrow-based vases from Switzerland. Bottom: Narrow-based vase supported by clay vase-holder. (after Donnelly)

to a funeral pile, whose rising flame proclaimed to the anxious people the promise of the god not to destroy the world for another fifty-two years. Precisely the same custom obtained among the nations of Asia Minor and other parts of the continent of Asia, wherever sun-worship prevailed, at the periodical reproduction of the sacred fire, but not with the same bloody rites as in Mexico. (Valentini, *Maya Archaeology*, p. 21.)

Fig. 11. The different races known to the Egyptians, as portrayed in Egyptian relief of the New Kingdom. On the right can be seen the Libyan, who is portrayed as white-skinned, with feathered headdress and tattoos. In Herodotus' time the Libyans of the Atlas Mountains called themselves Atlantioi (Atlanteans).

"To this day the Brahman of India 'churns' his sacred fire out of a board by boring into it with a stick; the Romans renewed their sacred fire in the same way; and in Sweden even now a 'need-fire is kindled in this manner when cholera or other pestilence is about.' (Tylor's *Anthropology*, p. 262.)"[1]

Superstitions about identical animals find echoes on both sides of the Atlantic: "Among both the Germans and the American Indians lycanthropy, or the metamorphosis of men into wolves, was believed in. In British Columbia the men-wolves have often been seen seated around a fire, with their wolf-hides hung upon sticks to dry! The Irish legend of hunters pursuing an animal which suddenly disappears, whereupon a human being appears in its place is found among all the American tribes.

"That timid and harmless animal, the hare, was, singularly enough, an object of superstitious reverence and fear in Europe, Asia, and America. The ancient Irish killed all the hares they found on May-day among their cattle, believing them to

---

1 Ibid., p. 146.

be witches. Caesar gives an account of the horror in which this animal was held by the Britons. The Calmucks regarded the rabbit with fear and reverence. Divine honors were paid to the hare in Mexico. Wabasso was changed into a white rabbit, and canonized in that form.

"The white bull, Apis, of the Egyptians, reappears in the Sacred white buffalo of the Dakotas, which was supposed to possess supernatural power, and after death became a god. The white doe of European legend had its representative in the white deer of the Housatonic Valley, whose death brought misery to the tribe. The transmission of spirits by the laying on of hands, and the exorcism of demons, were part of the religion of the American tribes."[1]

Social customs of even the most everyday kind seemed to find echoes on both sides of the ocean: "Customs. — Both peoples manufactured a fermented, intoxicating drink, the one deriving it from barley, the other from maize. Both drank toasts. Both had the institution of marriage, an important part of the ceremony consisting in the joining of hands; both recognized divorce, and the Peruvians and Mexicans established special courts to decide cases of this kind. Both the Americans and Europeans erected arches, and had triumphal processions for their victorious kings, and both strewed the ground before them with leaves and flowers. Both celebrated important events with bonfires and illuminations; both used banners, both invoked blessings. The Phoenicians, Hebrews, and Egyptians practiced circumcision. Palacio relates that at Azori, in Honduras, the natives circumcised boys before an idol called Icelca. (*Carta*, p. 84.) Lord Kingsborough tells us the Central Americans used the same rite, and McKenzie (quoted by Retzius) says he saw the ceremony performed by the Chippeways. Both had bards and minstrels, who on great festivals sung the deeds of kings and heroes. Both the Egyptians and the Peruvians held agricultural fairs; both took a census of the people. Among both the land was divided per capita among the people; in Judea a new division was made every fifty years. The Peruvians renewed every year all the fires of the kingdom from the Temple of the Sun, the new fire being kindled from concave mirrors by the sun's rays. The Romans under Numa had precisely the same custom. The Peruvians had theatrical plays. They chewed the leaves of the coca mixed with lime, as the Hindoo to-day chews the leaves of the betel mixed with lime."[2]

A SUPERABUNDANCE OF EVIDENCE

The above parallels are mainly concerned with religion and religious practices. Some undoubtedly found their inspiration and original source in cosmic

---

1 Ibid., p. 147.
2 Ibid., pp. 150-1.

events which affected the entire human race and which left an echo everywhere. It is possible too that some of them could have been introduced to the Americas via the Bering Strait. Yet others seem to be found only in the Americas and the western parts of the Old World, particularly in Europe and north-west Africa. Even mainstream academics, who almost universally rejected Donnelly's Atlantis explanation, were impressed by the sheer quantity of material he amassed, and not a few were prepared to concede that, whilst a sunken Atlantic island could not be invoked as an explanation, the parallels enumerated did indeed point to some form of transatlantic contact before the time of Columbus. Indeed, it is self-evident to any open-minded reader of Donnelly's work that he did prove — beyond reasonable doubt — the existence of frequent and significant contact across the Atlantic at some time in antiquity. It is a pity that such evidence was treated with hyperskepticism and we had to await the proof (as we shall see) of DNA and forensic science before being vindicated.

Although DNA and forensic science have made Donnelly's evidence superfluous, it is nevertheless worth repeating some more of it; for it displays in vivid detail the intimate nature of the ancient transatlantic links:

"Strabo (vol. iii., pp. 4, 17) mentions that, among the Iberians of the North of Spain, the women, after the birth of a child, tend their husbands, putting them to bed instead of going themselves. The same custom existed among the Basques only a few years ago. 'In Biscay,' says M. F. Michel, 'the women rise immediately after childbirth and attend to the duties of the household, while the husband goes to bed, taking the baby with him, and thus receives the neighbors' compliments.' The same custom was found in France, and is said to exist to this day in some cantons of Béarn. Diodorus Siculus tells us that among the Corsicans the wife was neglected, and the husband put to bed and treated as the patient. Apollonius Rhodius says that among the Tibereni, at the south of the Black Sea, 'when a child was born the father lay groaning, with his head tied up, while the mother tended him with food and prepared his baths.' The same absurd custom extends throughout the tribes of North and South America. Among the Caribs in the West Indies (and the Caribs, Brasseur de Bourbourg says, were the same as the ancient Carians of the Mediterranean Sea) the man takes to his bed as soon as a child is born, and kills no animals. And herein we find an explanation of a custom otherwise inexplicable. Among the American Indians it is believed that, if the father kills an animal during the infancy of the child, the spirit of the animal will revenge itself by inflicting some disease upon the helpless little one. 'For six months the Carib father must not eat birds or fish, for what ever animals he eats will impress their likeness on the child, or produce disease by entering its body.' (Dorman, *Prim. Superst.*, p. 58.) Among the Abipones the husband goes to bed, fasts a number of days, 'and you would think,' says Dobrizhoffer, 'that it was he that had had the child.' The Brazilian father takes to his hammock during and after the birth of the child, and for fifteen days eats no meat and hunts no game. Among the Esquimaux the husbands forbear hunting during the lying-in of their wives and for some time thereafter.

"Here, then, we have a very extraordinary and unnatural custom, existing to this day on both sides of the Atlantic, reaching back to a vast antiquity, and finding its explanation only in the superstition of the American races. A practice so absurd could scarcely have originated separately in the two continents; its existence is a very strong proof of unity of origin of the races on the opposite sides of the Atlantic; and the fact that the custom and the reason for it are both found in America, while the custom remains in Europe without the reason, would imply that the American population was the older of the two.

"The Indian practice of depositing weapons and food with the dead was universal in ancient Europe, and in German villages nowadays a needle and thread is placed in the coffin for the dead to mend their torn clothes with; 'while all over Europe the dead man had a piece of money put in his hand to pay his way with.'" (*Anthropology*, p. 347.)

"The American Indian leaves food with the dead; the Russian peasant puts crumbs of bread behind the saints' pictures on the little iron shelf, and believes that the souls of his forefathers creep in and out and eat them. 'At the cemetery of Pare-la-Chaise, Paris, on All-souls-day, they still put cakes and sweetmeats on the graves; and in Brittany the peasants that night do not forget to make up the fire and leave the fragments of the supper on the table for the souls of the dead.'" (Ibid.. p. 351.)

"The Indian prays to the spirits of his forefathers; the Chinese religion is largely 'ancestor-worship;' and the rites paid to the dead ancestors, or *lares*, held the Roman family together." (*Anthropology*, p. 351.)

"We find the Indian practice of burying the dead in a sitting posture in use among the Nasamonians, tribe of Libyans. Herodotus, speaking of the wandering tribes of Northern Africa, says, 'They bury their dead according to the fashion of the Greeks.... They bury them sitting, and are right careful, when the sick man is at the point of giving up the ghost, to make him sit, and not let him die lying down.'

"The dead bodies of the caciques of Bogota were protected from desecration by diverting the course of a river and making the grave in its bed, and then letting the stream return to its natural course. Alaric, the leader of the Goths, was secretly buried in the same way." (Dorman, *Prim. Superst.*, p. 195.)

"Among the American tribes no man is permitted to marry a wife of the same clan-name or totem as himself. In India a Brahman is not allowed to marry a wife whose clan-name (her 'cow-stall,' as they say) is the same as his own; nor may a Chinaman take a wife of his own surname." (*Anthropology*, p. 403.) "hroughout India the hill-tribes are divided into septs or clans, and a man may not marry a woman belonging to his own clan. The Calmucks of Tartary are divided into hordes, and a man may not marry a girl of his own horde. The same custom prevails among the Circassians and the Samoyeds of Siberia. The Ostyaks and Yakuts regard it as a crime to marry a woman of the same family, or even of the same name." (Sir John Lubbock, *Smith. Rep.*, p. 347, 1869.)

"Sutteeism — the burning of the widow upon the funeral-pile of the husband — was extensively practiced in America (West's *Journal*, p. 141); as was also the practice of sacrificing warriors, servants, and animals at the funeral of a great chief." (Dorman, pp. 210-211) Beautiful girls were sacrificed to appease the anger of the gods, as among the Mediterranean races. (Bancroft, vol. iii., p. 471.) Fathers offered up their children for a like purpose, as among the Carthaginians.

"The poisoned arrows of America had their representatives in Europe. Odysseus went to Ephyra for the man-slaying drug with which to smear his bronze-tipped arrows." (Tylor's *Anthropology*, p. 237.)

"'The bark canoe of America was not unknown in Asia and Africa' (Ibid., p. 254), while the skin canoes of our Indians and the Esquimaux were found on the shores of the Thames and the Euphrates. In Peru and on the Euphrates commerce was carried on upon rafts supported by inflated skins. They are still used on the Tigris."

"The Indian boils his meat by dropping red-hot stones into a water-vessel made of hide; and Linnéus found the Both land people brewing beer in this way — 'and to this day the rude Carinthian boor drinks such stone-beer, as it is called.'" (Ibid., p. 266.)

"In the buffalo dance of the Mandan Indians the dancers covered their heads with a mask made of the head and horns of the buffalo. To-day in the temples of India, or among the lamas of Thibet, the priests dance the demons out, or the new year in, arrayed in animal masks" (Ibid., p. 297); and "the 'mummers' at Yule-tide, in England, are a survival of the same custom." (Ibid., p. 298.) The North American dog and bear dances, wherein the dancers acted the part of those animals, had their prototype in the Greek dances at the festivals of Dionysia. (Ibid., p. 298.)

"Tattooing was practiced in both continents. Among the Indians it was fetichistic in its origin; 'every Indian had the image of an animal tattooed on his breast or arm, to charm away evil spirits.' (Dorman, *Prim. Superst.*, p. 156.) The sailors of Europe and America preserve to this day a custom which was once universal among the ancient races. Banners, flags, and armorial bearings are supposed to be survivals of the old totemic tattooing. The Arab woman still tattoos her face, arms, and ankles. The war-paint of the American savage reappeared in the woad with which the ancient Briton stained his body; and Tylor suggests that the painted stripes on the circus clown are a survival of a custom once universal. (Tylor's *Anthropology*, p. 327.)"[1]

Tattooing in fact is a crucial clue. Donnelly seems to have been unaware of the fact that tattooing was particularly associated with the Berbers of North Africa, the Atlantians of Herodotus and Diodorus Siculus. Egyptian portrayals of the Libyans consistently show them (and no other people) to be heavily tattooed. Mummified bodies found in the Sahara and Atlas Mountains confirm the accuracy of the Egyptian artists. Of interest too is the fact that these tattoos look strikingly similar to some of those found on the body of Ötzi, the Neolithic Age "Ice Man," found in a glacier on the Swiss-Italian border not too long ago. Furthermore, we note that body-painting (usually among women) continues to this day among the Berbers of the Atlas. Another striking feature of Libyan/Berber/Atlantian attire concerned hairstyle. On Egyptian monuments they are always shown with long hair and a classical "side lock," whilst on the top of their heads they typically sport two feathers, presumably ostrich feathers. Now, the wearing of feathered headdresses was not entirely unknown in the Old World. Aside from the Libyans, a few of the tribes of Africa wore such decorations. Yet the wearing of feathers on the head can hardly be described as typical of the Old World peoples. This was above all, and classically, a New World custom. Could it be, then, that this was one of the ideas picked up by the Atlantean/Berber/Amazigh sailors from their Amerindian hosts? We will never, perhaps, know for sure, but it is an intriguing possibility; and it should not be forgotten that the feathered headdress is shown on the earliest portrayals of Libyans from Egyptian art.

Let us continue with Donnelly's tour de force.

> "In America, as in the Old World, the temples of worship were built over the dead. (Dorman, *Prim. Superst.*, p. 178.) Says Prudentius, the Roman bard, 'there were as many temples of gods as sepulchres.'

> "The Etruscan belief that evil spirits strove for the possession of the dead was found among the Mosquito Indians. (Bancroft, *Native Races*, vol. i., p. 744.).

"The belief in fairies, which forms so large a part of the folklore of Western Europe, is found among the American races. The Ojibbeways see thousands of fairies dancing in a sunbeam; during a rain myriads of them bide in the flow-

---

1 Ibid., pp. 153-6.

ers. When disturbed they disappear underground. They have their dances, like the Irish fairies; and, like them, they kill the domestic animals of those who offend them. The Dakotas also believe in fairies. The Otoes located the 'little people' in a mound at the mouth of Whitestone River; they were eighteen inches high, with very large heads; they were armed with bows and arrows, and killed those who approached their residence. (See Dorman's *Origin of Primitive Superstitions*, p. 23.) 'The Shoshone legends people the mountains of Montana with little imps, called Nirumbees, two feet long, naked, and with a tail.' They stole the children of the Indians, and left in their stead the young of their own baneful race, who resembled the stolen children so much that the mothers were deceived and suckled them, whereupon they died. This greatly resembles the European belief in 'changelings.' (Ibid., p. 24.)

"In both continents we find tree-worship. In Mexico and Central America cypresses and palms were planted near the temples, generally in groups of threes; they were tended with great care, and received offerings of incense and gifts. The same custom prevailed among the Romans—the cypress was dedicated to Pluto, and the palm to Victory.

"Not only infant baptism by water was found both in the old Babylonian religion and among the Mexicans, but an offering of cakes, which is recorded by the prophet Jeremiah as part of the worship of the Babylonian goddess-mother, 'the Queen of Heaven,' was also found in the ritual of the Aztecs (*Builders of Babel*, p. 78.)

"In Babylonia, China, and Mexico the caste at the bottom of the social scale lived upon floating islands of reeds or rafts, covered with earth, on the lakes and rivers.

"In Peru and Babylonia marriages were made but once a year, at a public festival.

"'Among the Romans, the Chinese, the Abyssinians, and the Indians of Canada the singular custom prevails of lifting the bride over the door-step of the husband's home.' (Sir John Lubbock, *Smith. Rep.*, 1869, p. 352.)

"'The bride-cake which so invariably accompanies a wedding among ourselves, and which must always be cut by the bride, may be traced back to the old Roman form of marriage by *conferreatio*, or eating together. So, also, among the Iroquois the bride and bridegroom used to partake together of a cake of sagamite, which the bride always offered to her husband.' (Ibid.)

"Among many American tribes, notably in Brazil, the husband captured the wife by main force, as the men of Benjamin carried off the daughters of Shiloh at the feast, and as the Romans captured the Sabine women. 'Within a few generations the same old habit was kept up in Wales, where the bridegroom and his friends, mounted and armed as for war, carried off the bride; and in Ireland they used even to hurl spears at the bride's people, though at such a distance that no one was hurt, except now and then by accident — as happened when one Lord Hoath lost an eye, which mischance put an end to this curious relic of antiquity.' (Tylor's *Anthropology*, p. 409.)

"Marriage in Mexico was performed by the priest. He exhorted them to maintain peace and harmony, and tied the end of the man's mantle to the dress of the woman; he perfumed them, and placed on each a shawl on which was painted a skeleton, 'as a symbol that only death could now separate them from one another.' (Dorman, *Prim. Superst.*, p. 379.)

"The priesthood was thoroughly organized in Mexico and Peru. They were prophets as well as priests. 'They brought the newly-born infant into the religious society; they directed their training and education; they determined the entrance of the young men into the service of the state; they consecrated marriage by their blessing; they comforted the sick and assisted the dying.' (Ibid., p. 374.) There were five thousand priests in the temples of Mexico. They confessed and absolved the sinners, arranged the festivals, and managed the choirs in the churches. They lived in conventual discipline, but were allowed to marry; they practiced flagellation and fasting, and prayed at regular hours. There were great preachers and exhorters among them. There were also convents into which females were admitted. The novice had her hair cut off and took vows of celibacy; they lived holy and pious lives. (Ibid., pp. 375, 376.) The king was the high-priest of the religious orders. A new king ascended the temple naked, except his girdle; he was sprinkled four times with water which had been blessed; he was then clothed in a mantle, and on his knees took an oath to maintain the ancient religion. The priests then instructed him in his royal duties. (Ibid., p. 378.) Besides the regular priesthood there were monks who were confined in cloisters. (Ibid., p. 390.) Cortes says the Mexican priests were very strict in the practice of honesty and chastity, and any deviation was punished with death. They wore long white robes and burned incense. (Dorman, *Prim. Superst.*, p. 379.) The first fruits of the earth were devoted to the support of the priesthood. (Ibid., p. 383.) The priests of the Isthmus were sworn to perpetual chastity."[1]

It has to be admitted that the above is a rather idealized picture of the blood-drenched Aztec religion and priesthood. Nevertheless, there were real parallels with Old World practice, which may have had their origins in Neolithic times. Donnelly continues: "The American doctors practiced phlebotomy. They bled the sick man because they believed the evil spirit which afflicted him would come

---

1 Ibid., pp. 157-60.

away with the blood. In Europe phlebotomy only continued to a late period, but the original superstition out of which it arose, in this case as in many others, was forgotten.

"There is opportunity here for the philosopher to meditate upon the perversity of human nature and the persistence of hereditary error. The superstition of one age becomes the science of another; men were first bled to withdraw the evil spirit, then to cure the disease; and a practice whose origin is lost in the night of ages is continued into the midst of civilization, and only overthrown after it has sent millions of human beings to untimely graves. Dr. Sangrado could have found the explanation of his profession only among the red men of America.

"Folk-lore. — Says Max Müller: 'Not only do we find the same words and the same terminations in Sanscrit and Gothic; not only do we find the same name for Zeus in Sanscrit, Latin, and German; not only is the abstract Name for God the same in India, Greece, and Italy; but these very stories, these *Mährchen* which nurses still tell, with almost the same words, in the Thuringian forest and in the Norwegian villages, and to which crowds of children listen under the Pippal-trees of India—these stories, too, belonged to the common heirloom of the Indo-European race, and their origin carries us back to the same distant past, when no Greek had set foot in Europe, no Hindoo had bathed in the sacred waters of the Ganges.'

"And we find that an identity of origin can be established between the folk-lore or fairy tales of America and those of the Old World, precisely such as exists between the, legends of Norway and India.

"Mr. Tylor tells us the story of the two brothers in Central America who, starting on their dangerous journey to the land of Xibalba, where their father had perished, plant each a cane in the middle of their grandmother's house, that she may know by its flourishing or withering whether they are alive or dead. Exactly the same conception occurs in Grimm's *Mährchen*, when the two gold-children wish to see the world and to leave their father; and when their father is sad, and asks them how he shall bear news of them, they tell him, 'We leave you the two golden lilies; from these you can see how we fare. If they are fresh, we are well; if they fade, we are ill; if they fall, we are dead.' Grimm traces the same idea in Hindoo stories. 'Now this,' says Max Müller, 'is strange enough, and its occurrence in India, Germany, and Central America is stranger still.'"

Donnelly then provides us with four examples of fairy-tales, two from the Old World and two from the New, which are so strikingly similar that it seems extremely improbable the ideas encapsulated in them could have arisen separately. The first two stories are from the Ojibbeway people, from North America, and from Ireland.

THE OJIBBEWAY STORY	THE IRISH STORY
The birds met together one day to try to find which could fly the highest. Some flew up very swift, but soon tired, and were passed by others of stronger wing. But the eagle went up beyond them all, and was ready to claim the victory, when the gray linnet, a very small bird, flew from the eagle's back, where it had perched unperceived, and, being fresh and unexhausted, succeeded in going the highest. When the birds came down and met in council to award the prize it was given to the eagle, because that bird had not only gone up nearer to the sun than any of the larger birds, but it had carried the linnet on its back. For this reason the eagle's feathers became the most honourable marks of distinction a warrior could bear.	The birds all met together one day, and settled among themselves that whichever of them could fly highest was to be king of all. Well, just as they were on the hinges of being off, what does that little rogue of a wren do but hop up and perch himself unbeknown on the eagle's tail. So they flew and flew ever so high, till the eagle was miles above all the rest, and could not fly another stroke, he was so tired. "Then," says he, "I'm king of the birds." "You lie!" says the wren, darting up a perch and a half above the big fellow. Well, the eagle was so mad to think how he was done, that when the wren was coming down he gave him a stroke of his wing, and from that day to this the wren was never able to fly farther than a hawthorn-bush.

Donnelly then asks us to compare also the following stories:

THE ASIATIC STORY	THE AMERICAN STORY
In the Hindoo mythology Urvasi came down from heaven and became the wife of the son of Buddha only on condition that two pet rams should be taken from her bedside, and that she should never behold her lord undressed. The immortals, however, wishing Urvasi back in heaven, contrived to steal the rams; and, as the king pursued the robbers with his sword in the dark, the lightning revealed his person, the compact was broken, and Urvasi disappeared. The same story is found in different forms among many people of Aryan and Turanian descent, the central idea being that of a man marrying some one of an aerial or aquatic origin, and living happily with her till he breaks the condition on which her residence with him depends, stories exactly parallel to that of Raymond of Toulouse, who chances in the hunt upon the beautiful Melusina at a fountain, and lives with her happily until he discovers her fish-nature and she vanishes.	Wampee, a great hunter, once came to a strange prairie, where he heard faint sounds of music, and looking up saw a speck in the sky, which proved itself to be a basket containing twelve most beautiful maidens, who, on reaching the earth, forthwith set themselves to dance. He tried to catch the youngest, but in vain; ultimately, he succeeded by assuming the disguise of a mouse. He was very attentive to his new wife, who was really a daughter of one of the stars, but she wished to return home, so she made a wicker basket secretly, and, by help of a charm she remembered, ascended to her father.

These and other folk-legends provided by Donnelly are surely so strikingly similar than even the skeptic must pause to consider. But he is not yet finished. He continues:

> If the legend of Cadmus recovering Europa, after she has been carried away by the white bull, the spotless cloud, means that 'the sun must journey westward until he sees again the beautiful tints which greeted his eyes in the morning,' it is curious to find a story current in North America to the effect that a man once had a beautiful daughter, 'whom he forbade to leave the lodge lest she should be carried off by the king of the buffaloes;' and that as she sat, notwithstanding, outside the house combing her hair, 'all of a sudden the king of the buffaloes came dashing on, with his herd of followers, and, taking her between his horns, away be cantered over plains, plunged into a river which bounded his land, and carried her safely to his lodge on the other side,' whence she was finally recovered by her father.
>
> Games. — The same games and sports extended from India to the shores of Lake Superior. The game of the Hindoos, called *pachisi*, is played upon a cross-shaped board or cloth; it is a combination of checkers and draughts, with the throwing of dice, the dice determining the number of moves; when the Spaniards entered Mexico they found the Aztecs playing a game called *patolli*, identical with the Hindoo *pachisi*, on a similar cross-shaped board.[1]

At this point we must pause. The similarities between the Hindu *pachisi* and the Aztec *patolli* are truly striking. Over a century ago, Tylor (1896) compared details of the Aztec game (*e.g.*, the board's layout, the sequence of moves, and cosmic associations of the pieces and moves), with the Indian game. So precise were the parallels that "Even Robert Lowie, an influential anthropologist who was usually critical of diffusionist (voyage-dependent) explanations for such similarities, accepted that in this case 'the concatenation of details puts the parallels far outside any probability [of having been invented independently].'"[2]

Donnelly continues: "The game of ball, which the Indians of America were in the habit of playing at the time of the discovery of the country, from California to the Atlantic, was identical with the European chueca, crosse, or hockey.

> One may well pause, after reading this catalogue, and ask himself, wherein do these peoples differ? It is absurd to pretend that all these similarities could have been the result of accidental coincidences.
>
> These two peoples, separated by the great ocean, were baptized alike in infancy with blessed water; they prayed alike to the gods; they wor-

---

1 Ibid. pp. 160-3.

2 John L. Sorenson and Carl L. Johannessen, "Scientific Evidence for Pre-Columbian Transoceanic Voyages to and from the Americas," at www.maxwellinstitute.byu.edu/display.php?table=transcripts&id=154.

shipped together the sun, moon, and stars; they confessed their sins alike; they were instructed alike by an established priesthood; they were married in the same way and by the joining of hands; they armed themselves with the same weapons; when children came, the man, on both continents, went to bed and left his wife to do the honors of the household; they tattooed and painted themselves in the same fashion; they became intoxicated on kindred drinks; their dresses were alike; they cooked in the same manner; they used the same metals; they employed the same exorcisms and bleedings for disease; they believed alike in ghosts, demons, and fairies; they listened to the same stories; they played the same games; they used the same musical instruments; they danced the same dances, and when they died they were embalmed in the same way and buried sitting; while over them were erected, on both continents, the same mounds, pyramids, obelisks, and temples. And yet we are asked to believe that there was no relationship between them, and that they had never had any ante-Columbian intercourse with each other.

If our knowledge of Atlantis was more thorough, it would no doubt appear that, in every instance wherein the people of Europe accord with the people of America, they were both in accord with the people of Atlantis; and that Atlantis was the common centre from which both peoples derived their arts, sciences, customs, and opinions. It will be seen that in every case where Plato gives us any information in this respect as to Atlantis, we find this agreement to exist. It existed in architecture, sculpture, navigation, engraving, writing, an established priesthood, the mode of worship, agriculture, the construction of roads and canals; and it is reasonable to suppose that the, same correspondence extended down to all the minor details treated of in this chapter.

We can only concur.

LINGUISTIC CLUES

Both Donnelly himself and his numerous imitators listed a veritable plethora of linguistic clues pointing to ancient commerce across the ocean. Such evidence must, of course, be treated with caution, since there exist only a limited number of sounds that the human palate and vocal chords can pronounce and accidental parallels are therefore very likely to occur. Nevertheless, some of the parallels, especially those that concern words of religious, ritualistic or cultural importance, cannot be so easily explained; and indeed some of the resemblances are so specific and so precise that we must list them among the other proved cultural links.

First and foremost among these comes the word *atl* or *atla*, found, crucially, amongst both the Berbers of North Africa and amongst the natives of Mexico. In both regions, the word meant (among other things) "water".[1] The Berbers, of

---

1 Incidentally, *atl* is related to the English "water" through the Old Indo-European *watar*. "L" and "r" are easily confused in many languages, so the original word may as easily be written *watal*. This is yet an indicator that links exist between language groups which we are now confidently told have no connections whatsoever with each other. (See below).

course, have been identified by us as ethnically identical to the Atlanteans, and we may perchance trace in this word *atl* the source of the names Atlas and Atlantis. To the ancient Berbers/Amazigh "Atla" apparently meant "water-region," and we may guess that "atlant" or "atlantis" implied "island in the sea," or "land in the sea." We have already shown too that a word variously rendered as "Atlaya" or "Atalaya," implying a mountain or sacred hill, is found throughout the Iberian Peninsula, North Africa, and Mexico; whilst the ancient home of Quetzalcoatl, according to the Mexican legend, was Tulan, apparently a variant of Atlan. (The simple addition of an 'a' gives us the word 'Atulan'). The Spanish even found, upon their arrival on the Panama coast, a settlement named Atlan.

The mysterious founders of the first Mexican civilizations, the Toltecs, who were associated with the city of Tulan and who are said to have been white-skinned, also appear to have a name that is, in part at least, a variant of "Atlan." The first two consonants, 't' and 'l,' form the root *atl*.

Yet this is only one word, of very many, that appears to have made the voyage across the ocean in pre-Columbian times. Donnelly listed scores of these, pointing in particular to some striking parallels between the languages of the Sioux and Mandan and various Old World peoples. The linguist and author Charles Berlitz, following the trail blazed by Donnelly, listed dozens more of such terms. Vocabulary is a minefield, however, and there is no doubt that many of the parallels can be put down to pure coincidence. Thus the Nahuatl/Aztec word *teo*, meaning "god," sounds like the Greek *theos* and the Latin *deus*. The parallel may well be a coincidence. On the other hand, we need to remember that Indo-European peoples much closer to the Atlantic seaboard, such as the Celts, had a similar word for "god" (Gaelic *dia*), and so an influence cannot be ruled out.

Indeed, the early Celts, particularly the Irish Gaels, were in close contact with the Berber/Atlantean civilization, and the two may be said at one time and in one location (Spain) to have formed a common cultural identity.

Most of the vocabulary parallels identified by Donnelly were between Siouan/Mandan and European languages, particularly to the Celtic Welsh. There are also strange echoes of English, especially Old English, and many people are aware of the strange similarity between the Old English *wiccan* (from which we derive the word "witch"), meaning "sacred" or "magic" and the Sioux word *wakan*, meaning essentially the same thing. But it was the similarities with Welsh that caused most comment: So striking were some of these that a whole cottage industry developed claiming a Welsh origin for the Mandans and suggesting that this people were descendants of the medieval Welsh prince Madoc, son of Owen Gwynedd. These theories were given some weight by the very evident European features of some of the Mandans, as well as this people's own legend of a white ancestor who came to them in a canoe after surviving a great flood. This man, alone in his vessel, sent out a dove in hope of finding dry land. The creature returned carrying a twig in its beak. These traditions were held to prove that the white ancestor was a Christian, responsible for transmitting to the Mandans the biblical story of the Flood. A few of the wilder propagandists even began to suggest that the Mandans spoke Welsh and that Welshmen were able to converse freely with them, each using his own language. Such claims are, of course, complete nonsense. Nevertheless, the list of similarities, reproduced below, is indeed impressive, and needs to be viewed in the context of the very real DNA evidence (shortly to be examined) for an ancient European link with the Mandan/Sioux group.

ENGLISH	MANDAN	WELSH	PRONOUNCED
I	Me	Mi	Me
You	Ne	Chwi	Chwe
He	E	A	A
She	Ea	E	A
It	Ount	Hwynt	Hooynt
We	Noo	Ni	Ne
They	Eonah	Hona (Fem).	Hona
No, or there is not.	Megosh	Nagoes	Nagosh
No	Na	Na	Na
Head	Pan	Pen	Pan

Donnelly also listed the following resemblances, identified by Lynd, between the Dakota tongue and the languages of the Old World:

COMPARISON OF DAKOTA, OR SIOUX, WITH OTHER LANGUAGES.

LATIN	ENGLISH	SAXON	SANSKRIT	GERMAN	DANISH	SIOUX	OTHER LANGUAGES	PRIMARY SIGNIFICATION
	See, seen	Seon		Sehen	Sigt	Sin		Appearing, visible
Pinso	Pound	Punian				Pau	Welsh, Pwynian	Beating
Vado	Went, wend	Wenden				Winta		Passage

	Town	Tun		Zaun	Tun	Tonwe	Gaelic, Dun	Settlement
Qui	Who	Hwa	Kwas	Wer		Tuwe		
	Weapon	Wepn		Wapen	Vaapen	Wipe	Sioux dim., Wipena	
Ego	I	Ic	Agam	Ich	Jeg	Mish		Me
Cor	Core					Co	Greek, Kear	Centre, heart
Octem	Eight	Achta	Aute	Acht	Otte	Shaktogan	Greek, Okto	
Canna	Cane					Can	Hebrew, Can	Reed, weed, wood
Poc	Pock	Poc		Pocke	Pukkel	Poka	Dutch, Poca	Swelling
	With	With		Wider		Wita	Gothic, Gewithen	
	Doughty	Dohtig		Taugen	Digtig	Ditaya		Hot, brave, daring
	Tight	Tian		Dicht	Digt	Titan		Strain
Tango, Tactus	Touch, Take.	Taecan		Ticken	Tekkan,	Tan, Htaka.		Touch, take
	Child	Cild		Kind	Kuld	Cin		Progeny
	Work	Wercan				Woccas	Dutch, Werk	Labour, motion
	Shackle	Seoacul				Shka	Teton Sioux, Shakalan	To bind (a link)
	Shabby			Schabig	Schabbig	Shabaya		

Since the Sioux and even more so the Mandan have recently been shown to possess a substantial percentage of ancient European or Old World DNA, the above parallels may well be important. This is all the more likely when we consider the fact (to be elucidated in the final chapter) that the Atlantean culture did not predate that of the Indo-European Celts and Germans by many millennia and that, quite the contrary, the Celts formed a common Atlantic Neolithic culture with the Atlantean Berbers. This culture reached its apogee in the early part of the first millennium BC. On the other hand, if the Atlanteans were primarily of Berber stock, how do we explain the links between American and Indo-European languages? The language of the Berbers, recognized as part of the Hamito-Semitic group, is said to be unrelated to Indo-European.

In answer to this, we note that whilst the Hamitic/Semitic (or Afro-Asiatic) languages are not closely related to Indo-European, there is indeed an ancient connection; and it is now freely admitted that both groups had a common ancestor in the distant past. Thus words in ancient Egyptian and Hebrew (and Berber) have counterparts in Indo-European languages. The Hebrew *sabbat*, for example ("seven"), is clearly related to the Latin *sept*, or *septem* (German *sieben*); whilst the Egyptian *mu* ("water" or "sea") is evidently related to the Latin *mare* (German *meer*), and the name of the Egyptian phallic deity Min is apparently cognate with the Indo-European "man." In more ancient times the resemblances would have been even stronger and clearer. Thus the words common to the Siouan languages and the Indo-European would also have been common to the Hamito-Semitic tongues, and a comparison between Berber and Sioux would perchance unearth many more parallels than those observed above.

Having said all that, a skeptic might reasonably point to the increasing evidence that all of the world's languages go back to a common dialect at the very beginning of the Paleolithic Age, at the very birth of modern man. Hence a small set of words, not onomatopoeic, have been identified on every continent, including Australia; and the common language hypothesis seems to be supported by the evidence of DNA, which shows that the entire human race is very closely linked, probably descended from a single family originating in East Africa some time near the start of the Paleolithic.

Bearing all this in mind, we need to exercise great caution with regard to word- and even syntactical and grammatical parallels. And yet, when we find words like *atl* or *atlan* on both sides of the ocean, and when these are moreover directly associated (again, on both sides of the ocean) with ancient transoceanic travelers, then the significance cannot be stressed too strongly. In addition, if we find words of special religious or cult significance, such as the names of gods or deities, on both sides of the ocean, then we might be tempted to see these as significant. We remember that Donnelly found evidence of the god Pan and his wife Maia in Mexico, and that their cults were strikingly similar on either side of the ocean.

Since Donnelly's time, much new research has been carried out, particularly by Berlitz, who noticed an interesting list of parallels between ancient Egyptian, or its modern descendant Coptic, and the Quechua language of Peru, the language of the Incas. These are, importantly, often connected to religious and cosmic ideas. Thus the Inca festival of the sun, Ra-mi, calls to mind the Egyptian name for the sun-god, Ra. Thus too the Quechua word *andi* ("high mountain"), is identical to the Egyptian *andi*. Mountain tops were sacred places upon which were sacrifices offered to the celestial deities. Such sacrifices however did not commence until after the great catastrophe, in the age when men started constructing temples and cities. We should note too that the Araucanian word for the sun, *anta*, is identical to the Egyptian *anta*, also meaning the sun. The Araucanians dwelt just to the south of the Incas, and were noted for their European-like features.

Other words, connected with agriculture or technology, might also be significant. So, for example, the Quechua word *anta*, "copper," is reminiscent of the Coptic/Egyptian *homnt*. Copper, of course, was one of the first metals utilized by men. Still other words, which might be of agricultural import, need to be noted. Thus the Coptic/Egyptian *knaao*, a "sheaf," seems to be related to the Quechua *kinuwa*, whilst words for clothing, for example the Egyptian *chten* and the Quechua *kutuna*, may be of importance. Nor can we rule out the possible importance of similarities between the Egyptian/Coptic *chlol*, "people," with the Quechua word *cholo*, for the same thing.[1]

A great deal more research needs to be carried out in this field. Nevertheless, enough evidence has been found to suggest real and important contact between the peoples of the Old and New Worlds in the Neolithic and Early Bronze Ages.

THE COCAINE AND TOBACCO MUMMIES OF EGYPT

After the European rediscovery of the Americas in the late fifteenth century, many influences and ideas of various kinds flooded into the New World. Indeed, within a short time, Europeans completely transformed both North and South America. Yet the flow was not all in one direction. Many New World influences reached the Old. First and foremost among these were in the field of agriculture: a whole range of crops, hitherto unknown in Europe, began to reach the Old World and began to transform the lives of Europeans of all classes. Almost from the start, plants such as the potato, maize, tobacco, tomato, pineapple and many others, had a profound influence upon the entire economic and cultural life of Europe. Domestic animals too were imported from the Americas, the most important of which, perhaps, were the turkey and the guinea-pig.

As well as how to cultivate and exploit these new food sources, Europeans derived many other ideas, in differing areas, from the Native Americans.

Is it possible that in ancient times too, during the Neolithic and Early Bronze Ages, that ideas and concepts originating in the New World reached the Old?

---

1 There are indeed many striking parallels between the Afroasiatic languages (which include Berber and Egyptian) and the Quechua and Aymara tongues of the Andes.

Over the past decade sensational new discoveries, deriving from forensic science, have answered that question dramatically in the affirmative.

In 1992 a team of toxicologists from the Institute of Forensic Medicine at Ulm in Germany were asked by Egyptologists at Munich University to test for traces of narcotics in Egyptian mummies. The team, headed by Dr. Svetlana Balabanova, were soon to discover that one of their mummies, a queen of the Twenty-First Dynasty named Henut Taui, had a great surprise in store. Incredibly, and much to their own surprise, they found clear evidence of both tobacco and cocaine, two narcotic plants of American origin, in her tissues. Almost refusing to believe their own findings, Balabanova, who was "absolutely sure it must be a mistake," ran the tests again and sent fresh samples to three other laboratories.[1] But the results just kept being confirmed. Finally, after exhausting all possibilities, Balabanova and her colleagues went ahead and published a paper.[2] To say that her findings were not well received would be a gross under-estimate. The reaction was a "sharp reminder that science is a conservative world." According to Balabanova, "I got a pile of letters that were almost threatening, insulting letters saying it was nonsense, that I was fantasizing, that it was impossible, because it was proven that before Columbus there plants were not found anywhere in the world outside the Americas."[3]

And so the debate, often conducted in such ill-tempered tones, has raged back and forth for a decade-and-a-half. To absolutely exclude the possibility of error, tests have been repeated again and again, from every conceivable angle. But always, the results have been the same. Henut Taui, as well as other mummies, from other periods in Egyptian history, are found to contain traces of the offending narcotics.

The major, and indeed only, argument against Balabanova and her team, is the historical one. These substances couldn't be there, because transatlantic travel in pre-Columbian times didn't happen. The same arguments, we have found, were used to dismiss the transoceanic cultural parallels identified by Donnelly, as well as (of an earlier epoch) by Greenman and Stanford, and even (as we shall see in the next chapter) the devastating mitochondrial DNA evidence identified by Michael D. Brown and his team of geneticists.

---

1   See transcript of documentary, "The Cocaine Mummies" (Discovery Channel) at www.druglibrary.org/schaffer/Misc/mummies.htm.
2   Balabanova, S., F. Parsche and W. Pirsig, "First Identification of Drugs in Egyptian Mummies," *Naturwissenschaften*, 79, (1992) 358.
3   Transcript of "The Cocaine Mummies" loc cit.

A major review of the evidence was presented recently by Samuel A. Wells of Columbia State University.[1] Here Wells correctly identifies the major objection as historical rather than scientific, and proceeds to demolish it:

> The biggest criticism of the findings of Balabanova et. al. was not necessarily directed at the extraction process per se, although this was discussed. The biggest criticism was that cocaine and nicotine could not possibly have been used in Egypt before the discovery of the New World, and that transatlantic journeys were not known — or at least they are highly speculative. It is safe to say that the criticisms of the study would have been minimal or nonexistent if the findings had been made of Old World drugs. Such findings, in fact, would not have been at all unusual as the use of stimulants were known in Egypt. Poppy seeds and lotus plants have been identified for just this use in manuscripts (the Papyrus Ebers) and in hieroglyphs (as Balabanova et. al. show).

After discussing the techniques used by Balabanova and her team, Wells concludes,

> The initial reaction to the findings of Balabanova, et al., were highly critical. These criticisms were not based on a known failing in the authors' research methodology, rather they were attempts to cast doubt on an implication of the research — that cocaine and nicotine were brought to Egypt from the New World before Columbus. This conclusion is not acceptable to conservative investigators of the past. In fact it suggests a deep-rooted aversion to what Balabanova suggested might mean an unraveling of aspects of history contrary to basic reconstructions. This aversion, according to Kehoe (1998) stems from the conviction that Indians were primitive savages destined to be overcome by the civilized world — that the acme of evolutionary success resided in the conquering race itself. "Childlike savages could never have voyaged across oceans."

> Balabanova's findings bring yet other evidence forward that humanity is not so easily pinioned into the pre-conceived notions of primitive and advanced — even as this might be related to the presumed technology of earlier times. The quest for discovery — to find new worlds — is not just a modern selective advantage of our species. Perhaps it is the defining characteristic.

Since the publication of Balabanova's first paper, new impetus has been given to the study of botanical and zoological contacts between Old and New Worlds, and it has since emerged that as early as the 1970s traces of tobacco were discovered in the mummy of Ramses II.[2] At the time, the result was dismissed as impossible and put down to contamination or faulty methodology; though the evidence uncovered by Balabanova et al has caused a rethink. Admittedly, all the mummies

---

1 Samuel A. Wells, "American Drugs in Egyptian Mummies: A Review of the Evidence" at www.colostate.edu/Dept/Entomology/courses/en570/papers_2000/wells.html
2 "Fragments of tobacco were found about 30 years ago in the abdominal cavity of the mummy of Ramses II in a European museum (Bucaille 1990)." John L. Sorenson, loc cit.

so far found to contain tobacco and cocaine are of New Kingdom date, which, even allowing for the dramatically shortened chronology of Egypt proposed by the present author, still makes them around 250 years younger than the end of Atlantis and the island-bridge which formed the transatlantic link. This, however, may not present too great a problem or mystery. Both tobacco and cocaine were considered by the natives of the Americas to have been sacred plants, used in religious ritual. Presumably, any Berber travelers to the New World would have viewed the plants in the same way, and exported them to Egypt as such. It is quite possible, therefore, that Egyptian temples could have "stockpiled" supplies of tobacco and cocaine, sacred herbs from the ends of the earth, from the sacred land which lay beyond the setting sun (the Egyptians always viewed the abode of the gods as in the far west, where the sun set), for use in special rituals over the years.

Alternatively, it may be that the Egyptians actually cultivated, in special gardens, small quantities of the precious herbs, though it is more likely that such cultivation was carried out by the Berbers on the Atlantic coast.

As we shall see, tobacco and cocaine were not the only narcotics to have made it across the ocean from the Americas, and these sacred plants from the far west were to occupy a central role in the mystery cults which sprang up in many of the ancient cultures of the Mediterranean.

THE EVIDENCE OF BOTANY AND ZOOLOGY

As we have seen, the discoveries made by Balabanova and her team have given renewed impetus to a field of study which is rather actually old, but which has hitherto not been well-received in the halls of academia: this is the study of the migration and dissemination of plants and animals in the Pre-Columbian period.

It has long been known, of course, that some edible or crop plants made it across the Atlantic before Columbus. Perhaps the most famous example of this was the banana or plantain, a native of south-east Asia which in prehistoric times also appeared in Africa. Yet well before the voyage of Columbus the banana made it to the Americas, and the first Spanish explorers noted its cultivation and consumption among the Amerindians. The problem, of course, was that the banana is not a seeding plant, and needs human help for propagation. Floating and presumably rotting bananas, floating at random across the Atlantic, certainly cannot explain the presence of the plant in the New World.

Note, too, that the onion, garlic, and radishes were cultivated by the Aztecs when the Spaniards arrived.

A rather exhaustive study of the pre-Columbian distribution and occurrence of plants has now been undertaken by John L. Sorenson and Carl L. Johannessen, of the Maxwell Institute, Brigham Young University, Utah. Although Sorenson and Johannessen have an ideological agenda (both are Mormons), it cannot be denied that their research is first-class. Their recent extended paper, "Scientific Evidence for Pre-Columbian Transoceanic Voyages to and from the Americas," references all sources and allows the facts to speak for themselves. In the Abstract, Sorenson and Johannessen state their position thus:

> Examination of an extensive literature has revealed conclusive evidence that nearly one hundred species of plants, a majority of them cultivars, were present in both the Eastern and Western Hemispheres prior to Columbus' first voyage to the Americas. The evidence comes from archaeology, historical and linguistic sources, ancient art, and conventional botanical studies. Additionally, 21 species of micro-predators and six other species of fauna were shared by the Old and New Worlds. The evidence further suggests the desirability of additional study of up to 70 other organisms as probably or possibly bi-hemispheric in pre-Columbian times. This distribution could not have been due merely to natural transfer mechanisms, nor can it be explained by early human migrations to the New World via the Bering Strait route. Well over half the plant transfers consisted of flora of American origin that spread to Eurasia or Oceania, some at surprisingly early dates.
>
> The only plausible explanation for these findings is that a considerable number of transoceanic voyages in both directions across both major oceans were completed between the 7th millennium BC and the European age of discovery. Our growing knowledge of early maritime technology and its accomplishments gives us confidence that vessels and nautical skills capable of these long-distance travels were developed by the times indicated. These voyages put a new complexion on the extensive Old World/New World cultural parallels that have long been controversial.[1]

It would be impossible here to provide an exhaustive overview of what Sorenson and Johannessen have amassed. Their document comprises a volume of some one hundred eighty thousand words, and looks in great detail at enormous numbers of plants and micro-organisms. They note, mainly from ancient and early modern botanical records, almost one hundred species of plants which made it from the Americas to the Old World and vice-versa. Most commonly, the plants were of American origin, and the earliest and most extensive description of them comes, surprisingly enough, from ancient Indian texts composed in Sanskrit. There seems little doubt that at least some of the plants which made it from America to the Old World and vice versa did so by way of the Pacific; yet this is by no means always the case, and the question of the routes taken by these plants is one we shall return to in due course. For the present, we shall content ourselves here with mention of a few of the more outstanding examples, concentrating on

---

1 John L. Sorenson and Carl L. Johannessen, loc cit.

those which are definitely mentioned in Egyptian and Greek sources, and which most obviously had an Atlantic connection.

The entire genus Agave is of American origin, yet "it was represented in Old World biotas in several regions." Agave fibers were found mixed with pine resin as a watertight sealant in a 4th century BC Greek ship that had sunk at Kyrenia, in Cyprus. The discoverer, Steffy, confided that other Mediterranean archaeologists had excavated agave specimens, but had not reported the discoveries in print, presumably for fear of the hostility such a claim would generate.[1]

Most of the plants that made it from the New World to the Old had a medicinal or ritualistic function. Only rarely were they agricultural, a fact of great importance from a chronological point of view. Foremost amongst the medicinal herbs to cross the oceans was *Artemisia vulgaris*, a fragrant tree well-known in Europe and Asia anciently. "It was also present in Mexico, where it shared parallel cultural meanings (including medicinal use) associated particularly with the goddesses Artemis (Greece) and Chalchiuhtlicue (Mexico). Both of them were especially concerned with women and childbirth, as well as associated with water and marshes."[2]

Ananas comosus, the pineapple, is a native of America; yet there is good evidence that it was known in the ancient Near East, one of the very few strictly agricultural plants to make the crossing. "A pineapple fruit pictured in an Assyrian bas-relief of the 7th century BC was confidently identified by the Assyriologist Rawlinson ('The representation is so exact that I can scarcely doubt the pineapple being intended') and confirmed by Layard, the excavator of the relief (Collins 1951). The fruit is also represented on artifacts from Egypt (Wilkinson 1879) and in an Ankara museum (seen by Johannessen 1998). Its presence on a Pompeii mural has been claimed."[3]

Chili peppers (*Capsicum frutechens*), another American crop, seem to have been known in ancient Europe, for the Greek writer Theophrastus (370–286 BC) describes what appears to be them in his *Historia Planatarum*, whilst the Roman poet Martialis speaks of 'Pipervee crudum' (raw pepper), but says they are long and contain seeds, which seems to best describe chilli peppers.

The bottle gourd, *Lagenaria siceraria*, is a plant of African origin. Yet it was "discovered by Bird (1948) in pre-ceramic levels on the coast of Peru dating to the 3rd millennium BC. Its discovery was hailed by diffusionists as proof that ancient voyagers had crossed the Pacific (Carter 1950). Botanists previously had assumed that the species had not reached the Americas until imported by the Spaniards."

1 Ibid.
2 Ibid.
3 Ibid.

Whether or not the bottle gourd could have floated across the Atlantic or perhaps the Pacific has been a question of heated debate for decades. Yet, one way or another, it did reach the Americas. Interesting, "the species was found in 5th-Dynasty Egyptian tombs (Whitaker and Carter 1954, 697–700), and in India it bears Sanskrit names."

Purslane, *Portulaca oleracea*, was common in Roman gardens in Pliny's day (Leach 1982, 2). According to Sorenson, "It grew throughout the warmer parts of the Old World and was also mentioned in Egyptian texts. Nevertheless, Gray and Trumbell (1883, 253) demonstrated over a century ago that the species is actually of American origin. In North America, it was growing as early as 2,500–3,000 years ago (Chapman *et al.* 1974, 412). It thrives best in the disturbed soils of gardens, which indicates that the plant may well have accompanied a transoceanic transfer of horticulture."

Sonchus oleraceus in some sources is called 'chicory' although true chicory is *Cichorium intybus*. According to Sorenson, "It was a potherb and source of medicine among the Maya (Tozzer 1941, 146) and in Peru (Yacovleff and Herrera 1933–1934, 299). Chroniclers' accounts place it so early in the Americas that there is no question of the Spaniards having brought it. Yet, it was an Old World native that was extensively cultivated in Europe and Asia (Balfour 1871–1873, V, 482–83; Bretschneider 1892, 179; Watson 1868, 259; Watt 1888–1893, II, 285). Those facts can only be explained by supposing that it was carried from Eurasia to the Americas before Columbus."

In addition to these and many other plants, Sorenson and Johannessen also look at the origin and distribution of several species of fauna and micro-fauna. The microfauna, typically, are parasitical pests attached to humans, and could only have been spread by human agency. Once again, space permits mention of only a small sample of the species mentioned.

Ascaris lumbricoides is the large roundworm known to have infested an Egyptian mummy dating to 170 BC. It has been found also in other Old World locations in antiquity. According to Sorenson "Pictorial evidence exists for ascariasis in ancient Mesopotamia, and prescriptions in ancient Egypt have *A. lumbricoides* as a target of treatment (Kuhnke 1993, 457). Moreover, this nematode was known to ancient pre-Columbian writers in China, India, and Europe. It was also present in pre-Columbian America (Patterson 1993, 603). Although it was once thought to be a post-Columbian arrival, it has been shown recently to have plagued pre-Columbian South American populations (Verano 1998, 221)."

Bordetella pertussis is the bacterium that causes whooping cough. It originated in the Old World. However, as Sorenson notes, "antibodies for pertussis bacilli occur in the blood of isolated, unacculturated Brazilian Indians. Furthermore, it 'may have been present in the Southwest [of the United States] before arrival of the Spaniards' (Stodder and Martin 1992, 62). Van Blerkom (1985, 46-7) con-cludes, 'If not pertussis, then some close relative of it probably occurred in the New World as well as the Old.... Perhaps different strains existed in the two hemispheres.' But, as Sorenson notes, what close relative could that be unless one that also arrived from the Eastern Hemisphere where alone it would have evolved? Sorenson notes that to "Hare (1967, 119, 122), 'It is highly improbable that any of these organisms would have become established in a scattered com-munity with a Paleolithic culture' and thus that they could have crossed to the Americas with early hunters via Beringia. The transfer of *B. pertussis* would of ne-cessity have waited until an infected person from a more densely populated agri-cultural society crossed the ocean as a voyager."

Several species of domestic animals, as well as two species of shellfish, are also mentioned. First and foremost among these is the dog. This animal is generally thought to have accompanied the Amerindians into America via the Bering Strait, yet, according to Sorenson, "there is very slim evidence for this." He goes on to note that the dog was first domesticated in Europe and the Near East during the Mesolithic period, and that the dogs kept by the Amerindians were virtually genetically identical to these creatures. The evidence for dogs is not conclusive, yet it does strongly suggest an Old World origin for the native American breeds.[1]

And so it goes on. It should be emphasized here that the above represents only a small sample of the material amassed by Sorenson and Johannessen, and that the project is an ongoing one, with more evidence emerging almost by the day. Summarizing the history of the debate and the direction science has now pointed, Sorenson and Johannessen note that, "In the past, arguments for trans-oceanic contacts have relied mainly on evidence from cultural parallels (Sorenson and Raish 1996). Some of those parallels are indeed striking, but scholars gener-ally have rejected their value as evidence that significant pre-Columbian contacts took place with the Americas across the oceans ... tentative acceptance by some influential observers, like Lowie, of the possible historical significance of the cul-tural parallels has always ended up being rebutted by a demand from critics for 'hard,' or 'scientific' evidence for voyaging. Often, the sort of evidence demanded was demonstration that numbers of plants were present on both sides of the

---

1 We should remind ourselves here of the tradition which credited the Libyans of North Africa with the domestication of the dog, as well as the very real evidence of Mesolithic (Capsian) domestication of the dog in the same region. Also, strikingly, the dog is seen as the guide of souls into the underworld in the ancient religions of Europe and North Africa, as well as in the Americas.

oceans before Columbus' day (Kidder *et al.* 1946, 2). "Data from the life sciences now provide that desired evidence, not only for the flora, but for fauna as well."[1]

As noted earlier, the majority of the New World plants which made it to the Old are mentioned first and most extensively in Sanskrit texts from India. The Indian connection is indeed pervasive. But why should this be so? India is just about as far from the Americas as it is possible to be, without actually leaving the planet. Why such a strong Indian contact? This a question we shall deal with presently.

Before finishing, one important objection needs to be addressed: If so many plants made it across the Atlantic in ancient times, why not the extremely useful ones encountered by the Spanish in the sixteenth century — crops like the potato, tomato, and maize, that soon became so important in the Old World?[2] If Atlantean seafarers could bring back tobacco and cocaine, why not the above? We might also wonder why useful Old World crops, such as oats, barley, rye, etc. did not make it to the New World; and why domestic animals too, with the exception of the dog and the chicken,[3] failed to make the crossing.

There can be only one possible answer: The link between Old and New Worlds, which now seems beyond question, must have been severed either before the age of agriculture, or before knowledge of agriculture had reached an advanced stage. The potato, tomato, and maize, as we have them, all represent domestic strains of wild plants which were selectively bred by Native Americans over many years, perhaps many centuries. The high-yielding crops we now possess are the man-made descendants of low-yielding wild plants that took much time to produce. We hold that the Atlantis connection was broken at the end of the Early Dynastic Age (contemporary with the European Neolithic), a fairly remote period, even allowing for the radically-adjusted and shortened chronology proposed by the present author. In short, when Atlantis was destroyed the potato, tomato and maize had not been properly domesticated, or their domesticated varieties had not spread widely. The Atlanteans did not import them to Europe and North Africa because they couldn't: they didn't yet exist.

When the Atlanteans last sailed the seas, men had only recently invented the arts of agriculture; the great developments in this field were yet to take place. A few plants, and only a few, were raised as food. Among these were bananas, on-

---

1 Ibid.

2 According to Nikolai Zhirov however (op. cit., p. 52) maize appears to have been cultivated in a part of North Africa, namely Nigeria, in remote antiquity. Zhirov does not give his source for this information, which, if true, represents crucial evidence in favour of ancient transatlantic contact.

3 The chicken or domestic hen, a native of south-east Asia, could well have reached America via the Pacific, though this is by no means certain.

ions, peppers, radishes, etc., all of which were found on both sides of the ocean. More commonly used by them were the plants familiar to Stone Age hunters: herbs; and these, both medicinal and narcotic, were spread by them throughout the Atlantic littoral.[1]

SECRET KNOWLEDGE OF THE ATLANTEANS

The discovery of a truly enormous body of literary references to American plants in the ancient literature of India, highlighted by Sorenson and Johannessen, demands an answer. The most obvious response, perhaps, might be that the American plants reached the Old World not via the Atlantic but by way of the Pacific; and there is indeed strong evidence of some transpacific commerce in antiquity. An extreme view would be that all Pre-Columbian contacts were by this route, and that the "Atlantean" connection is untenable. Yet such an explanation is simplistic. The distance from India to Central America is actually about the same via the Atlantic and the Pacific, and it cannot be forgotten that the great Polynesian transpacific voyages only began around AD 300, when they reached Easter Island, for example. Hawaii was settled around AD 400, whilst New Zealand was not discovered until around the year 1000. On the other hand, both the Egyptian and Sanskrit references to American plants are much older; the Egyptian oldest of all.

Many of the American plants which made it to India had medicinal and/or narcotic qualities. We know that the Egyptians made use of tobacco and cocaine, whilst *Datura metel*, the notorious jimson weed, is mentioned in the Sanskrit sources. It is at least as likely that these plants reached India by way of the Atlantic as the other way round, especially in view of the fact that Egyptian references to them are usually considerably older than the Sanskrit ones. But if such be the case, why was knowledge of these varieties of flora lost to the west? Why did the people of India alone retain a knowledge of them?

From late antiquity the entire western world, including all the ancient centers of civilization, came successively under the influences of Christianity and Islam. Both these religions were intrinsically hostile to ideas such as herbalism and divination. The use of narcotic plants, in particular, was viewed as equivalent to sorcery or black magic, and carried with it heavy penalties. As such, much of the ancient knowledge of these plants disappeared from the western reaches of the Old World. Yet before disappearing, it is quite likely that it would have been transferred to India, a region far more tolerant in its attitude to divination, herbalism, and the use of narcotics. Transmission could easily have been through

---

1 So too would the dog, arguably the first animal to be domesticated — a creature invaluable in a world of hunter-gatherers. This animal did, of course, make it across the ocean.

the priests of Babylonia and the Magi of Persia. With the Islamicization of these regions in the 7th century, the cultivation and knowledge of these "shamanistic" plants would have disappeared, but it would have remained alive in India.

It may be that narcotic and hallucinogenic American plants were used all over the ancient world, from western Europe through Egypt to Babylonia, Persia and India. These plants were a central feature of initiation rites which were attached to many of the mystery cults among the Greeks and Egyptians (and apparently also among the Celts). I was first made aware of the significance of the mystery cults by English writer Paul Brunton, who spoke of them at length in the 1930s. Brunton was of the opinion that the initiate was granted a glimpse of the Other World through the use of psychoactive drugs.[1] One or several of these were believed by him to induce an out of body or astral projection experience, an experience which convinced the initiate that he was not a body but a spirit and that death was an illusion.

The knowledge of these plants and their use by the mystery cults forms an important part of what has been called the "Atlantean wisdom" so often spoken of both by ancients and moderns. Brunton himself actually used the term "Atlantean" to describe the hidden wisdom of the mystery cults, but it was a term used by the ancients themselves. The Atlanteans were reckoned to have possessed other kinds of wisdom, of a more astronomical and mathematical nature; but this knowledge too, like that of the narcotic herbs, they kept a closely guarded secret.

That the mystery cults were of "western" or "Libyan" or "Atlantean" origin was, as we have said, common knowledge in antiquity. In more modern times, various researchers have linked these to the cult of the dead, both of which are held to have reached Egypt from the west. Lewis Spence, for example, noted that Sanconiathon, the Carthaginian writer, spoke of the mysterious cult of the Cabiri (in Greek Kabeiri, or Kapheroi), twin deities of apparently Libyan origin, whose secrets were delivered to, among others, "the Egyptian Osiris."[2] And we note here that the cult of Osiris, Lord of the Dead, was one identified by the Greek writers as granting its initiates a glimpse of the Other World. It was the priests of Osiris who were responsible for mummification and therefore, presumably, with the placing of cocaine and tobacco in the bodies of their charges. Osiris was associated by the Egyptians with the West and was portrayed wearing the Atef, the white crown of Upper Egypt enclosed by two feathers. The feathered headdress

---

1 Paul Brunton, *A Search in Secret Egypt* (London, 1935).
2 Lewis Spence, *The Mysteries of Britain* (London, 1928) p. 31.

was, of course, the symbol of Libya, and Osiris is repeatedly associated in Egyptian writings with that region.[1]

In Greece, the most important of the mystery cults was that of Eleusis. This too had an apparently Libyan origin. The Eleusinian mysteries were said to have been founded by one Eumolpus, a son of Poseidon and Chione. The Atlantean connections of Poseidon need no restating (Herodotus ii, 40, actually states that the Greeks received their knowledge of Poseidon from the Libyans), whilst Chione was also, apparently, a Libyan deity. She was the daughter of Boreas and Oreithyia, and according to Robert Graves, "The Boreas cult seems to have originated in Libya."[2] We must note too that Lewis Spence found good evidence for connecting the Eleusinian mysteries with Gadir, or Gadeirus, also named Eumelus, son of Atlas and grandson of Poseidon.[3] Eumelus' portion of the Atlantean kingdom, said Plato, was that part which stood closest to the Pillars of Hercules (i.e., Europe), and his Atlantean name, Gadir, is preserved in the Spanish city of Cadiz. Robert Graves was in substantial agreement: "The myth of Erechtheus and Eumolpus" he said, "concerns ... the Thraco-Libyan origin of the Eleusinian mysteries."[4] The Eleusinian mysteries, it is now clear, owed their prestige to the state of altered consciousness attained by initiates: "Some scholars believe that the power of the Eleusinian Mysteries came from the kykeon's functioning as a psychedelic agent. Barley may be parasitized by the fungus ergot, which contains the psychoactive alkaloids lysergic acid amide (LSA), a precursor to LSD and ergonovine. It is possible that a psychoactive potion was created using known methods of the day. The initiates, sensitized by their fast and prepared by preceding ceremonies, may have been propelled by the effects of a powerful psychoactive protein into revelatory mind states with profound spiritual and intellectual ramifications."[5]

Yet the priests of Eleusis had no need to manufacture lysergic acid. The psychoactive plants necessary to induce the altered state of consciousness were brought to them, ready packaged, from the far west.

---

1 Robert Graves also was of the opinion that the cult of the dead, both in Egypt and Greece, as well as, to some degree, in Europe, was of Libyan origin. "Cerberus" he says, "was the Greek counterpart of Anubis, the dog-headed son of the Libyan Death-goddess Nephthys, who conducted souls to the Underworld. In European folklore, which is partly of Libyan origin, the souls of the damned were hunted to the Northern Hell by a yelling pack of hounds — the Hounds of Annwn, Herne, Arthur, or Gabriel ..." *The Greek Myths*, Vol. 1 (1955), 31.3.

2 Ibid. p. 171. Boreas is also connected with Hyperborea, anciently identified with Britain; and the name Boreas seems to be identical to the Arthurian (Sir) Bors, or Boras.

3 Spence, *History of Atlantis*, p. 102.

4 Graves, op. cit., Vol. 1, 47.1

5 http://en.wikipedia.org/wiki/Eleusinian_Mysteries.

That Libya, or north-west Africa, was associated with the use of psychoactive drugs is already recognized in the Odyssey, where we find the hero and his men seduced by the pleasures of the "lotus" plant which the Lotus Eaters of Libya give them.

Before moving on, we should note that even today, Native American shamans use many so-called "power plants" to gain access to the world of the spirits. Indeed, the use of these plants is central to Native American religious ideas.[1] We can easily imagine early transatlantic voyagers coming into contact with the shamanistic tradition in the New World and transporting the magical herbs to the other side of the ocean, where they became, naturally enough, a cause of wonder.

Interestingly, the Libyan Cabiri, who taught their mysteries to Osiris, are said by Sanchoniathon to have been the inventors of boats, the arts of fishing, building and agriculture, writing and medicine. Cicero called the Cabiri the "Sons of Prosperine," goddess of the Underworld, whilst Strabo regarded them as ministers of Hecate.[2] In Spence's words, "The Cabirian cult ... hailing from North-West Africa, is evidently nothing but a dim survival or memorial of the ancient civilized race of that region, which made its way into Spain, and after undergoing many phases there from Paleolithic to Neolithic times, gradually found its way, or sent its doctrine of the Cult of the Dead, to Egypt on the one hand and to Britain on the other."[3] Indeed, it begins to look as if a great deal of what we regard as the essentials of high civilization had their origin, not in the eastern Mediterranean, but along the Atlantic seaboard. As we shall see, a very high level of civilization was attained by the Mesolithic and Neolithic inhabitants of North-West Africa and Spain, and these people, it would appear, were closely connected to the high cultures of the Balkans which, at that time, possessed their own writing system.

There is one more point that needs to be stressed. The land we call Atlantis was never, at least during the Neolithic and Early Bronze Ages, more than a moderately-sized island. Evidence, both from geology and from Plato, indicates that it was roughly the size of Ireland. It was the Atlanteans' familiarity with a great continent further west, America, that gave rise to the notion of a "lost continent." The Atlanteans' knowledge of this great landmass, directly alluded to be Plato, led to their own home being confused with the western continent. And this ex-

---

1 Knowledge of this use became widespread after the appearance of Carlos Castaneda's books in the 1960s. Castaneda claimed to have been apprentice to a Yaqui Indian sorcerer named Don Juan Matus, who initiated him into the shamanistic use of drugs like mescaline. The books, though claiming to be factual, are undoubtedly fiction. Nevertheless, they give a real insight into some of the beliefs and practices of Native American shamanism.

2 Spence, *History of Atlantis.*, p. 32.

3 Ibid.

plains why Plato gives two diametrically opposed estimates of Atlantis' dimensions. In one (in the *Critias*), the island is described as a landmass comparable to Ireland; in another (in the *Timaeus*), it is described as "larger than Asia and Libya put together." Clearly Plato, or his sources, was also confused. The account given by Aelian too speaks of a "lost continent" across the ocean.

The confusion of Atlantis with the Americas explains too the statement of Plato that the island had "many elephants." Pleistocene America, both North and South, did indeed have great numbers of elephants, of various species. But we can hardly imagine a smallish island in the Azores region being home to such beasts.

The Atlantic islanders' knowledge of the Americas only enhanced their reputation as a race of sorcerers and men possessed of secret knowledge; and their use of American narcotic plants in religious rituals would have fitted well with that overall picture.

WITCHCRAFT AND MUMMIFICATION

It could be argued that witchcraft or sorcery, meaning a system of rituals and formulae intended to control aspects of the physical and spiritual world, has always existed in all human societies. Witches or sorcerers tended, among the more advanced civilizations, to form secret groups outside the priesthoods of the organized religions. Among the latter, the mystery cults offered perhaps the closest analogy to witchcraft, and there is no doubt that some groups of witches employed narcotic plants and herbs to enter a state of altered consciousness, just as did the initiates of the mystery cults.

Witchcraft and sorcery, we have said, are universal; yet the witches of European and North African tradition had a peculiar feature, one that they shared with many of the those of the Americas: they were female. Indeed the female witches of Europe and the New World were strikingly similar in many ways.

According to Lewis Spence, there existed a definite group of cultural and customary manifestations and practices, which he termed a "culture complex," that were unique to Europe and North Africa on the one hand and to the Americas on the other. This he called the "Atlantean Culture Complex" and listed, among its other defining characteristics, the female practice of witchcraft and the practice of mummification. According to him, "The relationship between European and American witchcraft is ... sufficiently clear, nor does either system show any great degrees of resemblance to the sorcery cults of Asia, most of which are essentially male organizations."[1] The female witches of Europe, with their broomsticks, pointed hats, cauldrons, magic circles and secret formulae need no description; yet these apparently had a long pedigree in both Europe and North Africa. Thus

---

1 Ibid., p. 225.

wall-paintings from western Europe of the Aurignacian Age (Paleolithic) show several depictions of what appear to be witches. In a rock-shelter near Lerida in Spain, for example, there is a painting which represents a number of women dressed in the traditional costume of witches, with peaked hats and skirts descending from the waist, dancing round a male idol or priest, who is painted black.[1]

The antiquity of the European witch-cult finds its reflection in myth. In British tradition, for example, Morgan le Fay, or Morgana, was head of a confraternity of nine priestesses on the mystical island of Avalon — the "Island of Apples," and these were mythologically linked to the Hesperides, the "Daughters of Evening," who guarded the sacred apple tree in the Island of the Blessed. These were connected to the Amazon queen Myrine, mentioned by Diodorus, who lived in the Isle of Hespera, by the Ocean Stream. Certainly the peoples of North Africa were matriarchal in many of their customs, as were a number of the peoples of western Europe, among whom we might mention the Basques of Iberia and the Picts of Scotland. Matriarchy was gradually replaced by patriarchy, and with it went the spiritual power of women. Nevertheless, a relic of their ancient authority survived in witchcraft, and even as late as the fourteenth century, in the Canary Islands, there existed a sect known as the Effenecs, whose virgin priestesses, the Magades, worshipped in stone circles. On the Barranco of Valeron the circle in which they celebrated their rites still stands. They engaged in symbolic dances and cast themselves into the ocean as a sacrifice to the waters which they believed would one day submerge their islands.[2] The power of these women was great. It was their duty to baptize children. Polyandry was in vogue among them, and it would seem that feminine rule obtained on the island.

Yet the cult of female sorcerers had its precise equivalent on the other side of the Atlantic. The Mexican witches, the *ciuateteo*, were supposed to wander through the air, to haunt crossroads, to afflict children with paralysis, and to use their weapons the elf-arrows, precisely as did the witches of Europe. According to Spence: "The witches' Sabbath was ... quite as notorious an institution in ancient Mexico as in medieval Europe. The Mexican witch, like her European sister, carried a broom on which she rode through the air, and was associated with the screech-owl. Indeed the queen of the witches, Tlazolteotl, is depicted as riding on a broom and as wearing the witches' peaked hat. Elsewhere, she is seen standing beside a house accompanied by an owl, the whole representing the witches' dwelling, with medicinal herbs hanging from the eaves. The Mexican witches, too, like their European counterparts, smeared themselves with ointment which

---

1 Ibid., p. 223.
2 Ibid., p. 226.

enabled them to fly through the air, and engaged in wild and lascivious dances, precisely as did the adherents of the cult in Europe. Indeed the old Spanish friars who describe them call them witches."[1]

Spence notes too that the witches of Mexico appeared originally to have linked to a "female cult of warlike tendencies and perhaps cannibalistic leanings," and "It is significant ... that we find the witches of Mexico behaving in precisely the same manner as the Amazons of classical tradition. In fact at one period of Mexican history a large force of Amazons or women warriors dwelling in the Huaxtec region on the eastern coast of Mexico invaded the Mexican valley. They sacrificed their prisoners of war, and it is noteworthy that their leader on that occasion was Tlazolteotl, the chief goddess of the witches. Their principal weapon, like that of the Amazons, was the bow, and it is clear from Camargo's account of their patron goddess that she came from the classical Gardens of the Hesperides. He says that she 'dwelt in a very pleasant and delectable place, where are many delightful fountains, brooks, and flower-gardens, which are called Tamoanchan, or the Place where are the Flowers, the nine-fold enchained, the place of the fresh, cool winds.'"[2]

Another feature of Spence's 'Atlantean culture-complex' was that of mummification. This again was a custom almost unique to ancient North Africa and to the Americas. (Europeans never practiced mummification, but there clearly existed a developed cult of the dead on the continent, as well as, in the Old Stone Age, the custom of painting the dead with red ochre; a kind of preliminary to mummification, in the opinion of Spence). There were, of course, connections between witchcraft and mummification. In Spence's words, "the witches of Europe prized above all things a piece of Egyptian mummy-flesh as a vehicle for their magical operations, and the same practice was in vogue in America, where the hands and fingers of dead women were employed by the sorcerer for magical purposes."[3]

Spence provides us with a valuable overview of the custom of mummification, in both hemispheres, that is perhaps worth repeating: "We have seen," he says, "that the ancient Aurignacians of Spain and France possessed the rudiments of the art of mummification, and it is also well-known that their kindred on the Canary Islands were acquainted with it in its more advanced stage. From the work of Alonzo de Espinosa, a friar of the sixteenth century, we learn that in these islands there existed a caste of embalmers who, like those in the Nile country, were regarded as outcasts. The corpse was embalmed with a mixture of melted

1 Ibid. p. 224.
2 Ibid. pp. 225-6.
3 Ibid. p. 224.

mutton-grease and grass-seed, stones and the bark of pine trees, the object being to give the shrunken frame the contours of life. The body was then placed in the sun until it was dried, and was later sewn up in sheepskin, which was then enclosed in pine-bark. Some of the more distinguished dead were placed in sarcophagi made of hard wood and carved in one piece in the shape of the body, precisely as were the Egyptian mummy-cases. It is also known that dressed skins were swathed round the body just as linen bands were wound round the Egyptian corpse. The Canarese custom further resembles the Egyptian in that the first incision in the body was made with a stone knife. Examination of the mummies found in the Canary Islands prove them to bear a close resemblance to those of Peru.

"The beginnings of mummification are thus found among the Aurignacians of Spain and France, and its later stage among the people of the Canary Islands. If we cross the ocean to the Antilles, we find that the art of mummification had at one time flourished there. In Porto Rico the skull and bones of the dead were wrapped in cotton cloth or in baskets and preserved for worship. Again the skulls were frequently attached to false bodies made of cotton and were kept in a separate temple. The Caribs likewise made cotton images which contained human bones ... One myth of the Haitian Indians told how a certain idol, Faraguvaol, was, like the mummified Osiris, discovered in the trunk of a tree. When wrapped in cotton he was able to escape from it as the Egyptian ba or soul could escape from its mummy-swathings."[1]

The resemblances between Egyptian mummies and those of other parts of the New World, especially in Mexico and Peru, are of course well-known. What is not so well-known is the fact that there exist striking parallels in the methods of preparation and the symbols and rituals attached to the process on both sides of the Atlantic. Again, we quote Spence: "Like the Egyptians ... the Maya associated certain colours with the principal bodily organs and with the cardinal points. In some cases colours and organs affected agree both as regards their Maya and Egyptian examples. We also find the dog regarded as the guide of the dead both in Egypt and Mexico. When a Mexican chieftain died a dog was slain, which was supposed to precede him to the other world, precisely as the dog Anubis did in the case of the Egyptian dead. A further striking similarity between Mexican and Egyptian funerary practice is the presence in Mexican manuscripts of the *tat* symbol in association with the mummy, the emblem which was believed to provide the dead with a new backbone on resurrection. This *tat* symbol, it may be

---

1 Ibid. pp. 219-220.

said in passing, bears strong resemblance to certain of the Azilian symbols found on painted pebbles and in caves in France and Spain.

> Certain Mexican gods were actually developed from the idea of the mummy. One of them, Tlauizcalpan-tecutli, the god and the planet Venus, is shown both in the Codex Borgia and the Codex Borbonicus as a mummy accompanied by the small blue dog, the companion of the dead.[1]

The mention here of Venus brings us to the fascinating topic of the cosmo-gonic associations of the mummification cult, both in the Old and New Worlds. It would appear that the mummy, in some regard, was viewed as a manifestation of one of the celestial deities. Earlier in the present chapter we saw how Spence linked the cult of the axe, or thunder-stone, with the practice of mummifica-tion. "In Mexico the planet Venus, the star Quetzalcoatl, was regarded as the thunder-stone, and this symbol in many American and West European localities was carefully wrapped in swathings of cloth or hide precisely as the mummy was wrapped.... This god, like Vulcan, had been lamed through a supernatural acci-dent, so that he had obviously a volcanic significance, like the god of Mount Etna, whose volcanic scoriae were regarded as thunderbolts.[2]

Spence goes on to note the occurrence, in some parts of the Antilles, of a number of strange-looking three-cornered stones. These are usually carved in the shape of a mountain, beneath which the head and legs of a buried Titan can be observed. Quoting a professor Mason, Spence concludes that the underlying myth might be analogous to that of Typhon, who was slain by Zeus and buried under Mount Etna, and that they seem to refer to an American belief in "a deity, whose duty it was to uphold the earth, but who, like Atlas, occasionally felt the immensity of his burden and cast it from him, causing universal destruction and catastrophe.

> It would seem, too, that in these three-pointed stones we find a combi-nation of the idea of Atlas and that of the world-shaping pick or hammer. Thus, in the thunder-stone symbol, it seems, the whole significance of the Atlantean culture-complex finds a nucleus. In it there centre, as in the hub of a wheel, the practice of mummification, witchcraft, and the mysteries and art of building in stone. The hammer of the thunder-god or creative deity with which he carved and shaped the earth was indeed identical with the implement by which the early sculptor fashioned his work. Manibozho, the god of the Algonquin Indians, shaped the hills and val-leys with his hammer, constructing great beaver dams and moles across the lakes. His myths says that 'he carved the land to his liking,' precisely as Poseidon carved the island of Atlantis into alternate zones of land and water....

1 Ibid. pp. 221-222.
2 Ibid. pp. 234-5.

It would seem that this sacred pick or hammer must have become symbolic of Poseidon in the continent [island] of Atlantis. In all likelihood it would have been kept wrapped up in linen in his temple, just as the black stone of Jupiter was preserved at Pergamos, or the arrows of Uitzilopochtli in the great temple-pyramid at Mexico. At the Kaaba at Mecca, the centre of the Mahommedan world, a similar stone is preserved wrapped in silks, and we have seen that in the Irish islands its counterpart was swathed in flannel and preserved in a separate house.[1]

1 Ibid. pp. 236-7.

CHAPTER 5. ANCIENT EUROPEANS IN AMERICA

A PERSISTENT RUMOR

Ever since the discovery of the New World by Columbus, there have been persistent rumors, until recently more or less dismissed as travelers' tales, of tribes of "white Indians," or at least of individual Native Americans who displayed apparently European characteristics such as light-colored skin, fair hair, and even, on occasion, blue eyes. Such reports came from as far apart as Chile in the south, where the Araucanians often had auburn or brownish hair and blue or green eyes, to Lake Superior in the north, where members of the Mandan and Menominee tribes were similarly reported. As late as the 1920s English traveler and surveyor Percy Fawcett heard reports of, and actually met, many white-skinned and blue- or green-eyed Amerindians in the rain forests of Brazil and Peru. He was convinced that, in almost all cases, these "white" traits could not be explained by recent contact with Europeans, and reported on the countless similar reports coming from the earliest Spanish and Portuguese explorers of the region.[1]

But it was not only European travelers who spoke in such terms. The Native Americans themselves, from the very beginning, attested to the presence, especially in former times, of white men with beards, who had visited them and interacted with them. Such stories played a crucial role in the unfolding of major

---

1 Fawcett speaks, for example, of a Tumupasa Indian called Medina from the Bolivian-Brazilain border, who had a daughter "who was one of the prettiest blonde Indians I have seen — tall, with delicate features, small hands, and a mass of silky golden hair." *Exploration Fawcett*, p. 85.

events, particularly with the conquest of the great civilizations of the Aztecs and Incas.

A large number of Native American peoples had both a legend of a white fore-father, plus numerous members of the nation who looked white. In very many cases the white forefather(s) were specifically linked to flood and catastrophe legends. Thus for example among the Navajo, the ancient "white people" are mentioned in relation to a myth of world-destruction during which men took refuge in a cave and had to dig themselves out. Thus we hear how:

> [A]t that time all the nations — Navajos, Pueblos, Coyoteros and white people — lived together underground, in the heart of a mountain, near the river San Juan. Their food was meat, which they had in abundance, for all kinds of game were closed up with them in the cave; but their light was dim, and only endured for a few hours each day.[1]

Sometime afterwards they successfully dug their way to the surface, only to find themselves on the outside of a mountain surrounded by water. Later the waters ebbed away, leaving a sea of mud; at which point,

> [T]he men and animals began to come up from the cave, and their com-ing up required several days. First came the Navajos ... then came the Pueb-los and other Indians ... [and] lastly came the white people, who started off at once for the rising sun, and were lost sight of for many winters.... When these nations lived underground they all spoke one tongue; but, with the light of day and the level of earth, came many languages. The earth was at this time very small, and the light was quite as scanty as it had been down below, for there was as yet no heaven, no sun, not moon, nor stars.

We recall at this moment how the bones of vast numbers of animals, as well as, on occasion, people, were found in caves in every part of the world; and how these underground places had apparently been used as refuges by both men and beasts during periods of upheaval in nature. The statement in the above narrative that the white people started off for the east ("the rising sun") may well allude to the fact that after this event the whites disappeared or at least became scarce.

Some of the natives of North America clearly intermarried with these ancient white people, for they retained many of their characteristics; including on oc-casion blonde hair and blue eyes. This was particularly the case with the Zuni Indians of New Mexico and the Mandans and Menominees of Great Lakes region. Thus in a footnote to Volume 3 of the U. S. *Explorations for a Railroad Route to the Pacific Ocean*, we are told that; "Many of the Indians of Zuni (New Mexico) are white. They have a fair skin, blue eyes, chestnut or auburn hair, and are quite good-looking. They claim to be full-blooded Zunians, and have no tradition of

---

1   H. H. Bancroft, *Native Races of North America*, Vol. 3 (London, 1875-6) p. 81.

intermarriage with any foreign race. The circumstance creates no surprise among this people, for from time immemorial a similar class of people has existed among the tribe."[1] Of the Menominees, John T. Short writes: "The Menominees, sometimes called the 'White Indians,' formerly occupied the region bordering on Lake Michigan, around Green Bay. The whiteness of these Indians, which is compared to that of the white mulattoes, early attracted the attention of the Jesuit missionaries, and has often been commented on by travelers. While it is true that hybridy has done much to lighten the color of many of the tribes, still the peculiarity of the complexion of this people has been marked since the first time a European encountered them."[2] It was the Mandans, however, a tribe with a strong tradition of a semi-mythical white ancestor who had survived a great deluge, who attracted the most comment. The Mandans only came into regular contact with Europeans from the 1830s onwards; yet long before that they were a source of wonder. They were, it was said, almost white, with very many of them having blue eyes and fair hair. These reports so intrigued one of the earliest and greatest explorers of the American interior, the Sieur de La Vérendrye (Pierre Gaultier de Varennes), that in 1739 he undertook an expedition to the Great Lakes specially to find the Mandans and either confirm or refute the rumors. When he arrived, he was able to confirm everything he had been told.

But such was the reputation of the Mandans that they continued to excite the interest of Europeans well into the nineteenth century. Thus in 1832, lawyer, frontiersman and pictorial historian George Catlin made a point of reaching the Mandans, who at that time resided near the site of present-day Bismarck, North Dakota. He remained with them for several months, and his description of the people is frankly astonishing: "The Mandans were distinctly different from all other native American tribes Catlin had encountered, not least for the fact that one-fifth or one-sixth of them were 'nearly white' with light blue eyes. Catlin deemed the Mandans to be 'advanced farther in the arts of manufacture,' than any other Indian nation, and their lodges were equipped with 'more comforts and luxuries of life.'

> Some Mandan women, especially, possessed almost Nordic features — characteristics clearly shown in Catlin's surviving portraits of Sha-ko-ka ('Mint') and Mi-neek-e-sunk-te-ka ('Mink'). Apart from their Indian clothing, these women might have been mistaken for Europeans. Catlin described Mandan women as having "a mildness and sweetness of expression, and excessive modesty of demeanor," rendering them "exceedingly pleasing and beautiful." He found Mandans in general to be "a very interesting and pleasing people in their personal appearance and manners,

---

1 From Donnelly, p. 184.
2 John T. Short, *North Americans of Antiquity*, (1882) p. 189.

differing in many respects, both in looks and customs, from all the other tribes I have seen."

As he got to know them better, Catlin became more and more intrigued by the Mandans' "peculiarities." They claimed to be descended from a white man who came in a big canoe, which their oral tradition said had come to rest on a high mountain after a great flood that destroyed everything on earth. A symbolical representation of this canoe occupied a religious shrine in their public square. This was the more remarkable inasmuch as the plains-dwelling Mandans had little use for canoes, and their own watercraft were primitive, round "bullboats" of wicker covered with hides, used only for crossing rivers.[1]

In Catlin's own words,

Their traditions, so far as I have learned them, afford us no information of their having had any knowledge of white men before the visit of Lewis and Clark, made to their village 33 years ago. Since that time until now (1835) there have been but very few visits from white men to the place, and surely not enough to have changed the complexions and the customs of a nation. And I recollect perfectly well that Governor [William] Clark told me before I started for this place, that I would find the Mandans a strange people and half-white.

Among the females may be seen every shade and color of hair that can be seen in our own country except red or auburn, which is not to be found.... There are very many of both sexes, and of every age, from infancy and manhood to old age, with hair of a bright silvergray, and in some instances almost perfectly white. ...

So forcibly have I been struck with the peculiar ease and elegance of these people, together with their diversity of complexions, the various colours of their hair and eyes; the singularity of their language, and their peculiar and unaccountable customs, that I am fully convinced that they have sprung from some other origin than that of the other North American Tribes, or that they are an amalgam of natives with some civilized race.[2]

Tragically, most of the Mandans (though not all), were killed by a smallpox epidemic in 1837. It is not, therefore, possible to verify the reports of De Varennes, Lewis, Clark, Catlin, and the rest, and the very graphic description of a people clearly sharing many of the physical attributes of Europeans have been generally dismissed, until now, by the scholarly establishment, bewitched by their own myth of a world inhabited by isolated and primitive peoples who could not possibly have any connection or any knowledge of a world outside their own immediate experience.

---

1 Charles W. Moore, "The Mystery of the Mandans" (1998) See internet article at, www. geocities.com/athens/aegean/9318/mandan/html.
2 George Catlin, *Manners, Customs and Conditions of the Indians of North America*, Vol. 1, (1841) p. 95

Yet stories of white tribes, often with blue eyes and fairish hair, continued to come out of the Americas, often, as the nineteenth century turned to the twentieth, from South America. Here, in the depths of the Amazon forest, the English explorer and surveyor Percy Fawcett heard many stories of, and actually on more than one occasion saw with his own eyes, Native Americans who were clearly white, or at least partly of Caucasian extraction.

The custom, as we have said, is to dismiss these stories as fantasy, or to put them down to recent intermarriage with Europeans. But the same cannot be said of the reports deriving from the earliest Spanish explorers of the region, the Conquistadores.

WHITE MEN IN MEXICAN LEGEND

Famously, the Aztecs worshipped a "white" god named Quetzalcoatl, who was said to have bequeathed many civilized customs to the natives of Mexico, and had sailed into the sunrise in a distant age. He had promised, it was said, to return some day.

The Mexicans counted their years in groups, or "sheafs" of fifty-two, and it was held that Quetzalcoatl would return on one of these anniversaries. By astonishing coincidence, Cortes' fleet made land at Veracruz precisely on the closing of one of these cycles. The progress of Cortes and his band through the Mexican countryside was watched carefully by Montezuma's spies, who tried desperately to discover whether they were in fact gods: whether Cortes really was Quetzalcoatl. And it has been surmised, not without good cause, that the history of the Aztec civilization would have been very different had the Mexicans not been paralyzed by this belief.

Whether or not the myth of Quetzalcoatl does refer to a race of primeval white travelers (there is much evidence that Quetzalcoatl, the "Feathered Serpent," can equally-well be identified with an ancient comet-deity which looked white), the legend is fascinating and carries with it intriguing linguistic clues. This is the legend respecting him, as quoted by Donnelly: "From the distant East, from the fabulous Hue Hue Tlapalan, this mysterious person came to Tula [originally Tulan], and became the patron god and high-priest of the ancestors of the Toltecs. He is described as having been a white man, with strong formation of body, broad forehead, large eyes, and flowing beard. He wore a mitre on his head, and was dressed in a long white robe reaching to his feet, and covered with red crosses. In his hand he held a sickle. His habits were ascetic, he never married, was most chaste and pure in life, and is said to have endured penance in a neighboring mountain, not for its effects upon himself, but as a warning to others. He condemned sacrifices, except of fruits and flowers, and was known as the god of peace; for, when addressed on the subject of war, he is reported to have stopped his ears with his fingers. (*North Amer. of Antiq.*, p. 268.)"

Quetzalcoatl also bequeathed to the natives the arts of metallurgy and writing, before returning to his homeland in the east. "He was skilled in many arts: he invented gem-cutting and metal-casting; he originated letters, and invented the Mexican calendar. He finally returned to the land in the East from which he came: leaving the American coast at Vera Cruz, he embarked in a canoe made of serpent-skins, and 'sailed away into the east.' (Ibid., p. 271.)"

We should note here that Tula, or Tulan, the destination of Quetzalcoatl, calls to mind the world Atla or Atlan, and there seems little doubt they were identical. We know of course from other sources that a place called "Atla" or Aztlan was regarded by the Nahua of Mexico as their original homeland. It would appear that Quetzalcoatl was a composite figure, part comet-deity (hence his "feathered serpent" identity), part ancient white traveler from across the ocean. This conflating of gods and people was characteristic of the earliest age of historical consciousness, when cosmic catastrophes still afflicted the earth, yet people had appointed kings, lived in cities and kept records. The fact that Quetzalcoatl sailed in a ship made of skins is a striking detail, for it agrees quite well with the seagoing vessels of Atlantic Europe, first attested by the Phoenician traveler Himilco, which were fashioned of animal skins over a wooden frame. Such vessels, named currachs, were, until recently, still employed in Ireland and Wales. The Carchiquel MS. says:

Four persons came from Tulan, from the direction of the rising sun — that is one Tulan. There is another Tulan in Xibalbay, and another where the sun sets, and it is there that we came; and in the direction of the setting sun there is another, where is the god; so that there are four Tulans; and it is where the sun sets that we came to Tulan, from the other side of the sea, where this Tulan is; and it is there that we were conceived and begotten by our mothers and fathers.

The Abbé Brasseur de Bourbourg, in his Introduction to the *Popol Vuh*, the Mayan holy book, presents a very remarkable analogy between the kingdom of Xibalba, described in that work, and Atlantis. He says (as quoted by Donnelly): "Both countries are magnificent, exceedingly fertile, and abound in the precious metals. The empire of Atlantis was divided into ten kingdoms, governed by five couples of twin sons of Poseidon, the eldest being supreme over the others; and the ten constituted a tribunal that managed the affairs of the empire. Their descendants governed after them. The ten kings of Xibalba, who reigned (in couples) under Hun-Came and Vukub-Came (and who together constituted a grand council of the kingdom), certainly furnish curious points of comparison. And there is wanting neither a catastrophe — for Xibalba had a terrific inundation — nor the name of Atlas, of which the etymology is found only in the Nahuatl tongue: it comes from atl, water; and we know that a city of Atlan (near the water) still existed on the Atlantic side of the Isthmus of Panama at the time of the Conquest.

> "In Yucatan the traditions all point to an Eastern and foreign origin for the race. The early writers report that the natives believe their ancestors to have crossed the sea by a passage which was opened for them. (Landa's *Relacion*, p. 28.)

> "It was also believed that part of the population came into the country from the West. Lizana says that the smaller portion, 'the little descent,' came from the East, while the greater portion, 'the great descent,' came from the West. Cogolluda considers the Eastern colony to have been the larger.... The culture-hero Zamna, the author of all civilization in Yucatan, is described as the teacher of letters, and the leader of the people from their ancient home.... He was the leader of a colony from the East. (*North Amer. of Antiq.*, p. 229.)"

The ancient Mexican legends say that, after the Flood, Coxcox and his wife, after wandering one hundred and four years, landed at Antlan, and passed thence to Capultepec, and thence to Culhuacan, and lastly to Mexico.

The identification of Aztlan, the original Nahua homeland, with Atlan or Atlantis, has recently been criticized on chronological grounds. It is said, for example, that since the Aztecs only arrived in the Valley of Mexico in the fourteenth century AD, Aztlan could not be the same as Atlantis. This argument is spurious: It is well-known that ancient peoples had little knowledge of real timescales; and events that happened thousands of years earlier were often believed to have occurred in the recent past — and vice versa. But the fact that "Aztlan" was related to an island or at least mountainous region surrounded by water lying in the east, and to the Flood legend, is beyond question if we care to examine the details of the story. Thus Donnelly invites us to read the words of a Professor Valentini, who "describes an Aztec picture in the work of Gemelli (*Il giro del mondo*, vol. vi.) of the migration of the Aztecs from Aztlan": "Out of a sheet of water there projects the peak of a mountain; on it stands a tree, and on the tree a bird spreads its wings. At the foot of the mountain-peak there comes out of the water the heads of a man and a woman. The one wears on his head the symbol of his name, Coxcox, a pheasant. The other head bears that of a hand with a bouquet (xochitl, a flower, and quetzal, shining in green gold). In the foreground is a boat, out of which a naked man stretches out his hand imploringly to heaven. Now turn to the sculpture in the Flood tablet (on the great Calendar stone). There you will find represented the Flood, and with great emphasis, by the accumulation of all those symbols with which the ancient Mexicans conveyed the idea of water: a tub of standing water, drops springing out — not two, as heretofore in the symbol for Atl, water — but four drops; the picture for moisture, a snail; above, a crocodile, the king of the rivers. In the midst of these symbols you notice the profile of a man with a fillet, and a smaller one of a woman. There can be doubt these are the Mexican Noah, Coxcox, and his wife, Xochiquetzal; and at the same time it is evident (the Calendar stone, we know, was made in A.D., 1478) that the story of them, and the pictures representing the story, have not been invented by the Catholic clergy, but really existed among these nations long before the Conquest."

Again, Donnelly calls attention to information in the Popol Vuh, which speaks of events subsequent to the departure from Aztlan: "The *Popul Vuh* tells us that after the migration from Aztlan three sons of the King of the Quiches, upon the death of their father, 'determined to go as their fathers had ordered to the East, on the shores of the sea whence their fathers had come, to receive the royalty, bidding adieu to their brothers and friends, and promising to return.' Doubtless they passed over the sea when they went to the East to receive the royalty. Now this is the name of the lord, of the monarch of the people of the East where they went. And when they arrived before the lord Nacxit, the name of the great lord, the only judge, whose power was without limit, behold he granted them the sign of royalty and all that represents it . . . and the insignia of royalty . . . all the things, in fact, which they brought on their return, and which they went to receive from the other side of the sea — the art of painting from Tulan, a system of writing, they said, for the things recorded in their histories. (Bancroft's *Native Races*, vol. v., p. 553 *Popul Vuh*, p. 294.)"[1]

THE VIRACOCHAS

According to Peruvian legend, the Viracochas were a race of tall, white-skinned, bearded folk who had formerly inhabited the Andes region. When the Spaniards arrived in Peru, they were informed by the Incas that the colossal monuments which stood deserted about the landscape were erected by this race of "white gods." They were said to have come from the north, in the morning of time, and to have built the ancient city of Tiahuanaco. Their leader, who was also a sun-god, was named Kon-Tiki Viracocha. At some stage, the legend continued, the bearded white men were attacked by a chief named Cari, who came from the Coquimbo Valley. There was a great battle on an island in Lake Titicaca, which resulted in the defeat and massacre of the Viracochas. Kon-Tiki however and

---

1 Interestingly, a number of writers have viewed the location and design of the Aztec capital Tenochtitlan — an island in a lake, connected to the mainland with causeways — as a deliberate imitation of the ancestral Aztlan. Yet it is also stange that Tenochtitlan, in its general concept, bears some resemblance to the Atlantean capital, as described by Plato. (See e.g., E. V. Andreyeva, *Vekoviye zagadki (Age-old Riddles)* (Moscow, 1954) p. 70.

his closest companions managed to escape and later arrived on the Pacific coast, where they embarked on ships and sailed westwards across the ocean.

Some of the Viracochas, however, were said to have remained, and the first Spanish explorers, struck by the light-colored skin and reddish hair of many of the Inca royalty, were informed that there were descendants of the Viracochas.

Nevertheless, there was indeed a strong tradition that the majority of this ancient white race had fled across the Pacific, and a great deal of adventurer Thor Heyerdahl's work was concerned with tracing their journeys after they left South America. He was able to show, for example, that Easter Island, as well as various other Pacific islands, was formerly inhabited by a race of white-skinned and red-haired people. On Eastern Island these were known as the "Long Ears," a race which had dominated the island until being overthrown and massacred by Polynesian newcomers. Heyerdahl was able to produce fairly convincing archaeological evidence of Pacific-South American links in the past. These included pottery and various other cultural parallels, as well as the use by the Pacific islanders of the sweet potato, a South American plant. Heyerdahl has been much criticized by various members of the academic establishment, who were quick to point out that both genetic and archaeological evidence proves the majority of modern Polynesians to be of South East Asian origin. Yet Heyerdahl never commented on the origin of the Polynesians, it was an ancient and white-skinned race that concerned him, and he did unquestionably demonstrate that there was at least some cultural input into the Pacific from South America.

But it is the origin and not the fate of the Viracochas that is most interesting, and most controversial. In his various publications, Heyerdahl, following a line of thinking pursued by other adventurers like Colonel Percy Fawcett, suggested that the Viracochas might be linked to the Atlantis legend. He suggested in particular that the white-skinned Viracochas might have been ethnically related to the white-skinned Berbers of North Africa, as well as their Guanche cousins in the Canary Islands. The Guanches, he emphasized, like many of the peoples of South America, mummified their dead and constructed small pyramids.

Heyerdahl made no reference to a catastrophic destruction of an island in the Atlantic that might have provided a link between the Berbers and South America, though Fawcett and others were not so demure, stating plainly their belief, based on the still-living traditions of South America, that some great cataclysm had afflicted the entire earth in the not too-distant past. So, for example, he wrote that " ... the connection of Atlantis with parts of what is now Brazil is not to be dismissed contemptuously, and belief in it ... with or without scientific corroboration ... affords explanations for many problems which otherwise are unsolved mysteries." (*Exploration Fawcett*, (1953), pp. 15-17)

The problem faced by Fawcett, as well as by other writers on the same theme such as Ignatius Donnelly, was that they tended to accept too uncritically the statement of Plato that Atlantis' destruction took place 9,000 years before his own time. In such a remote age, no one anywhere built pyramids, used metal, kept written records, or practiced mummification, so the apparent cultural links between the Old and New Worlds had to be discounted.

The new chronology outlined in Ages in Alignment answers the question. The Atlantis civilization must have been a Neolithic/Early Bronze Age one, and its destruction would have coincided with the event recorded in the Old Testament as the Exodus, an event which the evidence leads us to believe occurred much more recently than is stated in the textbooks. By that time, of course, men on both sides of the Atlantic were mummifying the dead and building pyramids.

KENNEWICK MAN AND THE EVIDENCE OF DNA

Given the unanimity with which early explorers, as well as the Native Americans themselves, spoke of a white race in the Americas, the reader may wonder whether archaeologists and anthropologists found any trace of such a folk. After all, if the "Viracochas" were as influential and powerful as the Peruvians said they were, they cannot fail to have left some genetic marker of their presence.

In fact, the "white Indians" of the Americas have left abundant proofs of their existence. But the proofs have, until recently, been ignored.

In 1996 a pair of sightseers at a hydroplane race near Kennewick in Washington State noticed part of a human skull exposed on the banks of the Columbia River. Subsequent excavation revealed an ancient skeleton belonging, apparently, to a Caucasian male about five foot ten inches tall. The body had a two inch-long Clovis spear point, of grey volcanic rock, embedded in his pelvic bone. Described as one of the most complete skeletons ever unearthed in the Americas, the remains were immediately the subject of a storm of controversy over their ethnic association and ownership. Here, at last, it seemed, was definitive proof of ancient contact between the Old World and the New. Then establishment academia had its say. With astonishing ineptitude, and in apparent violation of all the principles of scientific enquiry, anthropologist Joseph Powell of the University of New Mexico announced that "Kennewick Man" was indeed Caucasian, but not European Caucasian: he more closely resembled a south Asian, or perhaps an Ainu. This in spite of the Clovis spear point associated with the remains.

Thus another vital clue was discarded. In the controversy that raged over Kennewick Man it emerged that at least six other Caucasoid skeletons had previously been found at different locations in North America. These included an almost ten-thousand-year-old mummy of a Caucasoid male from Spirit Cave Nevada, and the skeletal remains of a nine year old Caucasoid female child found in Nevada of equal antiquity. Interestingly, the Spirit Cave body had, after initial discovery, been describes as "Caucasoid" but nearest to south Asian or Ainu Caucasoid.. However, in 2000 a new report found that the cranial features more closely resembled those of a "Norse" individual.[1] In fact, it is now clear that remains of Caucasoids with striking affinities to the ancient Aurignacians of Europe have been located throughout the Americas with some frequency for well over a century. In the prehistoric cities of South America were found mummies of apparently Caucasoid nobles buried in the bowels of temples. Peru, Chile, and Ecuador are all revealing long forgotten cities of ancient peoples classified as at least partly Caucasoid. In the early years of the twentieth century Professor J. L. Myers wrote the following in the *Cambridge Ancient History*. "The similarity between Aurignacian skulls in Europe and the prehistoric skulls in Lagoa Santa in Brazil and the other remote localities round the margins of South America suggests that this type had once almost as wide a distribution as that of the older types of implements."[2]

All of this evidence was ignored, or "reinterpreted," precisely in the way the remains of Kennewick Man had been reinterpreted. And before moving on, we should note that the decision to class Kennewick Man as a non-European Caucasian was made on the flimsiest of pretexts: In the words of anthropologist James C. Chatters, "Many of ... [Kennewick Man's] characteristics are definitive of modern-day caucasoid peoples, while others, such as the orbits, are typical of neither race. Dental characteristics fit Turner's (1983) Sundadont pattern, indicating possible relationship to south Asian peoples."[3] So, this body, which Chatters had earlier believed belonged to a modern European settler, has now been classified as "Ainu" or "South Asian" on the strength of a *possible* relationship" of the teeth with modern southern Asians. The fact that a Clovis spear-point was embedded in Kennewick Man's hip, and that Clovis culture was virtually identi-

---

1 See, http//www.nv.blm.gov/cultural/spirit_cave_man/spirit_cave_man2.htm It is much to be regretted that the waters of the debate have been muddied by the claims of both racists and anti-racists; the former using the early Caucasians to legitimize the conquest of the Americas by Europeans; the latter then doing everything in their power to deny the very existence of these American Caucasians. It cannot be stressed too strongly that even if the Clovis folk were entirely Caucasian, this in no way legitimizes European colonialism or the treatment of the Native Americans by the Europeans. The Clovis people were destroyed by the same natural catastrophe that annihilated the mammoth and mastodon, and the Siberian ancestors of the Native Americans arrived in an uninhabited continent. They were, and are, the only Native Americans.

2 Cited from Spence, *History of Atlantis*, p. 84.

3 James C. Chatters, "Kennewick Man," *Newsletter of the American Anthropological Association* (2004).

cal, in the testimony of archaeologists, to the Solutrean culture of Europe, was completely ignored.

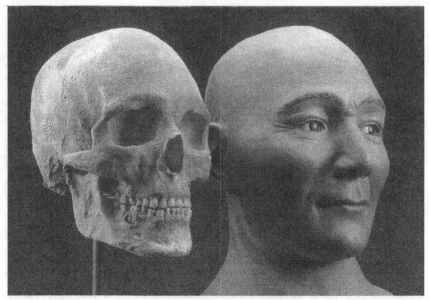

Fig. 12. Spirit Cave Man, showing skull and reconstructed features. Of Clovis age, he is clearly Caucasian.

With thinking of this type, it is doubtful if the academic establishment would ever have been able to look beyond dogma and *a priori* assumptions. But then, at last, came evidence that could not be so easily brushed aside.

In 1998, a team of geneticists, led by Michael D. Brown of Emory University, but comprising specialists from several universities on both sides of the Atlantic, published an article in the *American Journal of Human Genetics*. The article, entitled, "mtDNA Haplogroup X: An Ancient Link between Europe/Western Asia and North America?," made a sensational claim which created a storm of controversy that has not yet abated. In it, Brown and his associates claimed that, whilst the great majority of Native American mitochondrial DNA subtypes, (A, B, C, and D), can be traced to Siberia — where the origin of Native American populations has traditionally been sought — a small group, designated haplogroup X, cannot be so traced. The language used by Brown and his colleagues is the language of the specialist, but the message is crystal clear. Looking at the history of the debate, Brown et al. trace the course of their thinking: "For Native Americans, extensive RFLP and control region (CR; also known as the "D-loop") sequence analysis has unambiguously identified four major founding mtDNA haplogroups, designated 'A'–'D'(Torroni et al. 1992; 1993*a*). Together, these haplogroups account for ~97% of modern Native American mtDNAs surveyed to date (Torroni and

Wallace 1994; Merriwether et al. 1995). Apparent non–haplogroup A–D mtDNAs can result from reversion of key A–D markers, recent admixture with non–Native Americans, or represent additional Native American founding mtDNA lin-

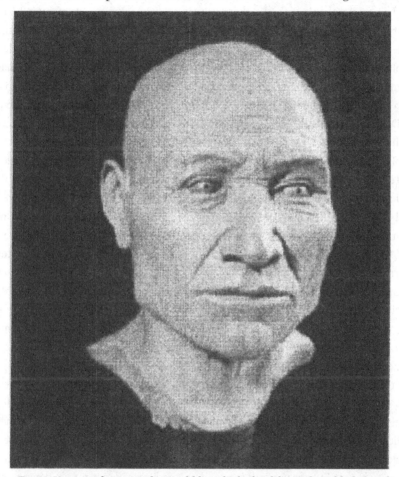

Fig. 13. Kennewick Man, as he would have looked in life. A Clovis blade was found embedded in his pelvis. He is clearly of Caucasian type, and strangely reminiscent of the actor Patrick Stewart.

eages. A striking example of the presence of non–haplogroup A–D genotypes in Native Americans can be seen in the Ojibwa, an Amerindian population from the Great Lakes region of North America. Using high–resolution RFLP analysis, Torroni et al. (1993*a*) found that 25% of the northern Ojibwa mtDNAs did not belong to haplogroups A–D and that nearly all of these 'other' mtDNAs encompassed four distinct but related haplotypes characterized by the RFLP motif -1715 *Dde*I and +16517 *Hae*III. This motif was also present in 4% of the Navajo, but it was not observed in 18 other tribes from North, South, and Central America. The high incidence of this motif in the Ojibwa has been confirmed recently by Scozzari et al. (1997), who reported its presence in 26% of the southeastern Ojibwa from Manitoulin Island, Canada."[1]

The origin of this "other" subgroup was surprising, even astonishing: "A recent survey of European mtDNAs has demonstrated the presence of the same 'other' haplotype motif in modern European populations, in which it is called 'haplogroup X.' Haplogroup X represents ~4% of European mtDNAs and has been found to be further characterized by C → T transitions at nucleotide position (np) 16223 and np 16278 of the CR (Torroni et al. 1996). Thus, haplogroup X mtDNAs are minimally characterized by a combination of RFLP and CR markers including -1715 DdeI, +16517 HaeIII, and the 16223T and 16278T mutations."

To say that geneticists were surprised by this finding is almost an understatement. It went against all they had expected and all they had been led to believe about the histories of the Old and New Worlds. As such, they checked and double-checked their results, trying to remove all possibilities of error or contamination. Above all, they were concerned to show that the "European" DNA had not entered into the Native American gene-pool through recent intermarriage. The evidence proved conclusive: "To investigate these issues, we performed high-resolution RFLP and complete CR sequence analysis for available Native American and Old World mtDNAs and found 22 Native American and 14 European mtDNAs that belonged to haplogroup X. Despite a shared consensus RFLP haplotype, substantial genetic differences exist between the Native American and European mtDNAs. Phylogenetic analysis indicates that the two groups are related — but only distantly — to each other and that considerable genetic substructure exists within both groups. Further, coalescence-age estimates for haplogroup X in the Americas, based on either RFLP or CR sequence data, clearly indicate the antiquity of this haplogroup in the New World. Overall, these data exclude the possibility that the occurrence of haplogroup X in Native Americans is due to recent European admixture and, instead, provide a rigorous demonstration that this haplogroup represents an additional founding mtDNA lineage in Native Americans."

So, although western Europeans and Native Americans shared haplogroup X, the differences in the two were so great that an ancient origin had to be postulated. The overall conclusion, astonishing as it may seem, is that, "some Native American founders were of Caucasian ancestry."

---

1 Michael D. Brown, Seyed H. Hosseini, Antonio Torroni, Hans-Jurgen Bandlet, Jon C. Allen, Theodore G. Schurr, Rosaria Scozzari, Fulvio Cruciani, and Douglas C. Wallace, "mtDNA Haplogroup X: An Ancient Link between Europe/Western Asia and North America?" *American Journal of Human Genetics*, 63 (October, 1998) 1852-1861.

Since the publication of Brown's article, the battle has raged to and fro. All kinds of tactics have been used, even the suggestion that the DNA specialists were somehow trying to justify European colonialism.[1] Yet none of the criticism has stood. On the contrary, further evidence has emerged supporting Brown. When the first article appeared, in 1998, the team was aware of haplogroup X only in certain tribes of North America, most especially amongst the Ojibwa, old neighbors, significantly enough, of the Mandan. Since that time, however, the group has been found throughout the Americas, including certain peoples of the Amazon and Orinoco regions, amongst them the Yanomamo. This alone goes a long way to confirming many of the traditions recounted by Percy Fawcett, of "white tribes" of that area.

Meanwhile, the evidence for an ancient "Caucasian" element in the Native populations, together with the well-publicized Clovis-Solutrean parallels, has prompted, very gradually, a movement towards abandoning the hitherto sacrosanct notion of an isolated New World in pre-Columbian times. In spite of the discoveries of Professor Ewing, the name "Atlantis" has not yet been heard; yet it is now cheerfully admitted that during the last Ice Age, presumably around ten or eleven thousand years ago, sailors, in small kayaks-like canoes, could have "hopped" between ice bergs along the southern shores of the great ice sheets, and somehow reached America that way.

The improbability of such a scenario needs no emphasis here.

It would appear that during the Pleistocene the Americas were inhabited by a Caucasian group with connections to south-west Europe and, more especially, north-west Africa. These "Clovis" people were almost certainly identical in terms of language and culture to the peoples of the Canary Islands. Their language would have been what we now call Berber. Then came the Deluge. The cataclysm which terminated the Pleistocene seems to have all but exterminated the Clovis folk, who were now largely replaced by new immigrants from Siberia. These, the ancestors of the Native Americans, mixed with the few survivors of the Clovis culture, whose genetic signature is found in the X haplogroup. The inhabitants of the Atlantic Islands, the Atlanteans, did re-establish contact with the Americas, and they helped to shape the great cultures of Mexico and Peru which now began

---

1 Haplogroup X was subsequently discovered in one western Siberian group resident in the Altai Mountains. The latter region, however, was the home of the ancient Tocharians, a Scythian people of Indo-European origin; and this region marked the easternmost reach of Indo-European settlement. That it was to the Tocharians that the Siberian X Haplogroup owed its origin was confirmed by the subgroup to which the DNA belonged. According to Wikipedia, "... the Altaian sequence are all almost identical (Haplogroup X2e), suggesting that they arrived in the area possibly from the South Caucasus more recently than 5,000 BP."

to develop. The contact continued until the Neolithic/Copper Age, when another, and final cosmic disaster, terminated the transatlantic link.

CHAPTER 6. RECONSTRUCTING A LOST HISTORY

THE NEOLITHIC AND EARLY BRONZE AGES

If the Atlantis civilization is to be placed in the Neolithic and Early Bronze Age, it means that, contemporary with Egypt's First, Second and Third Dynasties, there existed in the west a mighty seafaring culture, centered in the Atlantic Ocean. It is implied that these folk were in regular contact with the peoples of the Mediterranean, including, according to the legend, the peoples of the Aegean and the Egyptians; and that, at the other side of the scale, they made regular voyages westwards, exploring and perhaps trading with the peoples of North and South America. The evidence of archaeology, examined in the previous chapters, shows that from Old Stone Age times at least, a race of people originating in the Old World, probably from the region of Spain and north-west Africa, was in somewhat regular contact with the New. This contact has been put beyond question by the evidence of DNA, and archaeology proves that such links continued into the Neolithic and perhaps the early part of the Bronze Age. We have stated that after the catastrophic termination of the Pleistocene, which destroyed the mega fauna of the time, the link between the two worlds was disrupted but not terminated. Later voyagers had perhaps longer journeys to make to reach the shores of the New World, but they continued to make them.

Furthermore, if we are to give any credence at all to the testimonies of Plato and Diodorus, the Atlantic islanders not only kept up regular contact with the Americas, but they now formed themselves into something like an imperial power, which sought to dominate the whole Mediterranean.

Is this possible? Is it credible that at such an early date men made such journeys and conceived such ambitions? Could it be that by the time of Egypt's First Dynasty, the dynasty of pharaoh Menes, men had learned how to traverse great stretches of ocean water with impunity and to travel literally thousands of miles across the globe? If they did, they must surely, we might imagine, have mastered all the arts of seamanship, including, apparently, the use of the sail.

Could this be true?

Before looking at the question of maritime knowledge, we need first to stress that archaeology now confirms the existence of an advanced and technically refined culture in Europe and North Africa even before the advent of the Egyptian monarchy.

Perhaps owing to the existence until recently of the Iron Curtain, western scholarship has paid little attention to the astonishing civilization that we now know spread over much of eastern Europe in Neolithic times, where a flourishing Neolithic and Early Bronze (copper-using) culture seems to have established trading relations throughout Europe and the Near East. This culture, named after the Serbian region of Vinça, which is said to slightly predate the rise of dynastic civilization in Egypt and Mesopotamia, was apparently literate: throughout south-eastern Europe more than a thousand artifacts of the Late Neolithic and Early Bronze Ages are inscribed with mysterious pictographic-like signs, signs so similar to those of the earliest Mesopotamian ciphers that the name Old European Script has been given to them.[1] Marija Gimbutas, the renowned archaeologist, went so far as to declare that the inscriptions, of which the most famous are the Tartaria Tablets of Romania, represent the world's first writing system.

Evidence of this Old European Script is found in regions which in classical times were associated with the Thracians. And we note at this point that Robert Graves was convinced that the Thracians, with their matrilinear descent and other curious customs, such as tattooing, formed a single cultural entity with the Libyans of North Africa.[2] We should not be surprised at this connection, since the distance from Tunisia to Albania, via Sicily, is not a great one; and we know in any case that the Balkans folk traded regularly with North Africa, as the discovery of objects of Transylvanian gold in Second Dynasty Egyptian tombs makes all too clear.[3]

The Early and Middle Neolithic epoch in Western Europe was dominated by the so-called Azilian culture. The Azilians, who are placed immediately be-

---

1 See, e.g., http//en.wikipedia.org/wiki/Old_European_Script.
2 See Graves' *The Greek Myths*, also *The White Goddess*, for a lengthy discussion of the Libyan-Thracian link.
3 A. R. Burn, *Minoans, Philistines and Greeks* (London, 1930) p. 73.

fore the rise of the megalith-builders, achieved a high level of culture. They were skilled sailors, as the vast numbers of deer-antler harpoons they left behind show. That they fished the oceans is evidenced by the fact that in the Hebridean island of Oronsay, flat Azilian harpoons were found along with a mound of shells of deep-sea crabs.[1] The Azilians are known to have employed a series of symbols, many of which bear more than a passing resemblance to the Old European Script of the Balkans and at least one Neolithic potsherd from Portugal appears to be a fragment of true writing.[2] Lewis Spence noted that at Niebla in southern Spain there exists evidence of an Early Neolithic settlement of immense importance. He remarks on the discovery of vast quantities of "miniature darts of quartz, some less than half an inch long, beautifully chipped porphyry fish-hooks and small arrow-heads, and many other minute objects of the type usually classified as Azilian ... Enormous grain-crushers, too, have been excavated ..."[3] At Heulva, also in southern Spain, archaeologists found a great harbor, built of "cyclopean" stones, which was approached by a grand stairway, thirty feet wide, cut out of the rock above the harbor wall. This structure was dated to the Early Neolithic.[4]

Contemporary with and slightly preceding the European Early Neolithic there arose in North Africa a wonderfully innovative culture commonly known as Capsian, a culture which extended throughout present-day Algeria and Tunisia and reached Morocco and Libya, as well as northwards into Spain. The Capsian folk, recognized ancestors of the present-day Berbers, were the first to practice agriculture; and the rich pottery and art they left is rightly celebrated. Their material culture leaves little doubt that they were the descendants of the highly-gifted Old Stone Age Aurignacians of Spain and southern France, though their culture was superior to that of their predecessors in the domestication of the dog[5] and the use of the bow. "Like the Aurignacians, the Capsians were artists who left their paintings on the walls of their rock-shelters in the central parts of Spain, only these display a much more marked conventional treatment of the

---

1 Spence, *The History of Atlantis*. p. 78.
2 Ibid. pp. 166-7. "True writing is ... evident on a potsherd taken from a neolithic settlement at Los Murcielagos in Portugal." (Quotation from Dr. T. Rice Holmes, *Ancient Britain*, pp. 99-100).
3 Spence, *History of Atlantis* p. 115.
4 Ibid. Spence's source here was E. M. Whishaw, whose *Atlantis in Andalusia* (London, 1929) provides a wealth of evidence pointing to the existence of a mighty seafaring culture centered in southern and western Spain at the beginning of the Neolithic.
5 The dog, we recall, as an assistant to the hunter, was probably the first of all creatures to be domesticated. Legend, as well as archaeology, tells that it was first domesticated in North-West Africa; and we recall that it was one of the very few creatures to make it across the Atlantic in Pre-Columbian times.

subject and were nearly all of a religious or magical character."[1] These early Berbers ranged over a vast area. At that time, the Sahara was a fertile savannah, and the early Amazigh herders and farmers reached far into the interior of the continent. Impressive images of animals and human hunters are engraved and later painted on rock surfaces. Two styles of rock art, the "Large Wild Fauna" and the "Bovidian Pastoral" style have been identified. The former features hunting scenes with big game, including most of the animals now ranging across the East African savannah, as well as one or two extinct species, such as the giant buffalo. The latter, "Bovidian Pastoral," as its name suggests, features images of domestic herds, obviously executed by farmers. By this time, contemporary with Egypt's first monarchies, the communities of North and North-west Africa are: "part of trade networks and the cultural community of the western Mediterranean. Locally made pottery displays the same type of ornamentation found in the regions of modern-day Spain and southern France. Examples are cardial ware, a ceramic decorated with impressed seashells, and impressed ware, decorated with designs made by pressing string into the wet clay. Among the materials that come to western North Africa from abroad are obsidian blades from the Lipari Islands near Sicily."[2]

In time, Capsian and Azilian cultural features blended together, forming a common West-European-North African cultural complex.

Mesolithic cave-paintings from the Alps give us a glimpse of how these peoples looked, or rather how they dressed. And what they reveal is most instructive: Some of the figures "are represented as wearing plumed headdresses very like those still in use among Red Indian tribes."[3] Others wear "hats of high triangular shape, not unlike a Scots bonnet, and some of the women conical caps, made, perhaps, of bark or fur. Some of the men wear plumed bands beneath the knee and round the ankles like the Masai of south-eastern Africa; and probably both sexes wore ornaments of shells and teeth, painted or plain. Indeed, the general costume of the Azilians seems to have resembled that of the Aztecs of Mexico in some aspects ..."[4] Precisely the same could be said of the later Libyans, as portrayed on Egyptian monuments, whose cape, tied over one shoulder, and feathered headdress, give them a decidedly Aztec appearance.

It was after the convergence of the Capsians and Azilians, around the beginning of the Neolithic, that the peoples of western Europe and North Africa began to construct the great artificial mounds or barrows, an architectural style

---

1 Spence, *The Mysteries of Britain*, p. 22.
2 See "Western North Africa (Maghrib), 8000–2000 BC." www.metmuseum.org.
3 Spence, *History of Atlantis*, p. 165.
4 Ibid.

which has in many ways become the defining cultural characteristic of the whole "Atlantic" civilization. These structures, beginning first with the so-called Long Barrows, and eventually including stone circles and highly elaborate Passage Graves, were the western equivalent of the Egyptian pyramid. At this time too there arose the magnificent temple-building culture of Malta, where there are found the same spiral designs encountered throughout North Africa and western Europe; and it would appear that Malta formed the eastern extremity of a vast maritime cultural area; a cultural area described as "Atlantic Megalithic".

I should make it clear here that I do not subscribe to the idea, popularized recently by more than one author, that the Atlantic Megalithic culture was identical to the Atlantean "Empire." In fact, it is probable that the great majority of the European megaliths were constructed only after the subsidence of the Atlantis island — and most of the surviving structures were raised in the eighth and seventh centuries BC by the Druids. Nevertheless, the ideas and skills behind the Megalithic Culture Complex can certainly be traced back to the Atlanteans. These features, as we shall see, were absorbed by the early Celtic, Germanic and Iberian populations of western Europe and essentially made their own.

NEOLITHIC AND EARLY BRONZE AGE SEAFARERS

One of the skills "inherited" by the Celtic and Iberian megalith-builders was that of seamanship and maritime knowledge. We have already seen that the Neolithic Azilians of Europe were competent sailors, and we recall at this point that the importation by the Capsians of North Africa — in Early Neolithic times — of obsidian blades from the Lipari Isles near Sicily, speaks of regular sea-voyages. In actual fact, there is no question that, by the Late Neolithic at least, the peoples of the Mediterranean had mastered seamanship. We know that in the Eastern Mediterranean sailing ships were being constructed even before the founding of the Egyptian First Dynasty. Illustrations of such vessels are found on a number of predynastic rock carvings, as well as in various Early Dynastic contexts. The sail revolutionized travel by sea and made voyages of truly epic proportions possible. One of the chief concerns of Thor Heyerdahl, in his various expeditions, was to demonstrate just how effective were primitive sailing vessels, especially if they were assisted by favorable currents. During the Ra expeditions he showed fairly conclusively that it was possible to cross the entire Atlantic Ocean in nothing more than a basic reed boat fitted with a primitive sail.

So, from Predynastic times onwards, we must assume that those who lived on the shores of the Mediterranean had the ability to traverse immense distances, both by land and sea. Trade, it seems, was truly intercontinental.

We recall at this point how Carthaginian and Roman writers identified the Cabiri deities of North Africa as the inventors of the ship. The Middle Neolithic folk of Atlantic Europe and North Africa, descendants of the highly-gifted Aurignacians of Spain, were perhaps linked with the Cabiri "folk," who also, we remember, communicated their mystery-cult to the Egyptians on one hand and, in the opinion of Lewis Spence, the Britons on the other. Extensive cultural and economic contacts are in any case indicated by the material remains. Certainly the slightly-later megalith-builders ranged from Scandinavia to Spain and to the Aegean world at least, for their Long Barrows and Passage Graves are related in terms of general concept to the pyramids of Egypt. Their journeys thus took them many thousands of miles, and amber they acquired in the Baltic found its way into Egyptian and Greek burials. Indeed, the full scope and extent of commercial relations during these ancient times has only recently become apparent. And so, for example, it was discovered that lapis lazuli, found in the royal tombs of the Egyptian First and Second Dynasties, as well as in some tombs of the immediate Predynastic Age, could only have come from Badakhshan in Afghanistan.[1] This is fully admitted by archaeologists and denied by no one. In addition, it was discovered, much to the astonishment of academics, that gold from the tomb of Khasekhemwy, of the Second Dynasty, came from the Transylvanian Mountains in Romania.[2] Such materials, could, of course, have arrived in Egypt by overland routes, but the evidence for long sea voyages in this remote time is also there, and increasing.

As we shall shortly see, the rich and opulent (and maritime) Early Helladic culture of Greece, destroyed in a great cataclysm, was the society which must have faced the seaborne aggression of the Atlanteans. One of the greatest of the Early Helladic settlements was not actually in Greece, but on the other side of the Aegean — Troy II. This city, razed to the ground by a terrible conflagration, revealed weapons and tools of tin bronze — thus speaking of contact with western Europe, either Brittany or more probably Cornwall — and a lump of white nephrite, a type of jade that could only have come from the Kunlun Mountains on the borders of China.[3] Strikingly, at least one ancient tradition, recounted by

---

1 Michael Rice, *Egypt's Making* (London, 1990) p. 35.

2 A. R. Burn, op. cit., p. 73.

3 Ibid., p. 72. It is likely that the bronze in Troy II came from Britain, which would imply that it was not the product of a true Bronze Age. As John Dayton showed in his *Minerals, Metals, Glazing and Man*, Britain, uniquely, has deposits of copper and tin already mixed in ore form; and it is likely that these were the source of the first bronze, quite possibly worked for centuries before craftsmen came to realize that bronze could also be produced by mixing tin with copper.

Virgil, links Troy with the mysterious island of Hesperia, a land with the same name as Diodorus' volcanic Atlantic island.

We know that in early times Spain was the hub of a great trading network, and Greek sources talk of a city or country named Tartessus, often identified with Gades or Gadir, which controlled much of this. The same region is known in Hebrew sources as Tarshish, and is mentioned as a source of silver, tin, and lead.

The origin of the word "Tartessus" is interesting. A. Rousseau-Liessens assumes it to be derived from the Berber *tarserts*, meaning "columns of stone," and thus associates it with the "Pillars of Hercules."[1] If the name is indeed Berber, then Tartessus may well have been an Atlantean center, probably part of the kingdom of Eumelus, which survived the general catastrophe of Atlantis' submergence. In any event, it is clear that this part of Spain was a major cultural and economic center during the Neolithic and Early Bronze Ages, as the researches of E. M. Whishaw make abundantly clear.

The Tartessian, Berber, element in Spain seems to have survived into Roman times in the Spanish tribe known as Turdetanians.

By the first phase of literate civilization then we have clear evidence of a thriving international trade along the Atlantic seaboard and throughout the Mediterranean; a trade which brought products to the Aegean from as far away as the British Isles in the west, Scandinavia in the north, and China in the west. Much of this commerce was centered around the Iberian Peninsula. Tin, or at least a tin and copper mixture, was mined in western Britain, gold in Transylvania, lapis lazuli in Afghanistan and jade in China. The use of the sail made enormous sea journeys comparatively easy, and it needs to be stressed that, from the invention of the first sailing vessels at this time until the advent of the Late Middle Ages in Europe, very few improvements were made in the general design of sea-going vessels. In short, any journeys made by Phoenicians or Vikings could just as easily have been made by the "Atlantians" of North-West Africa and Spain in the Early Neolithic.

SECRETS OF THE MEGALITHS

The builders of the barrow graves, dolmens and menhirs which dot the Atlantic coast of Europe and North Africa left behind a mystery that has intrigued scholars for many generations. These monuments, often constructed of gigantic blocks of stone, now look gaunt and bleak amidst the wild moorlands and craggy heaths where they stand. Throughout the centuries, the natives of western Eu-

---

1 A. Rousseau-Liessens, *Les Colonnes d'Hercule et l'Atlantide* (Brussels, 1956).

rope have treated them with superstitious awe, and various lewd customs, often associated with semi-pagan fertility rites, have been attached to them.

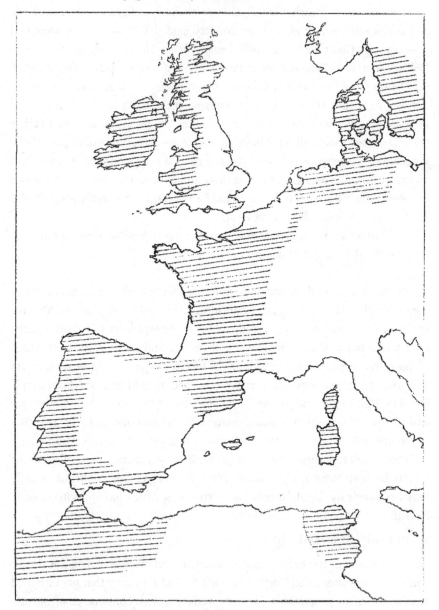

Fig. 14. The Atlantic Megalithic culture area.

Perhaps influenced by these peasant customs, scholars for a long time were not inclined to look favorably upon either the monuments or their builders. They seemed, quite simply, to be the work of primitive barbarians. True, there had been some voices raised in praise of the culture which could raise such structures, but these dissenters were not taken seriously.

All that changed in 1967, when there appeared Professor Alexander Thom's seminal *Megalithic Sites in Britain*. In this book, Thom, Emeritus Professor of Engineering at Oxford, presented the results of an examination of six hundred megalithic sites throughout Britain, conducted over a ten-year period. These monuments, almost without exception, were found to be designed geometrically and aligned astronomically to an astonishing degree of accuracy. Thom found that a common unit of measurement, the "megalithic yard" — 2.72 feet, had been used. With this the builders had constructed not just circles, but ellipses, egg-shapes and flattened circles, all based on an internal geometry that displayed the use of certain right-angled triangles whose discovery has always been credited to Pythagoras. As with Pythagoras, there was evidence that some of the integral numbers used in the dimensions of triangles — for instance, 5, 12, 13, or 8, 15, 17 — had a symbolic or magical significance. This in turn implied a knowledge of the value of π.

With larger structures, such as Avebury, Carnac, and Stonehenge, Thom found that the "megalithic rod" was used, a unit precisely two and a half times the megalithic yard.

Thom came to the conclusion that the megalith-builders were unmatched astronomers. They turned their stone circles into observatories that measured not just simple things, such as midsummer and midwinter sunrises, but a host of sophisticated movements that required an observation accuracy of one part in a thousand. They were even able, he said, to detect the Moon's "minor standstill," a phenomenon caused by its elliptical orbit that has a cycle of 18.6 years.

Thom's book caused a sensation and as might be expected there was initial resistance in academia. Nevertheless, his conclusions were at least widely debated and a new study in 1972 by C. A. Newham (*The Astronomical Significance of Stonehenge*) tipped the balance and won over the skeptics. As a result, it is now freely admitted that the megalith-builders were astronomer-mathematicians of the first order. Professor Richard Atkinson, of Cardiff University in Wales, who had earlier been a bitter opponent of Thom's ideas, explained why he had changed his mind. Thom's work, he wrote, upset, "the conceptual model of the prehistory of Europe, which has been current during the whole of the present century, and even now is only beginning to crumble at the edges ... In terms of this model, it is almost inconceivable that mere barbarians on the remote north-west fringes of the continent should display a knowledge of mathematics and its applications hardly inferior, if at all, to that of Egypt at about the same date, or that of Meso-potamia considerably later.

"It is hardly surprising, therefore, that many prehistorians either ignore the implications of Thom's work, because they do not understand them, or resist them because it is more comfortable to do so. I have myself gone through the latter process; but I have come to the conclusion that to reject Thom's thesis because it does not conform to the model of prehistory in which I was brought up involves also the acceptance of improbabilities of an even higher order."[1]

Acceptance of the achievements of the megalith-builders presented, in some ways, even greater mysteries: How, it was asked, did the astronomer-priests gain this knowledge? And how did they pass it on from generation to generation? As British astronomer Sir Fred Hoyle put it, "a veritable Newton or Einstein must have been at work," and there would have to have been a university or college where students could be taught. In 1967 Dr. Euan MacKie of the Hunterian Museum in Glasgow announced that the believed he had discovered this at a prehistoric site called Durrington Walls, near Stonehenge, where excavations had shown evidence of a diet much richer than usual, and the first evidence of woven cloth.

Scholars are baffled as to how this astronomical and mathematical knowledge could have been passed on without writing. As Atkinson put it, one has to suppose that "the *Astronomical ephemeris* is not published, but is transmitted by word of mouth from its compilers to its users in the form of epic verse which must be strictly memorized and reproduced."[2] Such feats are not impossible. Caesar wrote that the Druid priesthood "was taught to repeat a great number of verses by heart, and often spend twenty years in this institution; for it is deemed unlawful to commit their statutes to writing, for two reasons: to hide their mysteries from the knowledge of the vulgar, and to exercise the memory of their scholars."

Yet, although the master-astronomers may have exercised a prohibition against committing their knowledge to writing, there seems little doubt that writing as such was known to them. Even the practical tasks involved in the construction of a megalith would surely demand some form of record-keeping; and we know, in any case, from the Tartaria tablets, that a system of writing was known in eastern Europe at this very time. It seems probable then that no certain examples of a megalithic script have been found for the simple reason that the astronomers and priests forbade writing on anything but perishable materials, a prohibition we also know existed among the Druids.

---

1 Atkinson, quoted in Francis Hitching, *World Atlas of Mysteries* (Pan Books, 1978) p. 63.
2 Ibid. p. 64.

And the connection with the Druids is not coincidental: For the great majority of the megaliths of western Europe were actually raised by the Druids, as I have argued at length elsewhere.[1] Only the earliest of these monuments, the so-called Long Barrows, can be regarded as dating from the Atlantean period. The Celtic priests were the inheritors of a knowledge bequeathed to them by this earlier culture, one which nevertheless preceded them not by millennia, but by decades.

The Megalithic culture appeared along the western seaboard of Europe and North Africa at the start of the Neolithic Age, and, as E. M. Whishaw showed, had its beginning and its most brilliant manifestation in the south and west of Spain. Here are preserved magnificent temples and tombs, as well as large settlements; and it is to this region that we must turn in our search for surviving relics of the Atlantean culture spoken of by Plato. According to his account, Eumelus, one of the ten kings of Atlantis, was allotted a region near the Pillars of Hercules, which must surely mean Spain and part of North Africa. From the latter territories the custom of mound and megalith-building spread along the coastal regions of northern and western Europe, into the lands of the Celts and the Germans, who copied their more advanced neighbors.

THE ATLANTEAN WAR VIEWED AS HISTORY

It seems possible then, from the state of technology at least, that during the Neolithic a mighty power from the Atlantic, including in one way or another at its peak all the peoples of North Africa and Western Europe, from Spain to parts of Scandinavia, could have posed a threat to the peoples of the Eastern Mediterranean. But if such a power existed, and if it attempted to subdue Greece and Egypt, who did it face on the battlefield?

According to Plato, it was the Athenians who finally put an end to Atlantean ambitions, standing for a time alone against the invaders, before finally repulsing them.

Most commentators have not sought verification for this report from Greek legend, because they believe Plato in placing the action around 9500 BC. Locating the conflict in the Early Bronze Age however might lead us to expect Greek legend to recall it — if indeed the Greeks were involved. Yet the legends of Hellas (prior to Plato) apparently make no reference to any Atlantean war, and, as we saw, preserved only vague hints of a knowledge of Atlantis at all.[2] Nevertheless,

---

1 In my *Arthur and Stonehenge: Britain's Lost History* (2001).
2 One Athenian festival, the Panathenaea, has been suggested by various "Atlantean" writers, beginning with Donnelly, as a memory of the war with Atlantis. The festival, instituted by Theseus, was said to commemorate a battle between Athena and Poseidon. Since Poseidon was the chief god of the Atlanteans, there seemed to be a good match. Yet it was not a human but a divine war that the Panathenaea commemorated, and it

the cataclysm that destroyed the island — a world-wide event — may indeed have occupied a prominent place in Greek history. Hellenic tradition is full of accounts of devastating floods, often associated with vast earthquakes, which sent great tidal waves over the Greek mainland and the Aegean islands. Two of these, the Floods of Deucalion and Ogyges, were remembered for their extreme destructiveness. The Flood of Deucalion was said to have brought an end to the entire human race, excepting only Deucalion and his wife. The Flood of Ogyges was also devastating and apparently connected in the popular imagination with the Titan Atlas and his island, for we recall that Homer speaks of Atlas' daughter Calypso inhabiting an island named Ogygia.

Most probably, the Flood of Ogyges was contemporary also with the cataclysm otherwise known as the Conflagration of Phaeton.

Interestingly, early Christian authors found reason to believe that the Flood of Ogyges had been contemporaneous with the biblical Exodus. Julius Africanus, for example, wrote: "We affirm that Ogygus from whom the first flood [in Attica] derived its name, and who was saved when many perished, lived at the time of the Exodus of the people from Egypt along with Moses."[1] Again, he noted that "The Passover and the Exodus of the Hebrews from Egypt took place, and also in Attica the flood of Ogygus. And that is according to reason. For when the Egyptians were being smitten in the anger of God with hail and storms, it was only to be expected that certain parts of the earth should suffer with them."[2]

Virtually the whole of Greek myth and legend speaks of these vast upheavals of nature. The Heroic Age, an epoch apparently named in honor of the hero *par excellence* himself, Herakles (Hercules), was an age that directly preceded the historical epoch, an age in which gods and men interacted. During this time, Hercules and other semi-divine beings were involved in activities which radically altered the physical landscape. We have suggested that these events were contemporary with and directly related to the catastrophic destruction of Atlantis. Thus many of the deeds attributed to Hercules, we have seen, took place on the Atlantic seaboard, and at least two of them, the stealing of the Golden Apples of the Hesperides (the Hesperides themselves being the daughters of Atlas) and the plundering of the Cattle of Geryon, actually took place on an island in the Atlantic. It was during the expedition to retrieve the Apples of the Hesperides that Hercules took the weight of the heavens on his shoulders, temporarily relieving

seems quite certain that the assault of Poseidon (the Earthshaker) against Athens was a natural event. Nevertheless, there is reason to believe that the giant waves which Poseidon was said to have unleashed against Attica at this time was a local memory of the selfsame cataclysm which destroyed the Atlantic Island.

1 Julius Africanus in *The Ante-Nicene Fathers*, ed. A Roberts and J. Donaldson (1898), VI, 132.
2 Ibid. p. 134.

Atlas. In short, the celestial order, previously upheld by Atlas, was replaced. We note too that Hercules actually dispatches Atlas to steal the apples from his own

Fig. 15. A defeated Libyan chief from a bas-relief of pharaoh Sahura (Dynasty 5). Exactly the same portrayal, complete with the names of the chief and his sons, was copied by a number of later pharaohs, and it may well be that Sahura himself copied it from an earlier pharaoh, perhaps of Dynasty 2 or 3. The first foreign war mentioned by the Egyptian historian Manetho was against the Libyans, during Dynasty 2, and it seems that at that time the Libyans (or Atlantioi) posed the greatest threat to Egypt.

daughters. He, the titan who "knows the depths of the ocean" thereby plunders and denudes his own kingdom, his own island.

It was during this Labor too that Hercules defeated Antaeus in North Africa, a deity recognized as Anti, the Libyan (Atlantean) hero-god.

The theft of Geryon's cattle, from the Red Isle of Erytheia, was accompanied by the establishment of the great pillars at Gibraltar. According to some Greek sources, the hero pushed Europe and Africa apart, whilst others claimed that he had pulled the continents closer together, with the aim of making the channel narrower, thus keeping whales and other sea-monsters out of the Mediterranean.

These events then might well allude to the world-wide catastrophe that destroyed Atlantis. Their very magnitude could well have effaced the memory of prior events, especially human ones such as wars. Yet it appears that the Greeks did indeed preserve a memory of the Atlanteans and their assault on Hellas.

From before the time of Hercules, Greek tradition told of a race named the Telchines, a fierce breed of warriors said to be children of the sea.[1] They were connected with Rhodes, but also with Crete, to which land they migrated. They were the first inhabitants of that country. The goddess Rhea, it was said, entrust-

---

1 *Eustathius on Homer*, p. 771-2.

Fig. 16. Libyan (aka Amazigh, Atlantean) chief of Egypt's Early Dynastic Age; based on Egyptian illustrations. The Libyans of North Africa displayed many cultural features reminiscent of Native Americans, amongst which was the taking of mind-altering drugs for religious purposes.

ed the infant Poseidon to their care, and they forged his trident. Long before this, however, they had made for Cronus the toothed sickle with which he castrated his father Uranus, and they were the first to carve images of the gods.[1] Yet owing to their destructiveness, Zeus resolved to destroy them by a flood. Warned by Artemis, they fled overseas, including to various parts of the Greek mainland.

We might be tempted to regard the Telchines as little more than purely mythic furies, especially when we learn that they were dog-headed and flipped-handed. Nevertheless, there is good evidence to suggest that behind these grotesque images there was a real primeval race, a race to whom the dog was especially sacred. And we recall at this point the Libyan association with the dog and its domestication — an animal that played a special role in the Libyan cult of the dead — whether three-headed, like Cerberus, or dog-headed, like Anubis. We note too a strong Libyan influence on the early culture of Crete. All of which was enough to convince Robert Graves at least of a Libyan-Telchine connection.[2] Another writer, Specht Heidrich of Germany, went a stage further and specifically identified the Telchines as Atlanteans. He notes: " ... the Telchines were feared as the personification of evil. They were magicians who could at will raise clouds, rain, hail and snow and destroy vegetation and animals with Stygian waters ... Even in historical times the Greeks still named a malicious person a 'Telchine', and in Hellenistic Alexandria Kallimachos libelled his opponents as 'Telchines, a race to whom one thing alone is good, raising discord.'"[3] Although Heidrich placed Atlantis on Crete and accepted conventional chronology, he evidently hit upon a real and very old Greek tradition of a people named Telchines who were uniquely corrupt and evil, who were maritime, who were notorious sorcerers, and who were eventually destroyed by a flood. As Heidrich stressed, there seems little doubt that the Greeks of classical times believed the Telchines to have been a real people, a people who waged war against the early inhabitants of Greece. Thus Eusebius, bishop of Caesarea under Constantine, who had access to the literatures of the Greeks, Romans, Egyptians, Babylonians, Persians, and many others, remarked: "Telcisiis et Caryatiis adversum Foroneum et Parrhasios institit bellum." ('The Telchines and Caryatians started a war against Phoroneus [the first man of the Greeks] and Parrhasios.').[4]

If the Telchines were the Atlanteans, this constitutes a genuine native Greek tradition of the war waged against their homeland spoken of by the Egyptian priests. And yet it would appear that at least one other account from Athens tells of the same events. This was the story of Eumolpus. During the reign of king Erechtheus, who was slain by Poseidon, Athens was attacked in great force by a

1 See Robert Graves, op. cit., Vol. 1, 54, a.
2 Ibid. p. 189.
3 Specht K. Heidrich, *Mykenische Geschichten* (Mantis Verlag, 2004) p. 19.
4 Eusebius can. abr. 230.

confederation led by Eumolpus, a son of Poseidon himself and a native of North Africa. It was said that after quitting his homeland, Eumolpus made his way to Eleusis by way of Thrace, where he became priest of the Mysteries of Demeter and Persephone. (We have already seen that the Eleusinian mysteries were closely connected to Libya and the far west). After this, Eumolpus contrived to have himself made king of Thrace, and when war broke out between Athens and Eleusis, he brought a large force of Thracians to the Eleusinians' assistance, claiming the throne of Athens for himself in the name of his father Poseidon. The Athenians were said to have been greatly alarmed, and when Erechtheus consulted an oracle he was advised to sacrifice his youngest daughter Otonia to Athena, if he hoped for victory. Otonia was willingly led to the altar, whereupon her two elder sisters also killed themselves.[1]

In the ensuing battle, Ion led the Athenians to victory, and Erechtheus struck down Eumolpus as he fled. Poseidon appealed for vengeance to his brother Zeus, who at once destroyed Erechtheus with a thunderbolt. But some accounts say that Poseidon himself felled him with a trident blow at Macrae, where the earth opened to receive him.

This legend appears, rather obviously, to be connected with the mythic battle for Athens waged by Athena and Poseidon, which was commemorated in the Panathenia. Yet the conflict, which was marked by natural catastrophe (Poseidon flooded the entire Thriasian Plain and opened great chasms in the earth with his trident), was preceded by a human war involving a seafaring race connected with North Africa, home of Diodorus' and Herodotus' Atlantians. The fact that the invaders are led by Eumolpus, a Libyan and son of Poseidon, is telling, as is his involvement in the Eleusinian Mysteries. Strikingly, Eumolpus meaning "good melody," is almost identical to the name Eumelus ("sweet melody"), carried by one of the sons of Poseidon who reigned in Atlantis. According to Plato, Poseidon's son Gadeirus, who was given that portion of the European continent (Iberia, or Cadiz) closest to Atlantis, was named Eumelus in Greek.

Thus it would appear that the Greeks remembered not only the universal natural catastrophe which consigned the Atlantic island to the depths of the ocean, but several of the human events that preceded it, including the great war waged by the Atlantean invaders against the Hellenes in general and the Athenians in particular. But if this be the case then it raises the question of conditions in Greece at the time. What manner of civilization would the Atlanteans have confronted in the Aegean?

---

1 Apollodorus, iii, 15, 4; Hyginus, *Fabula*, 46.

We have stated that the destruction of Atlantis occurred near the end of the Early Bronze Age, and it so happens that the Early Bronze Age, known in Greece as the Early Helladic Age, was a period of high civilization. The second part of the Early Bronze epoch in particular, Early Helladic II, saw a great flowering of the civilized arts. In the words of one authority: "The second phase of the Early Bronze Age has left the greatest quantity of material evidence. The most striking types of objects, and the most impressive architectural monuments ... This was a prosperous era, a time of enterprising men who sailed the seas; sensitive imaginative people, one must think, who brought home wealth and new ideas from their journeys. Some were rich enough to attain a measure of power in their districts and presumably to rule as princes from their palaces at centers like Tiryns and Lerna, or from forts like the one at Chalandriani in Syros, maintaining contact with their royal cousins in the Hellespont."[1] Attica, named by the Egyptian priests as the power standing firmest against Atlantean aggression, was heavily populated at the time. These early "Hellenes," who raised massive fortifications in various settlements along the coast of southern Greece, were industrious traders with close contacts in Asia Minor and much further afield. In fact, by Late Neolithic times and especially by the beginning of the Early Helladic period they seem to have been in regular contact with the mighty and fabulously rich Vinça civilization of the Balkans (a civilization which we now know to be literate or at least proto-literate), and we can scarcely doubt that it was Greek traders who, acting as middlemen, brought gold from Transylvania across the Mediterranean to Egypt, gold used by Egyptian pharaohs of the First and Second Dynasties to beautify their palaces and tombs.

But this resplendent maritime culture, with its numerous coastal strongholds, came to a sudden and violent end. Thus for example the great settlement at Lerna in the Argolid, with its magnificent House of the Tiles, was razed to the ground in some terrible conflagration. And Lerna's fate was shared by all its contemporaries.

> An era was ended at Lerna with the burning of the [Early Helladic] House of the Tiles; and in the whole surrounding region there are evidences of a similar catastrophe ... it is extremely probable that the great round building at Tiryns, which has a roof of similar tiles, fell at the same time as the palace of Lerna III. There was a disaster also at nearby Asine, where one of the burnt buildings had been roofed likewise with tiles.... A few miles further north, at Zygouries in the valley of Cleonae, houses of the same age were destroyed in a general conflagration.[2]

---

1 John L. Caskey, "Greece, Crete, and the Aegean Islands in the Early Bronze Age," in *The Cambridge Ancient History*, Vol.1 part 2 (3rd ed.) pp. 805-6.
2 Ibid., p. 785.

The writer of these lines believed that the destruction had been carried out by a "foreign invader." Yet whilst human action may have played a part in some sites, the complete overthrow of Early Helladic civilization, not only in Greece itself, but in Asia Minor, cannot surely have been the work of people. And when we remember that the whole of Early Bronze Age civilization throughout the entire Near East suffered a similar fate at the same time, we must look to the action of nature and not of man. This is all the more certain when we recall — as described in Chapter 3 — that many of the Early Bronze sites show the unmistakable signs of earthquake and flood, as well as of fire. Fascinatingly, the Early Helladic settlement of Troy, which was likewise destroyed in a massive conflagration, seems to have had trading links to Atlantic Europe; for artifacts of tin-bronze, which can only have come from Britain or northern Spain, were found there.[1] And Troy was specifically connected to the far west in at least one tradition: Virgil writes that Dardanus, who gave the Trojans one of their generic names, was the grandson of Atlas and came to Asia Minor from Hesperia, a land in the extreme west. There seems little doubt that this Hesperia is identical to Diodorus' mystical isle of Hespera, located in the Atlantic. According to Virgil, Dardanus first settled on the island of Samothrace in the Aegean, but a mighty flood forced him to flee to the mainland. There, at the foot of Mount Ida, he founded the mythical town of Dardania.

We note too that Attica, which had been heavily populated during Early Helladic II, was almost deserted in the time of the rather short-lived Early Helladic III, a brief epoch during which the survivors of the catastrophe sought to re-establish some form of normality. And this of course calls to mind the legendary battle between Athena and Poseidon over possession of Attica, when the sea-god had sent huge waves to flood the Thriasian Plain, wherein stood the city of Athenae. After this, it was said, the goddess founded a new city nearby, also named after herself — Athens.[2]

Assuming then that the Atlantean war really happened, we might be tempted to ask: why? What was the motive? Such a question can never really be answered with any degree of confidence. The store of our knowledge is too meager. Nonetheless, it is right to say that the epoch in which these events took place — the Early Bronze Age — was one in which human sacrifice was still a widespread custom. This would have been particularly so with regard to a people such as the Atlanteans, who occupied a region ever threatened by the volcanic and seismic destruction. We know from other regions of the world that, where such conditions prevailed, human sacrifice continued to be practiced until very recent times, sometimes on an enormous scale. This was the case, for example, in Mexico,

---

1 Ibid., p. 807.
2 Herodotus, viii, 55; Apollodorus, iii, 14, 1.

where the Aztec Empire regularly conducted wars against its neighbors for the sole purpose of procuring hecatombs of victims for the altar.

The invasion of the Aegean and Egypt may therefore have been conducted for this reason. Perhaps it was not a "one-off" at all, but a long-standing tradition of slave-raiding and piracy. And we cannot doubt that the attack or attacks on Greece were by sea. Those against Egypt may well have been by land and sea: The Sahara was then a fertile and well-watered grassland, and the Libyan inhabitants of the region were of the same stock as the Atlanteans themselves. Plato asserts also that Atlantean power stretched across North Africa right to the borders of Egypt.

It is impossible to say what kind of ships the Atlanteans would have used; but that they were sail-powered seagoing vessels is accepted. It is possible, even probable, that they were similar to the sleek ships which we know the inhabitants of Crete and the Aegean used at that time. Indeed, Crete may well have borne the brunt of the Atlantean assault, though it is not impossible that this island was itself an Atlantean vassal, and a base for attacks against the Greek mainland. The striking parallels noted by many researchers between the culture of Minoan Crete and Atlantis, as described by Plato, is explained by the fact that they were contemporary civilizations in close contact with each other. The linguistic and racial affinities of the natives of Crete have never been established, though we know that from Neolithic times at least there were strong cultural links to Libya. It is unlikely however that the Minoans were primarily of Atlantean/Berber stock, though Atlantean outposts may have existed in other parts of the Aegean. Certainly Greek tradition suggests Libyan settlement in certain areas (as witnessed by the story of Eumolpus), and we need bear in mind too that the Etruscans, whose mysterious language has to this day defied interpretation, were at the same time believed to have originated in Asia Minor and to have formed part of the Atlantean confederacy.

Much more likely, however, is that the major Atlantean base in the region was the strategically vital island of Malta, whose magnificent megalithic monuments strike the visitor as the work of a highly cultured people.

All this however is speculation. What we can say is that attacks against the inhabitants of Greece by Atlantean raiders would probably have taken the form of lightning-fast raids, rather like those of the later Vikings. Siege-warfare would then have been unknown; and in this far-off time battles were fought with the bow, the spear, the club, and the stone (or copper) axe.

When then did all this happen? In considering this question we need to bear in mind the evidence, mentioned throughout the present volume, for a radical down dating of the whole of ancient civilization. Taking this into account, and bearing in mind also that the myths relating to Hercules seem to speak of events surrounding the catastrophe that destroyed the Island of Atlas, we note that Greek tradition placed Hercules just a few generations before the Trojan War. The traditional date of the fall of Troy is given as 1184 BC, yet (as I have also shown elsewhere) Hercules and his myth is precisely contemporary with Moses and the Exodus (Moses himself being clearly identifiable as an alter-ego of Hercules),[1] an event whose proper position in the chronology of the ancient world has long been controversial. I shall argue that the destruction of Atlantis was in fact precisely contemporary with the Exodus of the Israelites from Egypt; and that the two disasters were local manifestations of the same world-wide upheaval.

When exactly this occurred, in terms of dates, we shall discuss in the final chapter.

THE ATLANTEAN WAR IN EGYPTIAN TRADITION

According to the accounts of Plato and Diodorus the Atlantean/Amazon (or Amazigh/Libyan) war was a major event in Egyptian history. If it occurred within the historical period, as we claim, we must expect Egyptian tradition to have recalled it. The Egyptians of course preserved a written chronicle of their history dating back to the very foundation of the kingdom. If we cannot therefore find reference to the conflict in the Egyptian records, we must seriously question whether it is historical. But if we seek the event in the hieroglyphic records, where should we look?

According to the chronology proposed in these pages, the Atlantean power would have flourished during the time of the first three Egyptian dynasties. Since the account of Plato seems to suggest that the destruction of the island occurred very shortly after the great war of conquest, the present author is inclined to place the conflict during the period of the Third Dynasty. This epoch, as I have demonstrated in great detail elsewhere, was terminated by a catastrophic upheaval of nature.[2] It was a catastrophe recalled in biblical tradition as the Exodus and was simultaneous with the destruction of Atlantis.

Does Egyptian tradition during the time of the Third or perhaps Second Dynasty speak of a war against a great power in the west, of a war against the Libyans, perhaps?

---

1 As I have argued in great detail in *The Pyramid Age*. Moses, like Hercules, has a mysterious birth: he destroys the two serpents created by pharaoh's magicians, just as Hercules strangles the two serpents sent to destroy him in his cradle; he pushes apart the waters at the Sea of Passage, as Hercules pushes apart the Pillars that bear his name; he ascends a mountain (Horeb) at the end of his life, just as Hercules ascends Mount Oeta at the end of his.

2 In my *Genesis of Israel and Egypt* and my *Pyramid Age* (2nd ed. 2007).

Throughout her history, Egypt was involved in many wars against the Libyans. These peoples, highly civilized like the Egyptians themselves, are known by various names in the hieroglyphic monuments, the most common designation being Tjehenu, Tamahu, and Meshwesh. Other names were also used, though less frequently. The last-mentioned title, Meshwesh, would appear to be identical to the Maxyes of Herodotus, known to the Romans as Mazaces, or Mazax. It is generally agreed that this name is one and the same as the Berber Amazigh — the "Amazons" of Diodorus.

The first recorded conflicts between Egyptians and Libyans come right at the start of dynastic civilization. Thus from the First and Second Dynasties, we find mention of hostile action against the Tjehenu, and there is a suggestion that these encounters were part of an ongoing and bitter struggle. According to I. E. S. Edwards, "There can be little doubt ... that the traditional enmity between the Egyptians and both Libyans and the Asiatics of Sinai, which so often found expression in parallel scenes carved on the walls of later temples, originated at this time [Early Dynastic Period]."[1] But even though the Egyptians were at odds with the Libyans, this people seemed to be held in inordinately high esteem by the inhabitants of the Nile Valley. Thus for example right from the beginning of the Old Kingdom Egyptian queens were portrayed with blond hair, or blond wigs, obviously in imitation of Libyan hair or hairstyles. This is admitted by archaeologists, though why it should be so is not understood.[2]

Owing to the sparse and fragmentary nature of the hieroglyphic records, it is impossible to reconstruct the political history of Egypt during the Early Dynastic Age. Fortunately, the Hellenistic scholar Manetho provides us with rather more information. Although his history of Egypt, the *Aegyptiaca*, is lost, important fragments are preserved in the writings of Julius Africanus and Eusebius. And what we find here is telling. According to the account of Africanus, major conflict with the Libyans came during the Third Dynasty. Of Necherophes, the first ruler of the Third Dynasty, we are told that: "In his reign, the Libyans revolted from the Egyptians; when the moon waxed unexpectedly, they surrendered out of panic." In Eusebius' version, it is the sun that waxes (appears) unexpectedly.

It will not take a great stretch of the imagination to understand that the "revolt" of these Meshwesh, or Amazigh, is the "Amazon" war mentioned by Diodorus against Egypt. Nor will it be necessary to explain in detail how the "unex-

---

1 I. E. S. Edwards, "The Early Dynastic Period in Egypt," *The Cambridge Ancient History*, Vol.1 part 2, (3rd ed.) p. 47.
2 See e.g., W. Stevenson Smith, "The Old Kingdom in Egypt and the Beginning of the First Intermediate Period," *The Cambridge Ancient History*, Vol.1 part 2 (3rd ed.) p. 171.

pected" waxing of the sun or moon represents the cosmic event which was itself directly responsible for the destruction of the island empire.

Manetho's comment, brief though it is, is an unequivocal reference to the supposedly mythical war of Egyptians and Atlanteans mentioned by Plato. As such, we must now regard the Atlantean war as an historical event in the true sense of the term.

I do take issue with Manetho in one regard. He places the Libyan conflict in the reign of a Necherophes, described as the first pharaoh of the Third Dynasty. Yet the hieroglyphic monuments know of no king named Necherophes. Most now see Djoser, whom Manetho names Tosorthros and regards as the second king of the Third Dynasty, as the first pharaoh of the line. However, the monuments do speak of a ruler named Nefer-ka-ra (also written as Ka-nefer-ra) at the end of the dynasty. In another place, I have argued in detail that it was this Nefer-ka-ra, or Khenephres, who reigned during the Exodus, and in whose time a great natural catastrophe struck the earth.

It seems to me, then, that Necherophes should be regarded as identical to Nefer-ka-ra, and that the "Libyan" or Atlantean war should be placed at the end of the Third Dynasty, rather than the beginning.[1] The catastrophe which destroyed Atlantis was one and the same cosmic event that precipitated the Exodus.

Before finishing, it should be noted that the earliest monumental depiction of war with the Libyans comes in a bas-relief of Sahura, second pharaoh of the Fifth Dynasty. In it, he is shown smiting the Libyan leader, who is accompanied by his consort and offspring, all of whom are named. There are, however, serious doubts as to whether this is a record of anything actually accomplished by Sahura himself, for exactly the same scene, copied word for word and line for line, appears in a bas-relief of Neferirkara, also of the Fifth Dynasty, as well as in a carving of Pepi II (Sixth Dynasty) and later still in a monument of Tirhaka (Twenty-Fifth Dynasty). The scene is in all cases reproduced precisely, even down to the names of the sons of the defeated Libyan chief, Wni and Wsa. This naturally must lead us to suspect that the scene is formulaic, a venerated icon from the past, which Sahura himself may have copied.

If so, it can have only one source: It must be a record, carved originally by pharaoh Nefer-ka-ra of the Third Dynasty, of the epic battle for survival fought by Egypt against the greatest threat she ever faced.

---

1 The placing of Necherophes, or Nefer-ka-ra at the start of the Third Dynasty, rather than the end, may be explained by the very often confusing way kings and dynasties are listed on the Egyptian monuments. At the end of a line of rulers, it is not always easy to understand, at a glance, where the new line should begin.

CHAPTER 5. THE FINAL LINK

THE CHRONOLOGY OF THE ANCIENT WORLD

The Atlantic Megalithic culture, we have seen, must in some way be the material manifestation of the Atlantean civilization — or at least those parts of the Atlantean civilization which had spread beyond their island home onto the mainland of Europe and North Africa. The main flowering of this Megalithic culture is recognized as contemporary with Egypt's Early Dynastic Age, which itself is generally placed between circa 3200 and 2600 BC. A vibrant and powerful Early Minoan civilization existed at the same time on Crete; and it would have been the folk of this society, together with those of Second or Third Dynasty Egypt, who faced the Atlantean invaders on the field of battle.

The megalith-builders of the west, with their widely-attested seafaring abilities, their architectural skills, and their contacts with the eastern Mediterranean, are just the people who could have inspired the inhabitants of the Americas to erect their own megaliths, their own mounds and pyramids, and establish civilizations in many ways strikingly similar to those of the Old World. But here we encounter a grave problem. It is a problem which has bedeviled and stymied all serious debate on the Atlantis question for over a century. According to accepted ideas, the Megalithic civilization came to an end sometime in the early second millennium BC. If this marked the eclipse of Atlantis and its destruction, then it cannot have been the culture to inspire the early Americans, for they are known to have commenced their own pyramid- and mound-building only in the first millennium, or at the very end of the second millennium BC — say around 1100

BC. By this time, it is believed, the megalithic-building culture of Europe, as well as the pyramid-building culture of Egypt had long disappeared.

The answer to this problem has already been suggested in the third chapter of the present study, and is scarcely less dramatic than anything else we have asserted in the foregoing pages: The truth is, the chronology of the ancient civilizations of the Old World is distorted to an enormous degree. Contrary to what is stated in the textbooks, the literate cultures of the Old World had no 2,000-year head-start over those of the New. In fact, all the civilizations on both sides of the Atlantic arose more or less simultaneously around 1100 or 1200 BC at the earliest!

This may seem an astonishing statement to make. Egypt, for one, is said to have had a history beginning around 3200 BC, and historians confidently list the names of kings and dynasties to fill all the centuries stretching between 3200 and 525 BC, when the Persians conquered the country. If Egyptian civilization really only commenced around 1100 BC, what happens to all the rulers said to have lived in the two millennia beforehand? And, even more to the point: How was such a monumental mistake made?

It would be impossible to give a thorough answer to these questions in the space of a single volume, much less a single chapter. Over the past twenty years I have worked on a series of books, named "Ages in Alignment," which examine chronologies of the ancient civilizations in detail. There it is shown that the histories of Egypt and Babylonia, which we now possess, are based on the chronology of the Old Testament, and not upon an independent examination of Egyptian and Babylonian literature or archaeology. Thus by the early centuries of the Christian era, and even before, we already had a history of Egypt that was tied to the Bible, with Adam, for example, being equated with Menes, the first pharaoh. Since Jewish tradition placed the Creation around 3,750 BC, this was fixed as the date for the commencement of the First Dynasty, and the rest of Egyptian history was made to fall in behind, with important biblical events which involved Egypt forming anchor-points. Thus for example the Book of Exodus asserted that the Israelite slaves built a city named "Ramesses," and Bible scholars noted, from the lists of Manetho, a great pharaoh named Ramesses, who reigned over sixty years. It was therefore decreed that Ramses II was the pharaoh of the Exodus, and he was accordingly made to reign around 1,450 BC, a date he still occupies, more or less.

By the beginning of the sixteenth century, the "traditional" Bible-based history of Egypt had become firmly entrenched in European halls of learning. Refinements were indeed made by such scholars as Calvisius and Scaligar, but the essential biblical framework was not altered, and it is true to say that it has not been altered to this day. Illustration of this fact comes most famously from the lips of no less than Napoleon Bonaparte who, in 1798, just immediately prior to the Battle of the Pyramids, exhorted his men with the words "Forty centuries look down on you." The French commander therefore placed the building of the Great Pyramid around four thousand years before his time, i.e., around 2,200 BC — within little more than a couple of centuries of the date (c. 2550 BC) still found in the textbooks! Yet Napoleon made his speech over twenty years before Champollion had even read the first line of hieroglyphs and established the science of Egyptology!

In essence, then, the chronology found in the textbooks has nothing to do with science, and everything to do with the Bible. But this begs the question: What then is the true chronology of Egypt, and how to establish it?

TECHNICAL KNOW-HOW OF THE PYRAMID-BUILDERS

It is known that Egypt's great age of pyramid-building came shortly after the establishment of the first monarchy. Right from the beginning of the First Dynasty, smallish stepped-structures, part of the mastaba-tomb complexes, were being erected. By the Third Dynasty these had expanded greatly and, in the reign of King Djoser, acquired the aspect of real monumental architecture. Under him, the first true pyramid was erected. Less than a century after Djoser the pharaohs of the Fourth Dynasty were raising perhaps the greatest man-made structures ever conceived.

When we come to consider the pyramids erected by Cheops and the other pharaohs of the Fourth Dynasty at Giza we are presented with clue after clue about the true chronology of the epoch; clues which have tragically been overlooked in an almost willful fashion. Quite apart from the immense dimensions of Cheops' and Chephren's pyramids, a number of other features strike the modern observer as problematic in the extreme. Indeed, so strange are these that the recently-invoked intervention of aliens as a solution becomes almost believable.

To begin with, the pyramids were aligned precisely with the cardinal points of the compass, showing only an infinitesimal margin of error. Nineteenth century archaeologists were so impressed by these structures that they openly questioned whether they should be assigned to a remote antiquity at all. They were struck by various modern-looking features of the monuments. The arch, for example, which otherwise made its appearance in the 7th century BC, was already being employed in the temples and tombs of the pyramid-builders.[1] Partly influenced by such evidence it was then suggested that not all the work attributed to the Old Kingdom was genuine, and that the monuments of the time had been extensively renovated and modified during the 8th and 7th centuries BC. Flinders

---

1 Flinders Petrie, *Egyptian Architecture* (London, 1938) pp. 71-2.

Petrie considered this idea but rejected it because, "Not a hieroglyph, not a graffito, can be seen anywhere associated with these supposed reconstructions."[1] Thus the monuments of the Pyramid Age were not reconstructions, though they contained very modern-looking features.

Even worse was to emerge.

By the middle of the 20th century study of the Great Pyramid and its dimensions had become something of an obsession, both among mainstream archaeologists and the "fringe." Whether mainstream or fringe, it was clear to all that the architects and artisans who raised the structure were master craftsmen, whose methods and techniques remained mysterious. New discoveries only deepened the mystery. By the middle of the 1970s for example it became apparent that the architects had a knowledge of Pythagorean geometry. That, at least, was the conclusion reached by Peter Tompkins, whose *Secrets of the Great Pyramid* was the result of decades devoted to a study of the monument. According to Tompkins, the artisans had a knowledge of the value of π, the circumference of the earth, and the length of the year down to its 0.2422 fraction of a day. Tompkins, as conscientious a scholar as may be imagined, reached conclusions that were truly startling. The central burial chamber, for example, is said by him to have "incorporated the 'sacred' 3-4-5 and 2-3-5 triangles (a + b = c) which were to make Pythagoras famous, and which Plato in his *Timaeus* claimed as the building blocks of the cosmos."[2]

But the geometry employed by the architects is almost a trivial problem when we come to examine the materials used in the building. As is well-known, the inner chambers and corridors, including the great Ascending Passage, are carved of the finest Aswan granite. Indeed, granite was used with frequency by the pyramid-builders, as was the even harder basalt and diorite. The latter stone, which is of almost diamond-like hardness, was employed by sculptors during the Fourth Dynasty to fashion images of the pharaohs and the gods.

Now, the problem with all of these materials is that they cannot be worked without good-quality carbon-steel tools. That, at least, is the opinion of all modern artisans whose opinion has been sought. Over the years, there have in fact been many attempts to replicate the techniques and tools used by the pyramid-builders; and a fairly comprehensive overview of these attempts was provided by Charles Ginenthal in his 2004 book, *Pillars of the Past*. As Ginenthal notes, the debate on the technology employed by the Fourth Dynasty architects began at an early stage. Both I.E.S. Edwards and Flinders Petrie put forward their own suggestions, neither of which could be described as satisfactory. Petrie believed

1 Flinders Petrie, *A History of Egypt*, Vol. 1 (1894) p. 60.
2 P. Tompkins, *Secrets of the Great Pyramid* (London, 1977).

that the "granite and hard stones were ... cut with tubular drills." The saw blades were, he believed, of copper, in which were inserted abrasive gravels and sharp stones, often made of emery. "The is no doubt," he said, "that sawing and grinding with loose powder was the general method, but the use of fixed stones seems clearly shown [as well]."[1] But according to Ginenthal: "Petrie has made it quite clear that the saw markings are indicative of blades that cut, not with powder, but with hard teeth. He also offered that diorite, an extremely hard rock, was engraved by an extraordinarily thin point, 150th of an inch thick. His list of minerals to accomplish these tasks includes 'beryl, topaz, chrysoberyl, corundum or sapphire and diamond.' But did the Old Kingdom craftsmen possess these necessary materials as teeth for saws or points for punches or graving tools?"[2] This was a question also considered by Barbara Mertz, who could find no evidence that the Egyptians employed any of these.

It is fairly evident then that copper saws equipped with teeth fashioned from these types of gemstones cannot be invoked as a method of cutting granite and diorite. But, perhaps in desperation, historians have proposed copper saws fixed with abrasive powders as a solution (in spite of the clearly observed saw-teeth marks on many of the monuments). I.E.S. Edwards, along with several others, suggested that copper saws with quartz sand and gypsum as abrasives, which can in fact cut limestone, could also have been used on harder stones. Thus Lehner writes: "It is most likely that a copper drill or saw was employed in conjunction with an abrasive slurry of water, gypsum and quartz sand. The copper blade simply acted as a guide while the quartz sand did the actual cutting."[3] On this suggestion, Ginenthal writes, "The problem with this method is that copper is actually softer than quartz sand and also softer than granite, schist, basalt, and diorite. Rather than cutting into these stones the quartz sand will destroy the copper blade. While this method will work with soft limestone, it is not possible to use it with these harder stones."[4] The impossibility of using an emery abrasive attached to a copper saw was demonstrated years ago by the mineralogist H. Garland, who noted that, „By the use of emery powder anointed with oil or turpentine, no measurable progress could be made in the stone, whilst the edge of the copper blade wore away and was rendered useless, the bottom and sides of the groove being coated with particles of copper."[5]

---

1   F. Petrie, *The Arts and Crafts of Ancient Egypt*, (London, 1909) pp. 72-73.
2   C. Ginenthal, *Pillars of the Past* (New York, 2004) p. 200.
3   Mark Lehner, *The Complete Pyramids* (London, 1997) p. 210.
4   C. Ginenthal op. cit.
5   H. Garland and C.O. Bannister, *Ancient Egyptian Metallurgy* (London, 1927) p. 95.

In Ginenthal's words, "The test proved that the copper-abrasive method will not cut granite or diorite using emery powder or, as Garland stated, 'by any similar means.' Thus, sand-quartz will also destroy the copper blade and will fail to cut the hard stone."[1] Flint too is useless for the purpose.

Another hypothesis, one put forward regularly to this day, is that the Egyptian craftsmen pounded the granite with a hammer made of an even harder stone, such as diorite; and that this method, though extremely slow and laborious, would produce results. The softer granite, it is believed, crumbling under the hammer-blows, then simply had to be smoothed with a rough stone which acted as an abrasive. But, "Garland has shown that if one attempts to employ this method, say, on a granite sarcophagus, one will not be able to cut straight vertical corners inside the coffin; yet the insides of granite coffins exhibit straight vertical corners where the walls meet. 'Any rubbing process would surely have robbed the corners [of any stone] of all sharpness.'"[2] Denys Stocks further notes that, "The use of stone mauls for pounding calcite, granite, basalt, quartzite and graywacke from the interiors of sarcophagi is impracticable: the force of the blows would soon have cracked the shaped stone blocks."[3]

How then were the fine lines found on Pyramid Age sculptures achieved? Again, it was suggested that some form of hardened copper was used. It is true that hammering will harden copper, but the hardness achieved is quite insufficient to cut through granite, never mind diorite. Christopher Dunn, a master craftsman and engineer thoroughly familiar with metals and their qualities, comments on the belief of Egyptologists that hardened copper chisels could have done the work: "Having worked with copper on numerous occasions, and having hardened it in the manner suggested above, I was struck that this ... [belief] was entirely ridiculous."[4]

Yet some form of sharp, pointed tools *were* used. Petrie has described engraved diorite cut to "one hundred and fiftieth of an inch wide." Copper chisels will simply not do the job.

The early historians fully understood that steel was the only material capable of carving and engraving such hard stones. However, being unable to free themselves from the shackles of conventional chronology, they were incapable of even making an approach to a solution. Sir Gardiner Wilkinson long ago realized this but could not disentangle the problem because he also supported the long

---

1 Ginenthal, op. cit.
2 Garland and Bannister, op. cit. p. 96.
3 Denys A. Stocks, "Stone sarcophagus manufacture in ancient Egypt," *Antiquity*, vol. 73 (1999), p. 919.
4 Christopher Dunn, *The Giza Power Plant* (Santa Fe, New Mexico, 1998), p. 74.

---

chronology. He noted that, "No one who has tried to perforate or cut a block of Egyptian granite will scruple to acknowledge that our best steel tools are turned [blunted] in a very short time, and require to be re-tempered: and the labor experienced by the French engineers, who removed the obelisk of Luxor from Thebes, in cutting a space less than two feet deep, along the face of its partially decomposed pedestal, suffices to show that, even with our excellent modern implements, we find considerable what to Egyptians would have been one of the least arduous tasks."[1]

Wilkinson quotes Sir R. Westmacott that chisels "of strong tempered iron, about three-quarters of an inch in diameter . . . [can] resist the heat [of being pounded into granite before becoming blunted] sometimes half an hour, seldom longer . . . Tools of less diameter . . . of steel . . . will not resist 300 strokes...."[2] Yet, as Ginenthal notes, "we are expected to believe that copper chisels with edges much thinner than these engraved diorite with exquisite hieroglyphs."

Notwithstanding all this, scholars have not abandoned their attempts to explain the achievements of the Egyptians in terms of copper tools. This of course is inevitable, so long as the conventional chronology is unquestioned. As a rule, however, whenever an engineer, metallurgist or sculptor is asked to comment on the notion that granite and diorite were carved with copper tools, the result is always the same: Incredulity. Thus stonemason Roger Hopkins wrote:

> I am a stone mason by trade and in 1991 the PBS [Public Broadcasting System] series NOVA invited me to go to Egypt to experiment with building a pyramid; I quickly got bored with working the soft limestone and started to ponder the granite work. Here in Massachusetts my specialty is working in granite ...
>
> When I was asked by the Egyptologists how the ancients could have produced this work with mere copper tools, I told them they were crazy.[3]

In fact, the evidence, which I have explored in great detail in my *Pyramid Age*, shows conclusively that the Giza pyramids could not have been constructed before the 9th/8th century BC and that, if technology and culture, rather than the Bible, had been used to date Egyptian history, that is exactly where they would have been placed. *The Pyramid Age* is but one of a series of volumes, entitled Ages in Alignment, wherein there is presented manifold proofs that the chronology of the ancient civilizations is radically and dramatically wrong; and that all the Near Eastern cultures, the civilizations of Egypt, Syria, Mesopotamia and Ana-

---

1 Sir J. Gardiner Wilkinson, *A Popular Account of the Ancient Egyptians* Vol. 2 (London, 1878) p. 156.
2 Ibid. p. 157.
3 Cited from Ginenthal, op. cit.

tolia, began more or less simultaneously around 1100 or 1150 BC in the wake of a great upheaval of nature. The cultures of the Near East are thus, at last, brought into harmony with those of the Americas and the Far East, which have always been recognized as commencing around 1200 BC.

A NEW PERSPECTIVE

If Egypt's First Dynasty commenced around 1,100 BC, then the great Megalith-building culture of Atlantic Europe and North Africa commenced at the same time, or perhaps a little earlier. This means, of course, that the Atlantic sailors, who colonized the coastal regions of western Europe, could easily have influenced the first civilizations of the New World. Pyramid- and mound-building really did begin simultaneously in the Old and New Worlds. Finally, we can make sense of the detailed parallels observed by Donnelly, Spence, and the others.

It would appear that, immediately after the Deluge cataclysm the volcanic island which stood at the core of the Mid-Atlantic Ridge survived. It may have been reduced in size, but it was still there. As seen in Chapter 3, and as I have argued in greater detail elsewhere, it was at this time that in various parts of the earth men established the first civilized societies. It was the very cataclysm that they had so recently witnessed that impelled them to do so: Hence the advent of star-worship, temple building and sacrificial rituals, ideas completely unknown to the highly-intelligent and creative folk of the Paleolithic.

The first civilizations of the New World were thus contemporary with the earliest civilizations of the Old, and it now becomes clear, for example, that the great city of Tiahuanaco must have been raised at the same time as the monuments of Early Dynastic Egypt — before the final catastrophe which sank Atlantis, turned the Sahara into a desert, and allowed the Israelites to escape from Egypt. Most probably, Tiahuanaco was built around the same time as pharaoh Djoser's Step Pyramid at Sakkara in Egypt. It can thus claim to be among the oldest of all human monuments.

If Peruvian legend is anything to go by, Tiahuanaco would have been constructed by the Viracochas, the Atlanteans. Most probably, since the artwork is clearly native American in style, Atlantean wanderers worked alongside locals to produce the finished structures. Certainly nothing like Tiahuanaco was ever raised in Europe or North Africa. The nearest the megaliths of these regions come to Tiahuanaco, in terms of refinement, may be the temples of Malta. It is true, of course, that the great passage graves of Spain, especially around Los Millares, display a high degree of skill in stone-carving. Yet the quality of workmanship falls well behind that of the Andean structures. Much of course remains to be discovered in Spain and, more especially, in North Africa. Certainly there exists near the Moroccan port of Lixus cyclopean structures displaying a very refined stone-dressing capacity, and it is possible that many truly astonishing structures of the megalith age may yet await discovery.

Nevertheless, it is evident that the white-skinned Atlanteans, did not establish a unified empire with a single culture stretching from South America to Europe and North Africa. We remember that the white race was already established in the Americas before the cataclysm which ended the Paleolithic; and it was probably these people, not later Atlantean arrivals, who raised the walls of Tiahuanaco.

The final cataclysm of the age, the one which destroyed Atlantis, occurred around 850 BC and terminated once and for all the transatlantic connection.

But bringing the end of Atlantis down to 850 BC has dramatic consequences for our view of early European and Near Eastern history. It means, first of all, that the Atlanteans must have interacted with the early Celts and that, most probably, they influenced Celtic culture in a profound way. It means too that Celtic legends which spoke of a lost island in the ocean make perfect sense and no longer need to be viewed as an almost miraculous survival of a tradition going back nine thousand years.

ATLANTEANS AND CELTS

The Megalithic-building civilization of Western Europe was not, as we have seen, a manifestation of the Atlantean culture. The megaliths were raised after the destruction of the Atlantic island. Nevertheless, the knowledge, skills and science of the priest-kings who oversaw the building of these structures was indeed derived from the Berber-speaking Atlanteans, who, prior to the cataclysm that destroyed their Atlantic base, roamed far and wide throughout the western seaboard of Europe. Whether or not they actually conquered and colonized these lands is a moot point. Perhaps they did, though it is more likely that, in some places at least, they simply came as traders and left their cultural imprint behind in the local populations, much as they appear to have done in the Americas.

Placing the end of the Atlantis civilization around 850 BC, as we do, means that this point marks the eclipse of the Berber-speakers as a real power in Europe. Some groups of them no doubt survived, and it seems possible that the mysterious Ligurians of northern Italy and southern Gaul, as well as the Turdetanians of Spain, may have been of Berber speech. Yet by the time of Atlantis' destruction, the Berbers/Imazighen had already made a powerful impact upon the other peoples of the continent, most especially the Celts, who obviously interacted with them on many levels. As we shall shortly see, the Irish Celts in particular, who seem to have earlier inhabited the Iberian Peninsula, were heavily influenced by the Atlanteans, and, after their settlement in Ireland they erected monuments strikingly similar to those found in Spain, where Berber-speakers and Iberians seem to have interacted.

Precisely the same thing occurred throughout the British Isles, as well as north-western France and Scandinavia.

Not all of the interaction between Celts and Atlanteans can have been peaceful. Indeed, we must assume almost the precise opposite. The Carthaginian writer Himilco, of the late fifth century BC, left a detailed history of the Atlantic seaboard and its peoples. The bulk of his work is lost, though one or two fascinating fragments are preserved in some of the classical authors. Thus Rufus Festus Avienus provides the following excerpt, describing the invasion of the British Isles by the Celts.

> Whoever dares to push his ship beyond the Oestrymnic isles [probably Scilly isles] into the waters where under the northern constellation the air grows rigid reaches the land of the Ligurians, now uninhabited; for the bands of the Celts have long wasted it with many a battle. The Ligurians defeated — as fate so often brings about — came to these regions, which they hold amid the rough thickets. Thick in these parts lie rocks, stern cliffs, and mountains threatening the sky. Within such bounds the fugitive race long led a timid life, withdrawn from the waves; for because of the ancient danger they feared the sea. Afterwards repose and peace, when security had strengthened their courage, induced them to come down from their mountain lairs and descend again to the coastal lands.

The natives fled to the mountains at the time of the Celtic invasion. But it was not so much the Celts they feared as the sea, whence came an "ancient danger." What, we might ask, was this ancient danger that threatened the inhabitants of the coastal lands? The fragments of Celtic tradition which survived the Roman conquests have rather a lot to say about this danger. In a famous passage of Ammianus Marcellinus, where he quotes Timagenes, we read:

> According to ancient druidic teachings, the population of Gaul is only partly indigenous, and expanded at various times to include foreigners from across the sea, and people from beyond the Rhine who had to leave their home either because of the hardships of war, a constant problem in those countries, or because of the invasion of the fiery element that roars on their coasts.[1]

What, we may ask, was the "fiery element" that roared on the sea? Did the Druids here refer to tidal waves or fiery disturbances in the skies? Notably, disturbances in nature are here linked to tribal migration. This is an element in Celtic tradition that we encounter with great frequency.

---

1 Ammianus Marcellinus, xv, 9.

The Cimbri were one of the most renowned tribes of antiquity, and they too had a legend, alluded to by Strabo, of forced migration caused by the action of the sea:

> How are we to suppose that the Cimbri were driven from their original homeland by a high tide in the ocean when we now see them today living in those same places? ... Is it not absurd to suppose that a whole people could be driven from their homes by resentment against a natural and continual phenomenon which recurs twice a day? In any case, this extraordinary tide appears wholly fictitious, since variations in the level of ocean tides are quite regular and seasonal.[1]

Indeed the ocean tides are quite regular and seasonal, and it is just this fact that gives credence to the Cimbrian legend: for the Cimbri were no doubt well aware of the normal behavior of the tides, which strongly indicates that the tide of which they spoke was wholly abnormal. Continuing in his skeptical tone, Strabo exclaims:

> Neither do I believe ... that the Cimbri brandish their weapons at the mounting waves to drive them back, nor, as Ephorus says of the Celts or Gauls, that they train themselves to fear nothing by calmly watching the sea destroy their homes, which they later rebuild, and that the floods have claimed more victims among them than war.[2]

Another strong hint that these destructive waves from the sea were far from being normal tide-action or storms is provided by Aristotle, who specifically links them with earthquakes. Speaking of human courage, he muses: "When one goes to the extent of fearing neither earthquake nor rising waves, as the Celts claim to do ..."[3]

Small wonder that the evil Celtic goddess of death and battle, Morrigan/Morgana, was "born of the sea" (Muir-gen).

The legends of Ireland and Wales, as we saw earlier, spoke at length of cataclysmic inundations and other forms of natural disaster; and we shall have more to say on these presently. The important thing to remember here is that these traditions make it very clear that the destruction of Atlantis, as recounted in Plato and elsewhere, cannot be separated by any great stretch of time from the epoch of the Celts. The vast earthquakes, the inundations, the fiery disturbances in the skies: these were phenomena experienced by all the peoples of the earth at the same time.

There can be no question then that the dawn of the Celtic epoch corresponds precisely to the termination of the Atlantean. Earthquakes and giant tsunamis

---

1 Strabo, vii, 2.
2 Ibid.
3 Aristotle, *Nichomachean Ethics*, viii, 7.

devastated huge areas. Famine broke out, and populations were set in motion. War broke out, as desperate people fought for the few resources that were left. In Western Europe, remnant Berber-speaking populations survived along the Atlantic seaboard. These people mixed with and influenced the Celts, a people with whom they were probably in any case well acquainted. Many Berber/Atlantean ideas, including the erection of megalithic standing-stone structures, were adopted by the Celts. Amongst these can be counted the final phase of Stonehenge, Stonehenge 3. As I have shown elsewhere in great detail, Stonehenge 3, was probably raised by the Druids around 700 BC, and was intimately connected to the Arthurian myth.[1] Merlin, Arthur's Druid, was said to have built Stonehenge, but the monument occurs also in the guise of Arthur's Round Table — which also, incidentally, was said to have been fashioned by Merlin.

During the 8th century BC and afterwards Britain became immensely important to the great civilizations of the Near East as a source of tin and tin-bronze, and a flourishing trade developed between the island and the Levant. The central icon of British mythology, the Sword in the Stone, is well-recognized as referring to the creation of bronze swords which, unlike iron swords, are pulled fully-formed from a stone mould. Arthur, or more appropriately Artus (his name among the continentals), was actually a Celtic bear-god (Artos), a Hercules-figure who was portrayed with a bearskin over his head and shoulders and large oak club in his hand. The famous chalk figure, the so called Cerne-Abbas Giant, is a portrayal of this primeval Arthur. It can be shown that the Greeks were heavily influenced by the early Britons and incorporated many Celtic elements into their own mythology. Even Hercules, whom Herodotus claimed was the father of the Celts, was a direct derivation of the British Artus, and the Greeks themselves placed many of Hercules' adventures in the land of the Celts.

They even, on occasion, preserved Celtic names; and thus Hercules was said to have taken part in the hunt for the wild boar of Calydon. But Calydon (Caledonia), of course, was the ancient name of Scotland!

Megalith-building then continued among the Celts (and Germans) of the Atlantic seaboard, and there is evidence that some standing-stones were erected even in the post-Christian centuries. This is certainly the case in Scandinavia, where the standing-stones were often engraved with runic inscriptions, giving the name of the chieftain who had raised it.

The influence of the Atlanteans then upon the peoples of western Europe was profound and enduring. There seems little doubt too that many of the secret doctrines of the Druids, that priestly order said by Caesar to have originated in

---

1 In my *Arthur and Stonehenge* (2001).

Britain, contained much of the lore of the Atlantean priest-astronomers who had earlier spread the custom of star-worship and temple building throughout western Europe.

The Atlantean-Celtic link, long suspected by researchers, can at last be verified and vindicated.

IRISH AND WELSH TRADITION

The Irish, we have noted, had a strong tradition of a lost or sunken island in the ocean, an island they named Hy Brasil. But Irish legend had much else to say.

When the first Christian missionaries arrived in Ireland, they found a rich culture with a powerful oral and written tradition. The latter is not widely accepted, though it is freely admitted that the Celts of Spain knew how to write at least five or six centuries before Christ. In any event, it was said that the early missionaries examined many of the Druids' volumes, and Saint Patrick was related to have condemned and burned hundreds of them! What is not in doubt is that the Druids were charged with preserving the history and traditions of the nation intact, and that much of their knowledge was subsequently written down by Christian monks. These books, some of which have survived, often name the pagan volume from which the information was derived. Thus, by the beginning of the Middle Ages, the Irish could show travelers a written history of their nation claiming to stretch back some thirty-five generations (about 800 or 900 years) into the pre-Christian past. This history listed the names and deeds of the various High Kings of the island, from the first settlement of the land. According to these accounts, the ancestors of the Gaels had earlier inhabited north-west Spain — the region of Galicia — and, at a time of great disturbances in the natural order, had sailed northwards over the Bay of Biscay and colonized Ireland.

Various books tell the history of the island even before the arrival of the Gaels. These speak of the country inhabited by races of giants and demigods (Fomhor and Tuatha De Dannan), who had engaged in a titanic struggle. The Fomhor, or Fomorians (from the Gaelic meaning "beneath the sea") had threatened to submerge Ireland under the ocean; but they were defeated in a great battle at Magh Tuireadh (the "Plain of the Tower"). This is quite evidently a Celtic version of the universally-encountered myth of a clash between gods and giants (in Greek myth between Olympians and Titans), which in an earlier age had threatened the whole planet with destruction. The Greek myth also had a tower, for the Titans were said to have piled mountains one on top of the other in an effort to assault Olympus. The resulting tower was smashed when Zeus struck it with his thunderbolt.

The Irish legends also relate that on more than one occasion that entire island was swept by great tides from the ocean. These waves were said to have annihilated virtually the entire population.

Elsewhere I have examined the world-wide legend of the Tower (or World Tree) and the cataclysms associated with it.[1] Suffice to say here that this represents an event from natural history subsequent to the Great Deluge. As we indicated in Chapter 2, the Deluge itself must be placed sometime around the middle of the second millennium BC, probably near 1,300 BC, and was occasioned by the earth's close encounter with an enormous comet. Over the next few centuries, until circa 850 BC, the great comet periodically approached the earth, with cataclysmic consequences for our planet. The catastrophe recalled in the Tower Legend seems to have occurred around 1,100 BC.

Irish myth of course, like all ancient mythology, has localized the Battle of the Tower, and turned a cosmic event into something that took place in Ireland. In reality, of course, the Gaels probably still inhabited Northern Spain or, equally likely, the Celtic homeland in central Europe, during these events. Any human inhabitants of Ireland would likely have been swept away by enormous tides. It seems in fact that the colonization of Ireland by the Gaels occurred after 850 BC, and that it was the cataclysm of that time — the very one which finally destroyed the Atlantis Island — that impelled the early Hibernians out of Galicia.

The various accounts of how the first of the Gaels arrived in Ireland present a vivid description of a world in turmoil, of the forces of nature unleashed in a terrifying manner. So, for example, when the first ships of Lugaidh and his followers arrive off the coast, they are driven back out to sea by a mighty tempest, a tempest so powerful that it raises the gravel from the ocean-bed to the surface. And when the settlers do disembark, their troubles are not over: everywhere, in the months and years that follow, there are reports of rivers and lakes "erupting" (the Irish word used is *tomaidhm*), and it is clear that the land is beset by some major seismic disturbances, disturbances so powerful that rivers change their courses and lakes overflow. Occasionally, we are told of major inundations of the sea; inundations not so powerful as those spoken of in an earlier age, but terrifying enough.

Welsh tradition too, as well as that of the continental Celts, also speaks of major irruptions of the sea and terrifying seismic phenomena; and it should be noted at this point that at Stonehenge the massive stone lintels are secured to the uprights by mortise and tenon joints, as if to prevent them falling off in an earth tremor. In Welsh tradition the poet Taliesin, a contemporary of Merlin (Myrd-

---

1 In my *Arthur and Stonehenge* (2001).

din), who was credited with building Stonehenge, spoke at length of the destructive power of the sea, which is clearly related to earthquake activity.

Ho, that sound, is it the earth quaking?

Is it the sea overflowing from its usual banks to reach the feet of men?

Taliesin's utterances illustrate how the terrors of ancient times were incorporated into the colorful body of medieval Romance:

> When Amaethon came from the land of Gwyddyon, from Segon with the powerful gate, the storm raged for four nights at the height of the fine season. Men fell, even the woods no longer sheltered against the wind of the deep. Math and Hyvedd, the masters of the magic wand, had unleashed the elements. Then Gwyddyon and Amaethon held counsel. They made a shield so strong that the sea could not engulf the best of the troops.[1]

Other medieval Welsh poets of the old tradition gave an important place to the same theme. One of the most famous catastrophe stories from Wales is that of Cantref Gwaelod, or the "Submerged Hundred," which recounts how the Plain of Gwddeu, or Gwddno, was drowned. This story makes its first appearance in the Black Book of Carmarthen, written around 1200. The Plain, it seems, was overwhelmed by the sea by reason of the wickedness of its inhabitants. The person who let loose this judgment upon the land was a maiden, Mererid, who, at a time of feasting, suffered the waters of a magical well which was under her charge to escape and overflow the country. The "Triads of Britain" tell how Seithennin, son of Seithin Saidi, king of Dyved, "let in the sea, over Cantref Gwaelod, so as to destroy all the houses and lands in the place, where prior to that event, there had been sixteen cities, the best of all the towns and cities of Wales, excepting Caerleon upon Usk. This district was the dominion of Gwyddnau Garanhir, King of Cardigawn. The event happened in the time of Emyrs, the sovereign. The men who escaped the inundation came to land in Ardudwy, in the region of Avron, and in the mountains of Snowdon, and other places that had hitherto been uninhabited."[2] The Black Book of Carmarthen records the disaster thus:

> Seithenhin, arise, go from here and see the green battle-line of the waves.
> The sea has covered the land of Gwyddno again.
> Cursed be the girl, guardian of the spring, who sighed before freeing the fearful sea.
> Cursed be the girl, guardian of the spring, who sighed before freeing the ravaging sea.[3]

---

1 *Book of Taliesin*, poem xv.
2 Cited from Spence, *History of Atlantis*, pp. 125-6.
3 *Black Book*, poem xxxviii.

Events of this type occupy an altogether more prominent place in Welsh tradition than the general public is aware of. Indeed, in the words of Lewis Spence, "The native myths of Britain contain [numerous] ... references to cataclysmic insular disturbances ... associated more with volcanic or seismic upheaval than with flood."[1] This is precisely what we find in Ireland, where, as we saw, there are literally hundreds of accounts of seismic upheavals that changed the courses of rivers and emptied (or created) lakes. Evidently the "vast eruptive age" mentioned by Percy Fawcett, when speaking of the history of the Andes, came to an end only seven or eight centuries before the start of the Christian Age.

EARTHQUAKES AND *KLIMASTURZ* IN THE FIRST MILLENNIUM

Chapters 2 and 3 of the present volume were devoted to an examination of the physical, as well as literary evidence of cosmic catastrophes. These were clearly identified as events of the historical age, and their signature is found everywhere in the remains of the Bronze Age. We have suggested that the Bronze Age should be redated and that the great civilizations of this epoch only arose around 1100 BC or even later, and that the Bronze Age, as such, only came to and end in the Middle East in the seventh or even sixth centuries BC.

Such being the case, we might expect the catastrophic disturbances of nature, which in Chapters 2 and 3 we have said occurred throughout the early part of the Bronze Age, to have left their mark also in Europe. As a corollary to this, we might expect the catastrophes described so vividly in Celtic myth to have left their signature in the archaeology of western Europe.

In fact, the disturbances of nature recorded in Celtic tradition have left their mark clearly in the archaeological and geological records.

During the early Celtic Age, generally regarded as signified by the "Urnfield" culture, the peoples of central and western Europe frequently dwelt in villages constructed in the middle of lakes. R. Nordhagen and H. Gams were among the first to survey these lake dwellings in a scientific manner. To their great surprise, they found that those of the Alps and southern Germany were not abandoned gradually, but were overwhelmed, in the eight century BC, by massive inundations of water. These disastrous events were accompanied by powerful tectonic upheavals. Lake shorelines were tilted from the horizontal, in a manner that could only have occurred through the action of tremendously powerful earthquakes. Such, for example, was the case in the Ammersee and the Wurmsee in the foothills of the Bavarian Alps, as well as in other lakes on the fringes of the

---

1 Spence, *History of Atlantis*, p. 139.

Alps.[1] It was noted that Lake Constance had risen thirty feet at the time, whilst its bed was tilted dramatically. The same effects were observed in regions far removed from the Alps, especially in Scandinavia.[2] These disruptions also dated from the eighth century BC. A number of European lakes, such as the Ess-see and Federsee, were emptied of all their water as a result of these events. The Isartal (valley of the Isar) in the Bavarian Alps, was "violently torn out" in "very recent times." Around the Inntal in the Tyrol, the "many changes of river beds are indicative of ground movements on a grand scale." Apparently all the lakes of the Swiss Alps, as well as the Bavarian Alps, the Tyrol, and the Jura, were subjected to the same forces.

It hardly needs to be stressed that the overwhelming of lakes and disruption of rivers thus disclosed by science accords exactly with the great natural events recorded in the Celtic traditions.

Nordhagen and Gams presented extensive evidence demonstrating that these disasters were accompanied by sudden climatic changes. Analysis of flora and fauna showed there had been a marked deterioration of the European climate sometime in the eighth century. This evidence, together with the findings of other scholars, was placed before scientists gathered for the International geological Congress in Stockholm in 1910. It was demonstrated there that major climatic fluctuations had taken place throughout the globe over the past few thousand years.

Since the 1910 Congress much work has been done in this field, and it is now well accepted that a great climate "plunge" or Klimasturz happened throughout Europe, Asia and North America at the end of the Subboreal Period, i.e., in the eighth century BC. The most extensive work was carried out by Scandinavian scientists. One of these, Rutger Sernander, noted that "The deterioration of the climate must have been catastrophic in character."[3] G. Kossina, another prominent scientist of the period, agreed that the change had been brought about with suddenness. Scientists from many fields noted that changes in the flora were especially marked. Areas that had supported temperate deciduous forests of oak and beech were almost overnight denuded of their cover. In some areas these were replaced by pine, in others by peat. The latter was the case in the British Isles, and most especially in Ireland, where peculiar conditions resulted in the rapid formation of extensive peat bogs. It is still possible, in Ireland, to view the

---

1 R. Nordhagen and H. Gams, "Postglaziale Klimaänderungen und Erdkrustbewegungen Mitteleuropa," *Mitteilungen der Geographischen Gesellschaft in München*, XV, Heft 2 (1923), pp. 17-44.

2 Ibid. pp. 34, 225-42.

3 R. Sernander, "Klimaverschlechterung, Postglaciale" in *Reallexikon der Vorgeschichte*, ed. Max Ebert, VII (1926).

stumps of ancient oak forests which died in the eighth century BC, underlying the country's enormous peat bogs. On the continent too Nordhagen and Gams discovered, from analysis of pollen, a "radical change of life conditions, not a slow building of fens."[1]

This of course merely scratches the surface of a vast body of evidence relevant to our subject. Throughout the world, scientists have noted similar effects from the ninth, eighth and seventh centuries BC. In some places (as in Ireland and Scotland) beaches were raised, on occasion by hundreds of feet. In other places, but especially in England and Wales, land was submerged. Some coastal areas of Wales display drowned forests, thus giving spectacular confirmation to the Welsh legends which spoke of precisely these occurrences.

A NOTE ON RADIOCARBON DATING

Before concluding, we note that an objection of a most fundamental nature may be raised against the argument outlined in the foregoing pages. All the conclusions we have reached are heavily dependent upon a radical adjustment of chronology. If the Pleistocene epoch really came to an end over ten thousand years ago, and if this event had nothing whatsoever to do with the catastrophes which directly preceded the rise of the first civilizations in the Near East, and if, furthermore, the Old World civilizations are two thousand years older than those of the New, then none of the conclusions we have reached are valid. Thus we have argued that the six-thousand year gap between the end of the Paleolithic and the rise of the Near Eastern civilizations, plus the further two-thousand year gap between the Near Eastern and American civilizations, is a myth; and that all the world's civilizations arose simultaneously in the immediate aftermath of a great catastrophe which terminated the Paleolithic and Pleistocene epoch, and that this catastrophe occurred sometime near the middle of the second millennium BC. Yet according to the textbooks, the end of the Pleistocene, plus the rise of the Near Eastern civilizations, is accurately fixed by scientific proofs; and the most important of these involves the techniques of the nuclear age; that of radiocarbon dating.

It is indeed true that textbooks and other learned publications regularly publish radiocarbon results which seem to fix the Old, Middle, and New Stone Ages, as well as the Bronze Ages, in the places we have rejected. Actually, the confidence with which scholars quote radiocarbon and other dating systems leaves the average reader in no doubt that these questions are thoroughly settled, and that radical readjustments such as the one proposed by the present author are utterly impossible.

---

1 Nordhagen and Gams, loc cit. p. 94.

In order to see whether this is the case, we need to look briefly at radiocarbon dating and its application.

In 1949 Willard Libby, of the University of Chicago, suggested that since all living things absorb a radioactive isotope of carbon, known as carbon 14, and that since immediately an organism dies it ceases to take in carbon 14 — and the amount of radioactivity in the body then begins to decrease — this might be a useful tool to gauge when something died. According to atomic theory, the rate at which carbon 14 decays into normal carbon is constant, it is (or should be) comparatively simple to determine when the organism died by measuring the amount of radioactivity still in it.

Note that it is assumed that the proportion of carbon 14 in the atmosphere was always the same as it is now. This assumption is of course based squarely on the Uniformitarian supposition that conditions on the earth were always more or less the same. Yet if the catastrophes we have spoken of in the present volume actually happened, then atmospheric conditions in the past were most certainly not as they now are. Since these cataclysms were accompanied by the release into the atmosphere of vast amounts of gas and debris of all kinds, there is absolutely no way we can know what conditions were like earlier. By itself, this is more than enough to render the whole system virtually worthless. Since atmospheric disturbances continued into the ninth and even eighth centuries BC, it is highly likely that no radiocarbon data preceding the epoch of the Roman Empire could be accurate.

It is only the modern academic establishment, which, in its arrogance and blindness has dismissed the ancient accounts of cataclysms as worthless, who could take radiocarbon results seriously.

As a matter of fact, even establishment academics admit (though rarely publicly) that radiocarbon dating is at best a deeply flawed system. It is now widely accepted that a problem analogous to that of ancient catastrophes, namely the release into the atmosphere of large amounts of "old carbon," or carbon from fossil fuels, can seriously distort results. This is named the "Seuss effect" in honor of Hans Seuss, the Austrian chemist who first called attention to it. Since old carbon contains a depleted proportion of carbon 14, the plants and animals taking it in will consequently hold much less of the radioactive isotope in their bodies. This in turn will make them look much older than they really are; and the massive use of fossil fuels in the nineteenth and twentieth centuries — with their attendant release of great amounts of "old" carbon — has led to some startlingly anomalous results. In the words of one commentator; "We are told that plants in a rich old carbon environment were radiocarbon dated several thousand years older than they actually were, and a tree by an airport was actually dated to be 10,000 years old."[1]

Thus it is admitted that the first prerequisite of radiocarbon dating — the constancy of initial conditions — may not in fact always be a given. It goes without saying that ancient catastrophes would have released huge amounts of old carbon, as well as various other types of unusual gasses, into the atmosphere.

The second prerequisite — the constancy of rate of decay — rests on equally shaky grounds.

On a most obvious level, samples can be contaminated, and it is usually virtually impossible to know that they have been. Contamination comes in many forms, and can either increase or decrease the readings, making the sample under investigation appear either much younger or much older than it is. The most simple, yet possibly most pervasive form of contamination is that of water. Water can literally wash the radioactivity out of a sample, making it look older. There is absolutely no way of knowing whether a sample has been exposed to water; and we need only consider the traditions of great floods mentioned in the present volume to see that virtually everything in the ground has been thoroughly washed by the action of water on many occasions.

Just how much water contamination can affect radiocarbon results was dramatically illustrated in a Horizon documentary screened by the BBC.[2] An Englishman who, in a fit of remorse, had confessed to murdering and dismembering his wife, brought police to the spot where he had buried her head. Sure enough, the detectives soon uncovered the partial skull of a woman, complete with some still surviving fleshy tissue. They were astonished however when scientists from the British Museum, who had not been informed of the skull's provenance, radiocarbon dated it and declared it to be 1,500 years old! Other forensic scientists however, who reconstructed the woman's features from the skull, declared that in their opinion the body was indeed that of the vanished wife. The documentary concluded by offering the opinion that bodies found in boggy conditions take on the date of the sodden earth wherein they are interred. In short, the water had leeched the radiocarbon isotope from the remains, making them appear vastly older than they were.

Given this remarkable fact, one which in any case has always been well understood by the scholarly community, we may well wonder how esteemed academics can then propose to use radiocarbon readings of samples of wood, leather

---

1 Charles Ginenthal, "The Extinction of the Mammoth." *The Velikovskian* (special edition), Vol. III, 2 and 3 (1999) p. 184.
2 BBC 2, *Horizon*, 4th March, 1999.

and bone recovered from the ground that have endured millennia of rainfall and river floods. Yet such readings are still regularly published, without comment.

We should note that with wood there is an added complication: A tree can live for hundreds of years, but at any given time only absorbs carbon into its outermost layer. Thus it is necessary to know the age of the tree when it was cut down, as well as the part of the tree from which the timber was taken. Yet once again, timber is indiscriminately dated by laboratories and the results published without comment.

Another — and major — problem is the tendency of scientists to dismiss anomalous results that do not conform to preconceived ideas. Thus a very substantial number of results from Egypt and Mesopotamia have produced startlingly recent figures; yet these have not been published, or have at best been reduced to footnotes, because, ironically enough, the researchers have deemed them to be "contaminated." In the words of one eminent scholar: "Some archaeologists refused to accept radiocarbon dates. The attitude probably, in the early days of the new technique, was summed up by Professor Jo Brew, Director of the Peabody Museum at Harvard, 'If a C14 date supports our theories, we put it in the main text. If it does not entirely contradict them, we put it in the footnote. And if it is completely "out of date," we just drop it.'"[1]

An example of this pernicious practice is seen in the fate of samples from the tomb of Tutankhamun subjected by the British Museum to radiocarbon testing. The samples, consisting of fibers of a reed mat and a palm kernel, produced dates of 844 BC and 899 BC respectively. These were broadly in line with the date for Tutankhamun predicted by Velikovsky, but roughly 500 years too recent for textbook chronology. In spite of assurances given to Velikovsky that the results would be published, they never saw the light of day.[2]

The problems outlined above merely scratch the surface. The whole question of how we date the ancient past will need to be reconsidered in a fundamental way. Other "scientific" systems, such a dendrochronology, have entered the fray over the past couple of decades, only to confuse the picture even further. Ultimately, they have all been used very much as statistics unfortunately are: to prove whatever the researcher wishes to prove. And we note here the cautionary comment of scientist Gwen Schultz, who insisted on the necessity of acknowledging the possibility "that all methods [of dating] used today are wrong."[3]

---

1 David Wilson, *The New Archaeology* (New York, 1974) p. 97.
2 Velikovsky, *Peoples of the Sea* (1977) p. xvi.
3 Gwen Schultz, *Ice Age Lost* (New York, 1974) p. 28.

Finally, the reader may imagine it presumptuous of the present author to question the methods and techniques of so many eminent and highly respected scholars. Yet where does the real presumption lie? Does it not lie with those establishment academics who have systematically derided the value of tradition; who have scoffed at the notion that the catastrophes spoken of by the ancients could be real; and who have systematically suppressed the evidence of geology, of paleontology and of archaeology, which speak of those same catastrophes in a voice scarcely less eloquent than the writers of antiquity themselves?

EPILOGUE

We have completed, in the foregoing pages, a far from exhaustive survey of the relevant evidence. Indeed, the evidence available is so extensive that many volumes would perhaps be required to examine it properly. Nevertheless, what has been presented has been, I think, sufficiently persuasive to shift the burden of proof onto the skeptics. Of course, Plato could have invented the whole Atlantis story to make a political point; he could furthermore have been extremely lucky in placing a chain of volcanic islands due west of Gibraltar, where the volcanic Azores stand today. He could have been lucky too in stating that a great continent stood at the other side of the ocean.

By the same token, Diodorus could have lied when he said that in his time the people of the western Atlas region called themselves "Atlantians," and he could have been less than truthful when he told of their being conquered by a tribe of "Amazons" who lived on an enormous volcanic island in the ocean. That these "Amazons" conquered all of North Africa and attacked Egypt, just like Plato's Atlanteans, could have been coincidence. Coincidence too may explain the similarity between the word Amazon and "Imazighen," the name still used by the white-skinned and blue-eyed Berbers for themselves.

It could be that the Irish, Welsh, Bretons, Spaniards, Berbers and Canary Islanders all coincidentally decided to invent an entirely fictitious story of a lost island in the middle of the ocean.

The clear evidence discovered by geologists of a great sunken landmass in the Azores region may be explained as a feature of the distant past, long before people appeared on the earth; and coincidence too may explain why ancient men spoke of a sunken island in just the same place.

The cultural parallels between the Early Bronze Age civilizations of the Old World and the New, with pyramid-building, mummification etc., could likewise be just coincidental. And the parallels identified in an earlier age, the Paleolithic, may be explained away in a similar fashion. Alternatively, the Paleolithic culture-bearers may really have hopped (as many commentators have seriously suggested) in small canoes, from ice-floe to ice-floe, around the rims of a frozen North Atlantic.

Again, those who brought their western European/North African mitochondrial DNA to the shores of the New World may have reached there by the same channels; even women, it seems, in those far-off days dared to cross the frozen wastes of an Ice Age Atlantic in kayaks. And it may be only pure coincidence that the Native Americans, some of whom possessed the same fair hair and blue eyes as the Berbers/Atlantians, also told of a great island in the ocean that acted as a bridge to the lands on the far shores of the great sea.

Maybe the tobacco and cocaine found in some Egyptian mummies got to Egypt by some other route; or maybe these plants were brought to Egypt by later Phoenician traders, who nevertheless kept the great continent across the ocean a closely-guarded secret. Perhaps too the Libyans of North Africa, who almost unique amongst the peoples of the Old World, wore feathered headdresses, derived that idea not from the Native Americans, but from somewhere else.

And so it goes on and on. But just how many coincidences, lucky guesses and self-serving fictions (which also happen to be lucky) can an honest observer take? The geological and paleontological evidence, on its own, proves that cataclysmic upheavals of nature, involving massive movements of the earth's tectonic plates, occurred in very recent times. The evidence collected by Schaeffer, Velikovsky, and a veritable host of others, proved beyond question that these events continued until early in the first millennium BC. The geological evidence from the Atlantic Ocean, shorn of ideological preconceptions, proves beyond question that massive volcanic and seismic events occurred around the Mid-Atlantic Ridge in the very recent past. How else could vast beaches, still showing their original contours and features, lie over a thousand meters down and over a thousand miles from the present shore-line?

The geological evidence, by itself, should have been enough to end the debate. Yet it did not. Indeed, it faced the fate of many "anomalous" scientific findings which radically contradict the prevailing paradigm: It was noted in learned journals, declared to represent a "puzzle" and then quietly forgotten. The same fate, we may justifiably fear, might await the DNA evidence, the archaeological evidence and the forensic evidence. All of these are conclusive. Yet we should not underestimate the ability of the establishment to sweep uncomfortable facts under the carpet. Already we see signs of a closing of ranks. There have been strident attempts, for example, to explain the Clovis populations's Caucasian affinities and the European DNA in Native Americans in terms of a Siberian/Bering Strait link — completely ignoring the fact that Clovis culture has no affinities whatsoever with contemporary Siberian cultures. In the same way, there have been attempts to "explain" the tobacco found in the Egyptian mummies as another plant of the deadly nightshade family native to Africa — completely ignoring the fact that cocaine was found along with the tobacco. Paradigm shifts do not necessarily come about as a result of the accumulation of evidence. And should Atlantis be accepted, or even seriously considered, then many, very many, academic reputations will be in peril. Yet in this case even more than the egos of academics is at stake: For the Atlantis question brings us face to face with our whole view of the past, of life and its development and even of our future. We cannot even begin to consider Atlantis without asking fundamental questions about evolution, about catastrophes and extinctions, and about the age of the planet. To question what the textbooks say about these topics is not merely heresy; it borders on blasphemy. Here we tread not just on the egos of scientists and authors, but on the whole belief-system underpinning the Modern, or perhaps more accurately, the Darwinist Age.

The powers that be will surely not permit these dogmas to be questioned lightly. The tragedy is, it may in the end take nothing less than another "Atlantean" type catastrophe to change minds that are so closed.

CHRONOLOGY

Date, BC	EVENT	EGYPT	ISRAEL	GREECE	MEXICO
1400	GREAT FLOOD		Flood of Noah	Flood of Deucalion	Sun of Water catastrophe.
1100	CATASTROPHE	Catastrophe of Menes	Tower of Babel	Theomacy. War of Titans.	Sun of Wind. Destruction of Tower.
		First and Second Dynasties	Early Patriarchs		

950	CATASTROPHE	Famine of Djoser.	Famine of Joseph.		Sun of Earthquake.
		Third Dynasty	Exile in Egypt		
850	CATASTROPHE	Intermediate Age.	Exodus	Phaeton/ Hercules	Sun of Fire

Table 5

Date BC	Epoch	Culture	History
1350	Paleolithic Age	Flint-working and, in some places, pottery and early use of copper.	"Golden Age" before the Flood.
	GREAT FLOOD		
1300-1100	Mesolithic/ Neolithic	Some pottery. Invention of the bow.	Rise of priest-kings and temples.
	CATASTROPHE		
1100-950	Early Bronze 1	Some metallurgy and primitive writing.	Blood sacrifice.
	CATASTROPHE		
950-850	Early Bronze 2 and 3	Major structures in stone.	Age of pharaoh Djoser.
	CATASTROPHE		
850-		Giant megaliths and pyramids.	Pharaoh Cheops and Chephren.

BIBLIOGRAPHY

BOOKS:

Abbott, C. C., Haynes, H. W., and G. F. Wright, *The Paleolithic Implements of the Valley of the Delaware* (1881)

Alexander, H. B., *Latin American Mythology* (1920)

Allan, D. S., and J. B. Delair, *When the Earth Nearly Died* (London, 1994)

Andreyeva, E. V., *Vekoviye zagadki (Age-old Riddles)* (Moscow, 1954)

Bancroft, H. H., *Native Races of North America*, 5 Vols. (London, 1875-6)

Bellamy, H. S., *Built before the Flood* (1953)

Bogachov, V. V., *Atlantida* (Yuryev, 1912)

Bourcart, J., *Geographie du fond des mers* (Paris, 1949)

Brasseur de Bourbourg, C. E., *S'il existe des Sources de l'histoire primitive du Mexique dans les monuments égyptiens, etc.* (Paris, 1864)

Brunton, Paul, *A Search in Secret Egypt* (London, 1935)

Burn, A. R., *Minoans, Philistines and Greeks* (London, 1930)

Catlin, George, *Manners, Customs and Conditions of the Indians of North America*, 2 Vols. (1841)

Cuvier, Georges, *Essay on the Theory of the Earth*. (English trans. of *Discours sur les révolutions de la surface du globe, et sur les changements qu'elles ont produits dans le règne animal*) (Paris, 1822)

Dana, J. D., *Manual of Geology* (4th ed, 1894)

Darwin, Charles, *Geological Observations on the Volcanic Islands and Parts of South America*, (London, 1851)

Davies, Edward, *Celtic Researches* (London, 1804)

Dayton, John, *Minerals, Metals, Glazing and Man* (London, 1978)

De Camp, L. Sprague, *Lost Continents*, (New York, 1970).

Deloria, Vine, *Red Earth, White Lies* (1997)

Don Fernando de Alvara, "Ixtlilxochitl," *Obras Historicas*, 2 Vols. (Mexico, 1891)

Donnelly, Ignatius, *Atlantis: the Antediluvian World* (New York, 1882)

Donnelly, Ignatius, *Ragnarok: the Age of Fire and Gravel* (New York, 1883)

Dörpfeld, W., *Troja and Ilion* (1902)

Dunn, Christopher, *The Giza Power Plant* (Santa Fe, New Mexico, 1998)

Evans, Sir Arthur, *The Palace of Minos at Knossos*, 4 Vols. (1921-35)

Fawcett, Percy Harrison, *Exploration Fawcett* (London, 1953)

Firestone, Richard, Allen West and Simon Warwick-Smith, *The Cycle of Cosmic Catastrophes: How a Stone-Age Comet Changed the Course of World History* (2006).

Forrest, H. E., *The Atlantean Continent: its bearing on the Great Ice Age and the distribution of species* (2nd ed. London, 1935)

Garland, H., and C.O. Bannister, *Ancient Egyptian Metallurgy* (London, 1927)

Geikie, J., *The Great Ice Age and Its Relation to the Antiquity of Man* (London, 1894)

Ginenthal, Charles, *Pillars of the Past* (New York, 2004)

Graves, Robert, *The Greek Myths*, 2 Vols. (Penguin, 1955)

Hancock, Graham, *Underworld: The Mysterious Origins of Civilization* (Three Rivers Press, 2003).

Heidrich, Specht K., *Mykenische Geschichten* (Mantis Verlag, 2004)

Hitching, Francis, *World Atlas of Mysteries* (Pan Books, 1978)

Imbelloni, J., and A. Vivante, *La livre des Atlantides* (Paris, 1942)

Katz, Friedrich, *The Ancient American Civilisations* (English ed. George Weidenfeld and Nicolson, 1972)

Khain, V. E., *Proiskhozhdeniye materikov i okeanov* (*Origin of Continents and Oceans*) (Moscow, 1961)

Klenova, M. V., *Geologiya morya* (*Geology of the Sea*) (Moscow, 1948)

Lehner, Mark, *The Complete Pyramids* (London, 1997)

Lyell, Charles, *Principles of Geology* (London, 1830-33)

Machatscheck, F., *Das Relief der Erde* (2nd. ed. Berlin, 1955)

Malaise, Rene, *Atlantis en Geologisk Verklighet*, (Stockholm, 1951)

Malaise, Rene, *Sjunket land i Atlanten*, (Stockholm, 1956)

Markham, Clemens, *The Incas of Peru* (1910)

Mazarovich, A. I., *Osnovy regionalnoi geologii materikov* (*Fundamentals of the Regional Geology of Continents*), Part 2 (Moscow, 1952)

McEnery, J., *Cavern Researches, or discoveries of Organic remains and of British and Roman Relics, in the caves of Kent's Hole, Anstis Cove, Chudleigh and Barry Head* (London, 1859)

Merezhovsky, D. S., *The Secret of the West* (English trans. J. Cournos, London, 1933)

Mushketov, D. I., *Regionalnaya geotektonika* (*Regional Geotectonics*) (Moscow, 1935)

Petrie, Flinders, *A History of Egypt*, 4 Vols. (London, 1894-1905)

Petrie, Flinders, *Egyptian Architecture* (London, 1938)

Petrie, Flinders, *The Arts and Crafts of Ancient Egypt*, (London, 1909)

Petrie, Flinders, *The Making of Egypt* (London, 1939)

Pettersson, Hans, *Atlantis och Atlanten*, (Stockholm, 1944).

Posnansky, A., *Tiahuanaco, the Cradle of the American Man* (1945)

Reid, C., *Submerged Forests* (London, 1913)

Rice, Michael, *Egypt's Making* (London, 1990)

Rickard, T. A., *Man and Metals* (2nd ed. New York and London, 1932)

Rockenbach, Abraham, *De cometis tractatus novus methodicus* (Wittenberg, 1602)

Rousseau-Liessens, A., *Les Colonnes d'Hercule et l'Atlantide* (Brussels, 1956)

Rudbeck, O., *Atlantica, sive Manheim very Japhete posterorum sedes ac patria* (Uppsala, 1675)

Schaeffer, Claude, *Stratigraphie comparée et chronologie de l'Asie Occidentale (IIIe et IIe millénaires)* (Oxford, 1948)

Scharff, R. F., *European Animals* (London, 1907)

Schultz, Gwen, *Ice Age Lost* (New York, 1974)

Schweitzer, Bernhard, *Herakles, Aufsätze zur griechische Religion und Sagengeschichte* (1922)

Short, John T., *North Americans of Antiquity* (1882)

Spanuth, Jurgen, *Atlantis of the North* (London, 1980)

Spence, Lewis, *History of Atlantis* (London, 1927)

Spence, Lewis, *The Mysteries of Britain* (London, 1928)

Sweeney, Emmet, *Arthur and Stonehenge: Britain's Lost History* (Domra Publications, 2001)

Sweeney, Emmet, *The Genesis of Israel and Egypt* (2nd ed. Algora, 2008)

Sweeney, Emmet, *The Pyramid Age* (2nd ed. Algora, 2007)

Talbott, David and Wallace Thornhill, *Thunderbolts of the Gods* (Mikamar Publishing, 2005)

Thom, Alexander, *Megalithic Sites in Britain* (London, 1967)

Tompkins, P., *Secrets of the Great Pyramid* (London, 1977)

Vallaux, C., *La gographie generale des mers* (Paris, 1933)

Velikovsky, Immanuel, *Earth in Upheaval* (New York, 1956)

Velikovsky, Immanuel, *Peoples of the Sea* (New York, 1977)

Velikovsky, Immanuel, *Worlds in Collision* (New York, 1950)

Wallace, A. R., *Island Life* (3rd ed. London, 1911)

Whishaw, E. M., *Atlantis in Andalucia. A Study in Folk Memory* (London, 1929)

Whiston, William, *The New Theory of the Earth, from its Original to the Consummation of all Things* (London, 1696)

Wilkinson, J. Gardiner, *A Popular Account of the Ancient Egyptians*, 2 Vols. (London, 1878)

Wilson, David, *The New Archaeology* (New York, 1974)

Wright, G. F., *The Ice Age in North America*, (1891)

Zhirov, Nikolai, *Atlantis: Atlantology, Basic Problems* (English ed. 1968)

ARTICLES:

Alvara, Fernando de, "Ixtlilxochitl," *Obras Historicas* (Mexico, 1891), Vol. 1

Balabanova, S., Parsche, F., and W. Pirsig, "First Identification of Drugs in Egyptian Mummies," *Naturwissenschaften*, 79, (1992)

Berg, L. S., "Nekotoriye soobrazheniya o teorii peredvizheniya materikov" ("Some Considerations Regarding the Theory of the Movement of Continents"), *News of the USSR Geographical Society*, 74 (1947)

Blegen, C. W., "Excavations at Troy, 1936," *American Journal of Archaeology*, XLI (1937).

Brown, Michael D., Seyed H. Hosseini, Antonio Torroni, Hans-Jurgen Bandlet, Jon C. Allen, Theodore G. Schurr, Rosaria Scozzari, Fulvio Cruciani, and Douglas C. Wallace, "mtDNA Haplogroup X: An Ancient Link between Europe/Western Asia and North America?" *American Journal of Human Genetics*, 63 (October, 1998)

Caskey, John L., "Greece, Crete, and the Aegean Islands in the Early Bronze Age," in *The Cambridge Ancient History*, Vol.1 part 2 (3rd ed.)

Chatters, James C., "Kennewick Man," *Newsletter of the American Anthropological Association* (2004)

Clarke, W. B., "Remarks on the Sedimentary Foundations of New South Wales," *Annual Report of the Department of Mines, New South Wales* (3rd ed. 1875)

Easby, Elizabeth, "Seafarers and Sculptors of the Caribbean," *Expedition*, 14 (1972)

Edwards, I. E. S., "The Early Dynastic Period in Egypt," *The Cambridge Ancient History*, Vol.1 part 2, (3rd ed)

Emery, C., "On the Origin of European and North American Ants," *Nature*, Vol. LIII, (1895).

Ewing, M., "New Discoveries on the Mid-Atlantic Ridge," *National Geographic Magazine*, Vol. XCVI, No. 5 (November, 1949)

Gardner, E. W., and G. Caton-Thompson, "The Recent Geology and Neolithic Industry of the Northern Fayum Desert," *The Journal of the Royal Anthropological Institute of Great Britain and Ireland*, (1926)

Germain, L., "Le problème de l'Atlantide de la Zoologie," *Annales de Géographie, Paris*, Vol. xxii (1913) No. 123.

Greenman, E. F., "The Upper Paleolithic and the New World," *Current Anthropology*, Vol. 4, (1963)

Heinsohn, Gunnar, "The Rise of Blood Sacrifice and Priest Kingship in Mesopotamia: A Cosmic Decree?," *Religion*, Vol. 22 (1992)

Hibben, F. C., "Evidence of Early Man in Alaska," *American Antiquity*, VIII (1943)

Holmes, W. H., Willis, B., Wright, F. E., and C. N. Fenner, "Early Man in South America," *Bulletin of the Bureau of American Ethnology*, 52 (1912).

Kolbe, R. W., "Fresh-Water Diatoms from Atlantic Deep-Sea Sediments," *Science*, Vol. 126, No. 3282, 22 (November, 1957).

Mellis, Otto, "Zur Sedimentation in Der Romache-Tiefe (Ein Beitrag zur Erklärung der Enstellung des Tiefseesandes in Atlantischen Ozean)," *Geologischen Rundschau*, (Goteborg, 1958).

Moon, H. P., "The Geology and Physiography of the Altiplano of Peru and Bolivia," *The Transactions of the Linnean Society of London*, 3rd Series, Vol. 1. Pt. 1 (1939).

Nesis, K. N., "Puti i vremya formirovaniya razorvannogo areala u amfiborealnykh vidov morskikh donnykh zhivotnykh," ("The Ways and Time of the Formation of the Ruptured Areal of Amphiboreal Species of Sea Bottom Fauna") *Okeanologiya*, 2 (1962).

Nordhagen, R., and H. Gams, "Postglaziale Klimaänderungen und Erdkrustbewegungen Mitteleuropa," *Mitteilungen der Geographischen Gesellschaft in München*, XV, Heft 2 (1923)

Peratt, Anthony L., "Characteristics for the Occurrence of a High-Current, Z-Pinch Aurora as recorded in Antiquity," *Transactions on Plasma Science*, (December, 2003).

Piggot, Charles S., "Core samples of the ocean bottom," *Carnegie Institution of Washington News Service Bulletin* Staff Edition, 4 (no. 9), 6 (December 1936).

Rainey, F., "Archaeological Investigation in Central Alaska," *American Antiquity*, V (1940).

Sanderson, Ivan T., "Riddle of the Frozen Giants," *Saturday Evening Post*, No. 39, (January, 1960)

Scharff, R. F., "Some remarks on the Atlantis Problem," *Proceedings of the Royal Irish Academy*, sect. B, (1902) Vol. XXIV.

Sernander, R., "Klimaverschlechterung, Postglaciale" in *Reallexikon der Vorgeschichte*, ed. Max Ebert, VII (1926).

Smith, W. Stevenson, "The Old Kingdom in Egypt and the Beginning of the First Intermediate Period," *The Cambridge Ancient History*, Vol.1 part 2 (3rd ed)

Speicher, John, "Plate Tectonics — A Startling New View of Our Turbulent Earth," *Popular Science*, Vol. 200, No. 6, (June, 1972).

Stocks, Denys A., "Stone sarcophagus manufacture in ancient Egypt," *Antiquity*, vol. 73 (1999).

Tiede, E., "Atlas als Personifikation der Weltasche," ("Atlas as the Personification of the World Axis") *Museum Helveticum*, 2 (1945)

Whitley, D. Garth, "The Ivory Islands of the Arctic Ocean," *Journal of the Philosophical Society of Great Britain*, XII (1910).

Zhivago, A. V., and G. B. Udintsev, "Sovremenniye problemy geomorphologni dna morei i okeanov ("Modern Problems of the Geomorphology of the Floor of the Seas and Oceans"), *Herald of the USSR Academy of Sciences*, Geography Series, No. 1, (1960).

INDEX